8. Rounded Ascension Island
9. Rounded St Peter & St Paul rocks
10. Rounded Tristan da Cunha
11. Rounded Cape of Good Hope
12. Knockdown courtesy of Dera
13. Rounded South East Cape
14. Night of Lunacy
15. Arrived Newcastle 14th April 2001

NEVER, EVER GIVE IN!

Tony Mowbray

NEVER, EVER GIVE IN!
First published in Australia by Tony Mowbray 2025
www.tonymowbray.com.au

Copyright © Tony Mowbray 2025
All Rights Reserved

A catalogue record for this
book is available from the
National Library of Australia

ISBN: 978-1-7640853-0-4 (pbk)
ISBN: 978-1-7640853-1-1 (ebk)

Typesetting and design by Publicious Book Publishing
Published in collaboration with Publicious Book Publishing
www.publicious.com.au

No part of this book may be reproduced in any form, by photocopying or by any electronic or mechanical means, including information storage or retrieval systems, without permission in writing from both the copyright owner and the publisher of this book.

Dedication

I dedicate this book to all of my crew, both on land and at sea.

There were thousands of wonderful people that helped me in a multitude of ways, big and small, throughout our journey together.

No matter how many words I scribe, I will never be able to accurately convey my deep and abiding heartfelt thanks for all of the assistance I've received.

To family, friends, individuals, groups, companies and sponsors - I am indebted to you all!

I am eternally grateful and thank you from the bottom of my heart.

Thank you! Thank you! Thank you!

Contents

Solo Globe Challenger route

Chapter 1	What's that Mr. Snape?	1
Chapter 2	My 1st Sydney to Hobart yacht race	7
Chapter 3	A beer, a cigarette and a sexual encounter	13
Chapter 4	27 days. One pair of underpants	18
Chapter 5	Dream, Think, Talk, Commit, Act	28
Chapter 6	It's like climbing Mount Everest in Thongs	33
Chapter 7	The Bass Strait Eight locked and loaded	43
Chapter 8	At 4.03 pm it happened	52
Chapter 9	20 seconds can be an eternity	60
Chapter 10	Which one will I think of last	72
Chapter 11	I made promises to myself that night	82
Chapter 12	Well and truly fucking rooted	89
Chapter 13	Catastrophic or Phenomenal	101
Chapter 14	We can all be slow learners and fast forgetters	106
Chapter 15	A Nudie run with Cookie	117
Chapter 16	Proving ground - Race to New Zealand	127
Chapter 17	Its definitely not hot, dry or dusty out here	136
Chapter 18	How Much did it cost How do you pay for it	145
Chapter 19	How much toilet paper do I need	154
Chapter 20	Time to introduce my imaginary friends, Kevin and Frank	171
Chapter 21	Houston, we have a problem!	191
Chapter 22	Now I can wear an earring!	204
Chapter 23	Underpants off after 70 days	214

Chapter 24	It was like a Canary perched on my shoulder	237
Chapter 25	I could arrive back having gained weight	247
Chapter 26	Finally, I picked up the jagged outline of the rocks	253
Chapter 27	Hard on the wind	263
Chapter 28	The Indian Ocean is a Beast	279
Chapter 29	Oh Dera!	291
Chapter 30	Hunting down Tasmania	311
Chapter 31	It was lunacy out there that night	328
Chapter 32	This was my home turf	338
Chapter 33	It's over, stick with me, it's going to be okay	346
Chapter 34	Back to Bass Strait after '98	363
Chapter 35	Nic, Billy the Bear and other matters	366
Chapter 36	What happened to Solo Globe Challenger	373
Chapter 37	Books Read	375
Chapter 38	Food and other supplies	378

CHAPTER 1

What's that Mr. Snape?

My life began on 1st October 1955 weighing in at a hefty 4.82 kg (10lb 10ozs) with my paternal grandfather nicknaming me "Ten Ton Tony."

My Dad, William "Bill" Henry Mowbray was nearly 50 years old when I was born passing away in 1982, a day shy of 76 years of age. I think of him extremely fondly and wish I were more like him. My Mum, Beatrice May Stokes, passed away in 2010 aged 87 years old. They say opposites attract, and when I look at Mum and Dad, I see a striking contrast in their personalities. In myself, I recognise many of their traits, some distinctly from one or the other and others a blend of both.

The "old man" was 17 years older than the "old girl" and smaller in stature. I took after Mum in size, standing just shy of 1.8 metres by the time I was an adult, and continually needed to keep an eye on my weight.

The Mowbrays and Stokes have a long connection with underground coal mining, with nearly all of my uncles and grandfather spending all of their working lives down the pit. Dad started underground at 14 years of age in 1920, retiring compulsorily 46 years later at age 60. When he retired, I was 11 years old, and my sister Marina was just 8 years of age, so he had no choice but to keep working full time, most notably as a cleaner in a factory for a decade and other manual jobs well into his 70s.

In the 1950s and 60s, the norm was for fathers to be the breadwinner and mothers to be the homemaker and Mum attacked her role with gusto. She was a very, very determined person. Whatever she set her mind to, she pursued relentlessly until she got the result she wanted. I've inherited that same drive, which is something I'm grateful for, though I sometimes wonder what life would be like if I weren't quite so focused.

Mum and Dad instilled in us a very strong work ethic, demonstrating that there were no free rides. If you wanted to get ahead, you had to work for it. There was never any pocket money in our house, simply because there was none, so I was taught and encouraged to find ways to earn my own. I engaged in such entrepreneurial activities as growing mulberries, apple cucumbers, flowers and vegetables, selling them door to door.

Lawn mowing was also a good earner. Dad was always happy to drop his mower to my various clients so that I could ride my pushbike there after school to give their lawn the once over. A great way to maximise profits was to use Dad's mower fuel, when I could get away with it!

On the shores of Lake Macquarie, a canoe hire business operated and another of my jobs was hiring them out. "#73 come on in! Your time is up!" I would shout across the lake – they didn't have a chance of running over time on my watch!

At Belmont Tennis Club I maintained the lawn, kept the grounds tidy and had to hammer back in place the numerous timber fence palings that had been belted off by flying tennis balls. For 6 hours per month, I was paid the king's ransom of $1 per hour. To compensate for being underpaid (in my opinion) I regularly gave myself a bonus free soft drink, as I just happened to have the fridge keys!

I thrived on schoolboy's Rugby League playing under 7's to under 14's. Cricket had a brief look in as did a bit of tennis, just don't mention the drinks fridge! Golf (spoils a good walk) got a run as well but at the end of the day my inner young passion was ignited by sailing.

I enjoyed a wonderful carefree upbringing that I look back on extremely fondly, however if I put a foot out of line, I knew what to expect.

In this day and age, disciplining of children is cause for much lively debate but in our house, there was absolutely NO debate. Discipline in our house was almost always meted out by Mum and when she dished it out she took no prisoners.

Growing up in Belmont it is impossible not to have some sort of relationship with the water, whether it be fleeting or, as is the case with me, lifelong. Absolutely glorious Lake Macquarie measures about 160 km around its circuitous perimeter and is connected to the open ocean by the relatively narrow and shallow Swansea Channel.

One day in early 1961 Mum shoved a tearful, 5 year old Tony through the gate of Belmont Infants School on my first day in kindergarten with strict instructions to eat my lunch. I had no trouble doing so, and still don't.

I don't recall ever being taken to or picked up from school after that first morning. From the first afternoon I caught the bus there and back every day until eventually, at about 8 years of age I was allowed to ride my pushbike. I never, ever had a new push bike, having to bolt various parts together from 2 or 3 old bikes to get a working model.

Before long I was up at the "big school", Belmont Primary, with things going pretty well academically for the first couple years however when I was 11 years old a decline set in as I discovered my first great love.

I've always had an affinity with the Lake, splashing around in it as a toddler, then swimming, fishing, prawning, catching squid, crabbing, and just plain mucking about in all sorts of boats.

My family were not sailors. Dad was an avid fisherman as is my brother Trevor who did sail as well but never became addicted as I did.

When I was around 12 years old, as my interest in water activities increased my academic efforts and results tapered off in the same proportion. An ever vigilant, proactive ("we don't take no for an answer") Mum shipped me off for after school mathematics tutoring.

So, I found myself seated at the dining table of High School Maths Master, Bob Snape, trying to make sense of Pythagoras' Theorem - of which I still haven't got a clue. It was at my first tutoring session that a life defining moment occurred for me. I spied a vaguely familiar item leaning against the wall in the corner of his dining room.

Me: "What's that long skinny thing leaning against the wall Mr. Snape?"

Bob: "That's a spinnaker pole off my yacht that I need to repair."

Me: "You own a yacht do you?"

Neither had any inkling as to how interwoven our lives would become from that point on.

Being salt of the earth coal miners, we Mowbrays never ever thought about going to the yacht club. It just wasn't on our "to do" list. At Bob's invitation, the next Sunday I rode my beat up old "pushie" down to Lake Macquarie Yacht Club so I could check out his yacht, and the die was cast.

There was to be no going back. My life was impacted forever.

Bob was 22 years my senior, but a pivotal lifelong friendship began that saw "Snapey" become my teacher, mentor, friend, counsellor, guiding influence and surrogate father.

Right from the first time I laid eyes on his little 26 ft yacht "Odin", I was hooked. She was a small timber planked yacht built in the 1940's suited to 3 crew. It was not the sort of yacht that you "go below" on as there was no below. From the first time my young eyes saw her I thought she was huge, and I loved her. I signed on as crew immediately.

With Snapey, I started racing against, meeting and mingling with a variety of really good quality people. Not just good at sailing, but quality human beings, many of whom have had a major impact on my life. I was an eager pupil. I just loved the whole experience.

I was 14 years old when I ventured onto the open ocean for the first time in a day race from Moon Island (at the ocean entrance to Lake Macquarie) to Newcastle and return. It was a huge day in my life. As we approached the end of Nobbys breakwater at the entrance to Newcastle Harbour, I had no idea how this rock wall would come to mean so much to me 32 years later. As we rounded the end of the break wall in 1969, a wave threw me off balance and I was pitched overboard. To say I was not keen on being in the water would be a massive understatement. I reckon I only got wet up to my midriff as I scrambled back aboard.

So, there you have it. On my first open ocean trip I fell over the side.

My first ever "Big" boat ride was on the 37 ft. "Rival" in about 1968. It was a lake race, and the course that day took us around a headland to the unfamiliar, for me, southern reaches of the Lake.

As we rounded the headland, I lost all of my reference points and became disorientated. I felt nervous but excited and an awakening struck me deep within – there was a big wide world out there just waiting for me to explore.

At 16 years of age, a happy event occurred when I left Belmont High School after not exactly "leading the Fleet" academically.

We all have dreams.

Sometimes a dream will stay a dream forever, locked away in the inner recesses of the mind.

Some classrooms at Belmont High had a view of the ocean. I always claimed a seat with a view of the water, spending much of the class day dreaming as I stared out of the window. The lake and ocean captured me, and a dream began to form, though I was years away from being able to crystallise it.

Meanwhile, back at the yacht club, I came to an agonising decision to leave Snapey and join another crew. With Snapey's blessing, I signed on with the man that I came to regard as "The Legend of Lake Macquarie", Jack Morgan, and his father Ben, aboard "Pleasure II". It is unbelievable how many young kids (and not so young) that Jack taught to sail, be a better sailor or better human being. Always included in their crew was a young person to whom they imparted their extensive knowledge in a fun way. If you were one of Jack's "boys" you were extremely lucky. Jack and Ben taught me how to sail smart, push hard when appropriate but back off when prudent amongst a whole lot of "stuff". Their lessons have stood me in excellent stead for all of my life.

Jack and Ben operated a reward system where young members of the crew would get a jelly bean if they did a good job, and the older crew were rewarded with a beer. I thought it was an excellent reward. The beer, that is!

In early 1972 I started an Electrical apprenticeship with BHP at their Apprentice Training Centre in Mayfield. I was there for the first year before moving to BHP owned, Lambton Colliery, Redhead for the supposed last 3 years of my apprenticeship. I thoroughly loved underground coal mine work but became increasingly dissatisfied with some of the more repetitive unrelated tasks I was ordered to do as a 3rd year apprentice. As an example, I had to paint the yellow safety lines on the concrete workshop floor.

In my usual timid style (not) I had no qualms telling the Electrical Engineer that if I had wanted to be a painter then I would have done so. I wasn't exactly in a position of influence, so this didn't go down too well! Though I was frustrated with some of the work that was asked of me and wasn't as keen as I could have been. Towards the latter part of my 3rd year the manager suggested that I might like to ponder my future as an electrician.

That evening at the dinner table, in a watershed moment, I told Mum and Dad that I had decided to terminate my apprenticeship. FFThe next day I told the Manager (our nickname for him was "Gyro Gearloose" so what chance did we have?) that I was prepared to relinquish my apprenticeship if he would employ me as an underground coal miner to which he readily agreed.

CHAPTER 2
My 1st Sydney to Hobart yacht race

As I approached my 18th birthday, while still apprenticed (but only just), sailing dominated my thoughts and activities. I reached an extremely difficult decision to sign off from Jack Morgan's crew in order to actively pursue ocean racing.

I set my sights on doing a Sydney to Hobart yacht race.

There are many, varied and some indefinable reasons why men and women from all over the globe feel the need to compete in the 630 nm (nm stands for nautical miles) annual race. Some are happy to do it just once, whilst others, like me, become addicted and can't wait to go again and again. It is justifiably acknowledged as one of the toughest ocean races in the world. To finish is an achievement.

In 1973, most boats took between 3.5 - 5 days to complete the course and would usually get at least one serious "belting" along the way from the weather gods, and often two or three. I couldn't wait to experience my 1st race to Hobart. (I am an idiot).

Peter Rundle owned a pretty, tiny by today's standards, 30 ft yacht, "Cardinal Puff", and I was lucky enough to secure a berth (a bed) in the 5 man crew. I was 18 years and 3 months old on start day and as excited as I have ever been in my life. I soaked up the experience like a huge sponge. It took us 5 days to get there, finishing in the 60's on handicap out of about 100 starters. I was a little disappointed with the result, but had learned a great deal from Peter including the need for a good preparation and when racing: Attack, attack, and then attack some more! Another massive learning was to never ever, ever give in no matter how tough it gets.

Something happened on that race that irks me to this day.

On the last night, we were bashing into some big breaking seas on a very cold, dark, wet miserable night. I too, was cold and wet, plus a little scared. At the late evening change of watch, I hopped into my bunk and didn't surface until morning, having completely missed my turn on deck. I find it very confronting to recall that, at times I pretended to be asleep to avoid getting up. The crew had sensed I was struggling and had left me there.

After all these years, I still feel embarrassed.

At the conclusion of the race I promised myself that for as long as I sailed, I would never ever miss another watch. I swore I would always get up on deck, take it on and have a go, no matter how bad the weather was or how scared I might be.

I have NEVER missed a watch since.

A keen sense of adventure had kicked in and there was no fighting it. I resigned from the pit and headed to Auckland, New Zealand for an extended working holiday. Whilst in Auckland, I used to get up at 5.30 am each day on the weekends to catch 3 different buses to get me to the Yacht Club for a 9.30 am race start.

After 8 months of my living in Auckland, Dad fell down the back steps at home smashing heaps of ribs, puncturing a lung, and his life suddenly hung in the balance. I dropped everything and flew back. The "old fella" was in a bad way for a long time, but he fought back strongly and got through it.

As 1974 rolled along, most weekends were about sailing. I used to drive to Sydney on Saturday mornings in my beat up old panel van, sail all day, sleep in the back of van, sail Sunday and then drive back to Belmont. I started in my 2nd Hobart race in December 1974 on "Sirocco" but failed to finish after breeching the hull and nearly sinking.

Life was pretty simple. Life was good.

My dream had started to take form. I now visualised sailing long distances, solo, but the dream lacked clarity. It would be nearly 20 years before it would have definition.

I met John "Stanno" Stanton, when I was 14 years old and he was 41 years of age. He was a great guy, an excellent sailor and became a lifelong close friend.

As a young person, I gravitated toward older guys as mates. I had a lot of friends my age but it is interesting to note the age differences between me and some of my very close friends with Snapey 22 years my senior, Jack Morgan 26 years and Stanno 27 years. These blokes had a few more birthdays than I and had much to offer in terms of wisdom, humour, and were fantastic role models for me in addition to my own father. I loved spending time in their company.

Stanno passed away at 83 years old in 2011, and as he took his last breath, I held his hand and stroked his forehead.

What about female company? For the record, I think they are a great invention. At this time in my life there were many that caught my attention but my interest was generally not reciprocated!

Now, turning my attention to the more pressing matters in my life at this time, "Polaris" was a drop dead beautiful yacht. Jack, Stanno and Snapey were crewing on her in 1975 Hobart race and I managed to get a berth. As a warm up, we competed in the 380 nm Gosford to Lord Howe Island race, crossing the start line in a "smokin'" 50 knots of wind with our pocket handkerchief storm sails up and we crew hanging on tightly. Later, the breeze backed off a little and we cracked a multi coloured spinnaker and charged off on a "harem scarem" ride surfing big breaking seas.

Jack, always the mentor, handed me the steering wheel. I was very tentative, but he insisted I steer and then sat close by tutoring me as I added to and refined my skill set. I eventually "wiped out" massively, laying her over sideways. My fuck up lead to the end of the spinnaker pole snapping off as the spinnaker dragged in the water with the boat on her ear. I had let her get too close to the edge of a cliff and over she went, pinned on her side in a whitewashed ocean with the crew scuttling to restore sanity.

I felt very apprehensive and out of my depth. It was mayhem for a while, and I really hoped that I could get off the wheel and moved to do so, but Jack kept me there. He ordered the sail re-hoisted, using the spare pole and off we careered again.

"But Jack? I reckon it's time for someone else to have go?" I ventured, my voice an octave or two higher than usual.

"Tony, you'll be right. Learn from your mistakes" came the authoritative reply. He was right. Jack was a great teacher and a great man. I think of him very fondly and often.

Continuing the momentum, in December 1975, I did my 3rd Sydney to Hobart on Polaris, sharing a very enjoyable and fast ride, placing 8th on handicap.

In my wildest imagination, I could have never anticipated that one day I would own "Polaris" or that one of her sister ships would have such a profound impact on my life, almost defining it.

I helped sail Polaris home and in early January 1976, Stanno and I were bobbing around Sydney Harbour when we came across an old mate of his who told us he had a berth available on a yacht that he was about to deliver from Auckland to Perth via the northern coast of Aussie. His question: "Would you like to join, Tony?"

Bugger me. The next week I flew across the Tasman to New Zealand for another adventure. We sailed the boat into Queensland waters and, as we travelled north through the maze of islands that make up the Great Barrier Reef, we had a bloody unbelievable time. Systematically and without bias, we wreaked havoc on as many Island resorts as we could. I seem to recall something about swimming nude in the pool at Dunk Island and being thrown off the island? Who can say. It was a long time ago!

We stopped in Cairns for a weekend and whilst having a cooling ale (read: lots of beer) I met a girl that amazed me by seeming willing to talk to me, and – unbelievable to me at that time – actually seemed interested in me. Bloody hell, how long has this been going on?

I left with the boat after a couple of days and by the time we arrived in Darwin, a couple of months later, I had become disgruntled with Stanno's mate so it was time for me to depart.

"What next?" I thought, strolling along the dock, gazing out at the mighty big blue in front of me. I dug around in my pocket and found the phone number of "that girl" in Cairns and rang her, casually enquiring about the possibility of her speaking to me again if I were to fly back?

After a positive reaction from her, in September 1976, I stepped onto the tarmac of Cairns airport with 2 sailing bags of clothes and $200 to my name.

Queensland: perfect one day, bloody marvellous the next!

I slipped back home for my 21st birthday on the 1st October 1976 but couldn't wait to get back to Cairns. On my return up north, I hit the streets looking for work and for a time was a bartender in a pub, before moving "upwards" into the cab of a truck as a truck driver for a Wine and Spirit merchant. "That girl" was still talking to me so I thought "Why not hang around?"

Then I thought, "It's time to get a grown up job".

I looked for a sales role, hoping to be rewarded on results and a chance to be master of my own destiny sort of thing. Just about the first vacancy I came across was selling Life Insurance. Before I could say "Death cover" I was shipped off to Brisbane for a three-week training course with twelve other unsuspecting recruits. I had absolutely no idea about the social stigma associated with Life Insurance salesmen.

I returned to Cairns blissfully ignorant that everyone (including your mother) hates insurance salesman, however, I caught on after what seemed like the thousandth door was slammed in my face in the first week alone. I considered that this was going to be a bit harder that I had originally thought.

Around the end of my 3rd year in the role, I started to get a bit jaded selling life insurance. I had tried (unsuccessfully) to sell a policy to the CEO of Quaid Real Estate, Ian Beattie. I was very impressed with Ian and I met with him to chat about real estate sales. I enquired about the level of hate of real estate salesman by the general public, and he assured me it was better than the insurance industry. He said there was even a chance that my mother would get to like me again, and offered me a job.

When I resigned from the Life office, 3 days later, I was the second last one left of the original class of thirteen. I could be a determined bastard when I wanted to be.

I had a wonderful 3 years in residential real estate sales. I loved it and worked with a great bunch of people of whom I have very fond memories. All up, I sold Insurance, Real Estate and a high end commercial product for the first 10 years of my adult life being remunerated strictly by commission only. There was NEVER a base wage or an advance on possible sales. I am a firm believer in being rewarded for results and not just for showing up. These days everyone seems to get a prize even if they're bloody hopeless or come last.

Dinghy racing was popular in Cairns and I took the opportunity to sharpen my skills racing a one man Laser dinghy and was lucky enough to win some Queensland and North Queensland titles and a Papua New Guinea National title.

"That girl" finally wised up and stopped talking to me and early one morning in 1982, as I stared at the bedroom ceiling, I decided it was time to go home.

I headed back to my coveted Lake Macquarie and Belmont.

CHAPTER 3
A cigarette, a beer and a sexual encounter

Back home, I renewed a lot of friendships including that of Doug Coulter with whom Snapey was racing on Doug's 42 ft. yacht, "Fiona". I hitched a few rides with the boys including the 1983 Sydney to Hobart.

My renewed friendship with Doug led to a very close, strong business and sailing partnership for the next ten years, and a close personal friendship until Doug's passing in 2023.

In 1984 I purchased my first yacht, an Adams 31 ft called "Capsicum", which I acquired for the sole purpose of cruising socially and it turned out to be very social with the occasional (read: lots of) beer being consumed with friends on board.

I joined Doug's crew, sailing regularly with them. In 1984, we competed in the 320 nm (595 km) Sydney to Montague Island and return ocean race. We got absolutely smashed big time. The wind speed indictor went to a maximum of 60 knots (110 k/h) and for 12 hours the needle was jammed hard on 60 knots. We collectively agreed that the wind strength was 80-90 knots (150-170 k/h). It was freezing cold as well, and we were genuinely concerned about our survival prospects.

Sometimes, if it can go wrong, it will.

The rudder fell off, leaving no steerage. A storm sail got jammed half way up and flogged itself to shreds, all the while threatening to bring the mast down. At one point, we were one wave away from being smashed into the side of a tanker. The motor was disabled because a rope had become entangled around the propeller and the propeller shaft coupling was broken. In the end, we were towed to safety by water police with two of the officers later awarded bravery medals for rescuing us in such treacherous conditions.

That Saturday afternoon I said to Snapey, "If I'm going to die out here there's three things I'd like".

"What would they be?" says he.

"A cigarette, a beer and a sexual encounter".

He thought about it in his usual deliberate, contemplative way and replied, "I can help you with the first two but you'll have to see one of the other guys for the last one."

Because of the damage to the boat (and Doug's cheque book), we scratched the Hobart race for that year.

In early 1985, at Doug's invitation, I became joint owner with he and another, as well as managing director, of Newcastle Answering Service. The core business was a 24/7, 365 days a year, communications control room with staff processing thousands of messages via telephone, 2-way radio, pagers etc.

Doug had been a part owner for some time, but other business interests precluded him from being involved closely. It had been bumping along for a while, losing money, so the staff and I set about rebuilding it. Along the way, we added other services like typing, word processing, fax bureau, photocopying, selling and renting of pagers (beepers) etc. We also sold mobile phones when launched in Australia in the late 80's.

I remember being urged to "look into" a new system of an electronic letter box where the owner of the "box" could receive electronic messages. It all sounded a bit "airy fairy" to me, and I dismissed the idea as not having much merit.

That "airy fairy" idea was EMAIL! Who's a goose?

In early 1988, I added to the portfolio when I kicked off Around Town Couriers, specialising in "Hurricane" urgent deliveries. Eight months later we acquired the pre-eminent Crosstown Couriers and suddenly we were in the deep end of the pool. The courier business was fast moving and a lot of fun. When the pressure was on to deliver urgent medical equipment or a part to get a multimillion dollar piece of mining equipment operational again, there was no time to stop and powder your nose.

Turning my mind to sailing once more, I sailed on Fiona in the 1985 Hobart, the 1st of an unbroken run of 9 races for me during that time. I've always thrived on setting challenges and tests for myself, as my personality doesn't lend itself to mediocrity. When I take on a challenge, I have to be absolutely full on with it. There is rarely any middle ground or "things in moderation" in my book of life.

There must be a medical term for my "condition".

I smoked cigarettes intermittently from my late teens, getting really hooked at times. In January 1987, I was sailing home after the '86 Hobart when I lit a "lung buster" and a wave broke over us leaving a sodden "ciggie". I blurted out, "That's it, when I get home I'm giving these bloody things up!"

On the 19th January 1987, I smoked my last cigarette. It is a killer addiction.

My health was becoming of more interest, plus I definitely do not like to be controlled by a habit like cigarette smoking. I want to be strong and control it. There are some wonderful experiences to be had in life and believe me, you do not need cigarettes. Get high on life. No matter how desperate I might be for sponsorship to finance an adventure I would NEVER, EVER accept money from, nor promote, a tobacco company.

In September 1987, the rugby league grand final took place, and I was at the yacht club joining in the festivities. I'd had a couple of drinks (read: a truckload more than 2) when I spied a petite, attractive female. With plenty of Dutch courage, I decided to chance my arm and wandered over, striking up a conversation with the "chick" in the black and white dress, Lorraine Newell.

A day or two later, I called to invite her out to dinner, and she wasn't that keen. However, using my charm and usual determined attitude, I managed to persuade her to give me a chance and the rest is history, as they say. We quickly became close and started living together soon thereafter. Our relationship was going along nicely (or so I thought) for 3 years or so when one day she caught me completely unawares when she blurted out something like "If you want to have a child then let's do so, otherwise piss off and I'll find a bloke that does."

Bloody hell. Okay, I'll have to think about that.

A couple of weeks later we committed to starting a family and the most glorious thing that can ever happen to a human happened in January 1992 when our 1st child, a beautiful daughter, Holly was born. In August 1993, another glorious thing happened when we rounded things out with a "pigeon pair" when our champion son Jordan made an appearance.

Lorraine and I married in February 1993 and at the beginning of 1994, I was as happy and fulfilled as a father could be.

However, back in 1987 I was off the "ciggies" and started to pack on the weight as a result of another of my loves - eating far too much of the wrong food. It's taken me a LOT of years but I now recognise myself as a "Yo Yo" eater. Put it on. Take it off. Put it on. Take it off.

Cigarette free, I bought myself a pair of jogging shoes and started to run around the block in an attempt to slow down my weight gain.

I can remember being so excited when I was able to jog for 20 minutes continuously. Not content, wanting more, I started to run more often and further. Before you could say "sweat soaked headband" I had entered a 10 km fun run. As an athlete, I will never win anything more than a kind smile, but I just loved the training, the participation and the feeling of belonging. I got addicted to fresh air and went in boots and all.

In July 1988, just 18 months after my last cigarette, I lined up for the 42 km Gold Coast Marathon. The longest period of time that I had previously run was 2 hours and now I was staring down the barrel of probably 4 hours or more.

A marathon is about a lot of things and one of them is pain. At the 30 km mark, I was hurting really badly. At 35 km dehydration and blistered, bleeding feet were giving me plenty. From then on, I alternated between a "quickish" shuffle and a slow walk crossing the line in 3 hours 37 minutes. I was elated to have achieved my goal, and my newest addiction now had its hooks firmly embedded.

I had to have more. Training began in earnest. Over the next 12 months I progressed to running 140 kms per week, training twice some days. Sunday morning might be a long run knocking out 32 km in 2.5 hours.

In April 1999, I ran the Canberra Marathon taking 3 hours 17 minutes. I immediately switched to my next goal: I wanted to do a sub 3 hour run. I trained the house down as my weight dropped to the lightest I have ever been in my adult life, 78 kgs. In my 3rd Marathon, on the Gold Coast in 1999, at the 1 hour mark I flew past the 15 km marker, running strongly on schedule to do 2 hours 55 minutes. I was feeling great.

At 16 km I was in agony with stomach cramps, mostly walking and ready to pull out. My brain, however, would not let me pull to the side or give in, and I punished myself, taking 3 hours 43 minutes. I never did another marathon.

I then became addicted to the multisport of triathlon combining swimming, running and cycling and I loved it. A standard triathlon consisted of a 1.5 km swim and a 40 km bike ride topped off by a 10 km run.

Over the years my addictive personality has manifested itself in many ways and the need to test myself by giving them up eventually flows thereafter.

I gave up sugar in 1975
I gave up cigarettes in 1987
I gave up coffee in 1990
I gave up Diet Coke (that was hard) finally, in 2015
I gave up McDonalds fast food in 2016
I gave up alcohol in 2016
I gave up all carbonated soft drinks in 2017
I gave up fruit mince pies in 2022
I gave up lollies, chocolates deserts, cakes, sweet biscuits in 2023
I gave up Black tea in 2024 (strictly a decaf green tea guy now! bloody hell!)

My current addiction is chai latte. No doubt one day I'll feel the need to give that up too!

In 1990, Doug had built a 45 ft. racing yacht and I was intimately involved with its construction. We campaigned "OzFire" very successfully, hitting the start line of the '90, '91 and '92 Hobarts. We retired in 1990 but were 3rd in 1991 and 4th in 1992.

There was a time that I would have nearly given my left arm to win a Hobart race but it was not meant to be and I've decided I like having 2 arms.

In 1993, we competed in the Sydney to Mooloolaba and Brisbane to Gladstone races. Doug had decided to sell the boat and so as I sailed her back home from Queensland I wondered what might be next for little Tony Mowbray from Belmont?

CHAPTER 4

27 days. One pair of underpants

In April 1993, Glen "Cyril" Picasso and I sailed OzFire back home. He and I were clueless at this formative stage of our friendship as to how close we would become. Cyril's dry sense of humour appealed to me, plus he is a damned good sailor and a great bloke. For my 60th birthday (I can't be that old!) a number of my so-called mates, including Cyril, were asked the same set of questions about me.

"What three words would you use to describe Tony?"

Cyril: "Shy, unassuming, introverted"

"What three words do you think Tony would use to describe himself?"

Cyril: "Fucking smart bastard!"

I recently read that a good mate is someone who will listen to your bullshit, then tell you that it's bullshit but then settle back quite comfortably to listen to some more bullshit from you. Cyril is a good mate.

Cyril would become one of the Bass Strait Eight.

In April 1993, I charged through the back door at home, probably didn't even put my sailing bag down, and blurted out to Lorraine: "I've got this great idea! I'm going to sail around Australia, non-stop, two-handed blah blah blah blah. It's going to be fantastic!"

Her subdued response (extremely subdued) was, "Yeah, right."

"Yeah, oh yeah. It's going to be wonderful blah blah blah blah blah"

Lorraine was 5 months pregnant with Jordan and Holly was a 15-month-old toddler. We were a single-income family with me earning a reasonable income but not a king's ransom. We had a mortgage and not much cash on hand. To say Lorraine was disinterested would be a vast understatement.

Many years prior I had read of John Gleeson from Mooloolaba, who, in 1978, had sailed non-stop around Australia with 3 others in a voyage apparently prompted by national pride. When John heard that it hadn't been done, it is rumoured that he said "We better do it before a Frenchman or a Pom does" and just two months later they headed off. The story of their adventure had stuck with me, and as Cyril and I sailed past Mooloolaba on the way home I had reflected on John and his achievement.

I liken life to being like the chapters of a book. Some chapters are longer than others, some are shorter than others, some are more interesting than others and some you want to get the fuck over so you can move on. I was about to embark upon a very long and different chapter of my sailing life. The racing chapter that started in 1967 and went to 1993 had come to a close without me realising.

I am often asked, "How have you gotten to where you are?"

"Where is where?" I have wondered on many occasions.

I now realise that from 1993 to present I have come to many forks in the road, as we all do from time to time. Sometimes a fork has taken me down the path of business, conservative behaviour and the need to be a "grown up". The other fork has been in pursuit of my passion.

Many times, I have consciously chosen the passion path.

Many times, I have unconsciously chosen that path also.

Following my passion is one of the reasons that I have got to wherever I am today. Wherever the hell that is.

By 1993 the shine had worn off racing, and I wanted a change.

I wanted a new challenge. I tracked down John Gleeson, who was still working as a Pharmacist at the 67 years of age. He told me that he and 3 good mates had simply wanted to do the trip around Australia to "go for a good sail". I was inspired and once again, the die was cast.

Doug and I had been divesting ourselves of the various businesses that I shared in and by 1993 only the courier business remained. My plan was simple. Or so I thought:

- Find a suitable yacht that needed refurbishing and borrow it.
- Find a sponsor who will pay for said refurbishment and the cost of the trip.
- I enjoy the trip.
- At completion, the owner has their refurbished vessel returned to them.

- The sponsor gets a return on their investment.
- We would all be happy.

At the time, I thought I was an absolute genius. At the very least, I just knew I was an ideas man and a lateral thinker.

Lorraine didn't agree! A few weeks after barging through the back door I told her that I had found a boat to buy (the borrow idea didn't quite work out) and I was pulling it out of the water a couple of days hence to inspect it. I invited her to come and have a look. I knew she would be super keen.

The answer was a curt, resounding, "NO!" (read: Fuck right of!) Shock, horror. You don't want to come look at the boat?

Polaris, the boat that I had sailed the 1975 Hobart race on was now under different ownership and in a sad state of decline. If I were to buy her, a substantial refurbishment would be required. 18 years prior, not in my wildest dreams did I ever think I would ever own her BUT in June 1993 I bought Polaris for $68,500.

"How do you pay for it?" "It" being a necessary part of turning a dream into reality.

Finding the answer to that question is bloody hard and has been one of the almost soul destroying aspects of my dream chasing over the years. I needed to get $68,500 from somewhere. I spoke to some banks and the cookie cutter generic excuses preceded a polite, "No" which was code for "Fuck off, you idiot".

I outlined my plan to one stereotypical conservative bank manager who was vaguely interested (very vaguely).

Question: "How much do you need?"

Answer: "If you can lend me $68,000, I've got $500.

I was serious.

I ended up borrowing $15,000 as an unsecured personal loan, which I part paid for the boat with, plus the vendor provided $50,000 of vendor finance. I had to pay monthly interest only to him for a maximum of 2 years. I had to pay the full $50,000 to him within 2 years. I had the other $3,500. Financially, I was all over it.

Endeavour Credit Union came on board as naming rights sponsor for a reasonable contribution which was way less than what was needed (as is so often the case with sponsors). The project was christened "Hunter Life Ausail '94" and the boat temporarily renamed "Hunter Endeavour".

We all experience moments of great poignancy, moments that you will never forget when something particularly special and unforgettable happened. In July 1993, a moment of poignancy etched itself in my memory. I know exactly where I was and the vehicle I was driving when Lorraine called. Up to this point, she had been understandably nonplussed by my enthusiasm. She was a woman with a young toddler at home, and in the late stage of her second pregnancy. She had a husband who was proposing to fuck off to sea for a lengthy period of time, a husband that was working hard on finding the finances to undertake the voyage, let alone support a young family.

It was a straightforward conversation. She said that if this was what I really wanted to do then she would support me 100%. Let's go do this "thing."

In the latter part of 1993, another poignant moment occurred when, for the first time, I said out loud that I was thinking about attempting to sail solo, non-stop and unassisted around the world. This would mean raising the bar to a whole new level, but Lorraine was unwavering in her support. She said that she would leave it to me to decide as she felt that I would make the correct decision.

I decided that I would put my best foot forward with the around Australia sail and see how that turned out, before making a decision re: a world attempt.

Over the years there were many tough times for Lorraine to endure because of my drive to pursue my dreams. Very rarely did she ever complain. I told her that I didn't know how long it would take or how I would be able to do it BUT I promised her that one day I would repay my debt to her, Holly and Jordan for sticking by me.

Hunter Life Ausail '94 was a two handed, non-stop and unassisted sail around Australia. The goal was to sail out of Newcastle with me and another on board, turn left and keep land to the left all the way around Australia (including Tasmania) and sail back into Newcastle without receiving any help or stopping. At departure, everything had to be on board to sustain two of us for however long it took. I thought that the 6400 nm (11850 km) journey would take 50 to 60 days but I allowed for 80.

I needed to find someone with the appropriate skills, mindset, and critically, a person who could put up with me plus be able to have a couple of months away to sail with me. Morrie Morgan was perfect.

I first met Morrie in 1985 and right from the get go, I was super impressed with his no-nonsense, down to earth approach to life, his seafaring abilities and personality. We were very close friends for 40 years and my life is richer for having had Morrie in it.

Sadly, he passed away in 2024

As departure loomed, the courier business was sold and so I was unemployed and bloody happy to be so. I knew that when I got back I would have to put my nose firmly to the financial grindstone but for time being I was professionally free and unencumbered. Yahoo!

In March 1994, Morrie and I charged out of Newcastle Harbour and headed north. We rocketed up the NSW coast, into QLD waters, threading our way through the thousands of coral reefs and islands that make up the Great Barrier Reef.

At Cape York Peninsula, we turned left for the westbound leg across the top of Australia. We inched our way past Darwin and as we paralleled the northern coast of Western Australia, Tropical Cyclone Vivien formed behind us and began to hunt us down. Over the next three days, Vivien got closer and closer and by the time she was within striking distance the forecast sea state was "High to Phenomenal" so Morrie and I thought discretion would be the better part of valour.

In other words, let's get the fuck out of here.

The rules of a non-stop attempt allow you to seek shelter and anchor if necessary, to rest or make repairs so long as no outside assistance whatsoever is received. You are definitely not allowed to go ashore. My mindset was (and still is) that once you are out there, you stay out there until the job is done, however Vivien and her vicious winds and crazy seas demanded common sense. We headed to land to seek shelter and sailed into King Sound, a 60 nm long V shaped body of water at the base of which sits Derby, WA. We found a beautiful, protected anchorage and stayed there for three nights until Vivien's wrath and fury dissipated.

We continued on, passing the North West shelf oil rigs belching their flames into the night sky. We bashed our way south for days into very strong headwinds before turning left near Albany and entering the Great Southern Ocean, setting course for the bottom of Tasmania about 1500 nm (2800 km) and 10 days away.

The underlying ocean swell increased dramatically and were easily 40 feet (ft) high. We would rise to the crest of each one, hover and then surf off with a mountain of swirling green water hard on our heels.

The Southern Ocean is no place for the fainthearted. It was exhilarating, scary, beautiful and mesmerising all at the same time. One needs to be very careful in that part of the world as the ocean can chew you up and spit you out in the blink of an eye.

I felt that Jack, Snapey, Stanno and all my other teachers were there with me in spirit, still guiding me.

Morrie and I had a fantastic time. We did a lot of talking, thinking, relaxing, reading and got to know each other extremely well. Morrie would politely laugh at my hopeless jokes, even when I told him the same one for the 5th or 6th time.

At North West Cape, I had a wash and put on clean clothes including fresh underpants. A week or so after my tub up, I still had the same clothes on – including the underpants. Somehow the subject of 7 days in the same undies came up and Morrie was distinctly unimpressed at my lack of personal hygiene. It became a running joke, and I decided to see how long I could keep them on without changing. I was curious to see how disgusted I could get Morrie. The more he urged me to change my undies, the more determined I was to not. If the sign says "Don't walk on the Grass", what are you going to do?

A day or so from the finish I finally had a wash and changed undies. I had kept my underpants on for 27 days and was quite proud of the achievement for a number of reasons, including the fact that they were in quite reasonable condition.

Morrie was mortified and shook his head whenever the subject came up over the years, trying to act bemused but never succeeding. I was unsure as to whether I should be proud of my effort and so didn't share my "achievement" with too many outside of my mates, who predictably were in absolute awe whilst their wives/girlfriends were absolutely aghast.

Years later, when Jordan was able to fully appreciate the enormity of what I achieved, he upgraded my status to "legend".

We were in the grip of a major storm as we tracked to the bottom of Tasmania. Conditions were hostile with wind of 50 + knots, and we were running under bare poles (no sail up) in dangerous 40 ft breaking, cresting seas. We were streaming a drogue from the stern to act as a handbrake, slowing us down, preventing full blooded out of control surfing down the face of the waves. We were okay but seriously bloody apprehensive.

At lunch time I asked Morrie what he wanted to eat? No answer.

A few minutes later I asked again. No answer.

At the third request, he finally blurted out that he "had been thinking about it and what he really wanted was a hot meat pie BUT he was only going to eat it if he could sit in a concrete bus shelter at a bus stop."

Morrie Morgan was a great mate.

We crossed the finish line on 12th May 1994 after spending 54 days at sea. As we prepared to enter the harbour, I said, "Well, what do you think about that Morrie? There's another 54 days that we haven't had to go to a real job". We both laughed long and loud.

As I write, revisiting 1993/94, it is surreal to think that just 13 months after barging through the back door and blurting out my grand plan we had bought a boat, refurbished it, found a sponsor, Jordan was born and I was at sea for nearly 2 months having left our 26 month old daughter and 5 month old son on the dock with their mother.

I shake my head for a number of reasons. Pride is not one of them.

As has been clearly evident many times over the years, I actually work harder at avoiding a real job than if I actually had a real job. Hardly had the dust settled or from a nautical viewpoint, or the salt spray crystalised, and it was onwards and upwards.

What might the next chapter be?

I had a huge decision that I was grappling with.

Many times, after the around Oz trip, I would lay wide awake at 4 am staring almost unblinkingly at the black void of the ceiling thinking: Will I or won't I? Will I or won't I?

Will I have a crack at a solo around the world?

On the positive side of the ledger:

- I owned a boat suitable to the task. I used the word "owned" loosely as I still owed a tad under $64,000.
- I didn't have a job to go to, although some may not see that as a plus.
- There were a large group of supporters that had worked tirelessly with me on the around Australia campaign that were ready to fire up again.
- I was in the groove.

On the negative side of the ledger:

- It would require a huge effort to prepare the boat for such an arduous journey, up to four times longer than the around Australia trip.
- It would be in much more inhospitable, life-threatening and boat breaking conditions for much of the time.
- There would have to be a lot of attention to detail.
- It would require a lot of time.
- It would require a lot of money.
- I would be an absentee husband and father for a very long time.

I thought long and hard about whether or not I would have a crack, but the one thing I kept returning to was my family. Over the preceding 15 months or so I had subjected Lorraine and the kids to some difficult times.

As a husband, I had been absent in a lot of ways.

As a father, I had been absent in a lot of ways.

As a breadwinner, I had shortchanged my family.

In July 1994 I said an emphatic NO to an around the world attempt and walked away.

In 1994 plans were underway for the 50th Sydney to Hobart yacht race, scheduled for that December. It was to be a milestone event and would be celebrated appropriately by the sailing community. A huge, all-out effort was to be made to attract boats from yesteryear. Ian Chant from Endeavour Credit Union had been the decision maker to sponsor the around Australia trip. He was dynamic, proactive and loved sailing. He was delighted with the exposure that Endeavour had received so came to me with another idea. Ian asked if I be interested in participating in the 50th race, and if so, he might be able to squeeze the Endeavour Credit Union budget a little further. A proviso was that he and his mate David Cutcliffe, be in the crew.

The opportunity to compete as owner/skipper of my own yacht was too good to pass up, so I accepted.

The squeezing of the Endeavour Credit Union budget produced a fast trickle as opposed to a torrent of money so the eternal question arose. How do I pay for it?

I put an advertisement in our local newspaper to try and attract some paying crew. From about 30 enquiries I ended up with two guys who met the criteria. At that point, we three had absolutely no inkling that we would become lifelong friends and blood brothers. Keith Molloy and Keir Enderby did not know each other, and I did not know them.

Keith is a couple of years older than me. In 1994, he owned a small cruising yacht. Upon meeting him, I posed an important question.

"Keith, why do you want to do this race?" He looked me in the eye and with obvious emotion welling to near tears, he shared, that recently his mother, to whom he had been very close, had passed away. She knew of his passion for sailing and before dying she had made him promise that he would do a Sydney to Hobart for her.

That was good enough for me. How could I say no? Keith was in.

Keir Enderby is the artistic one amongst us and a world class rum drinker. He will also tell you that he is the world's sexiest man, however I am yet to see any evidence of this and don't believe such evidence has been seen by anyone else. He is a couple of years older than me and in 1994 owned a beautiful traditional timber yacht, "Bissy Girl" that he was devoted to.

The following are responses from Keir to my 60th birthday questionnaire.

Censorship has been necessary to protect the young, old, females, males, sailors, non-sailors. Anyone really.

"Where did you meet?"

Keir: On my yacht. I was younger then, quite naïve and didn't know what I was letting myself in for.

"How has Tony influenced/ruined/made a difference in your life?"

Keir: He hasn't really. Or maybe he has? I've done stuff with Tony that I only dreamed of because of his capacity to make things happen and take certain people along for the ride. I'm one of those people.

"What three words would you use to describe him?"

Keir: Over the top. Bald, ego, flatulent, loyal, determined, horny, committed, friend, true, there, quite incredible.

Keir was also to become one of the Bass Strait Eight.

It is said that you can count your really close friends on one hand.

I need both hands plus have to remove my shoes and socks.

Ian Chant and David Cutcliffe, were in. I was taken (in?) by Keith and Keir and they signed on. Doug Coulter was in as was another "brother", Mark Schroder, a sailor of great pedigree and a bloody good bloke. Rounding out the crew of 8 was my long time sailing mate, Ralph Carlier, fellow crew from my 1st Hobart in 1973.

For years I've asked Ralph, "Who would name a baby "Ralph"?" Imagine a parent saying to a one day old baby, "Here Ralph, have your bottle". His short, sharp come back on every occasion is, "It's the second most popular dog's name."

We had a great team.

On Boxing Day 1994, we crossed the start line of the much celebrated 50th race as one of a record-smashing, 371 entries, of which 309 finished, including us in a little over 4 days. It was a very special experience.

I then needed to consolidate our position as a family in a number of ways. I had stretched the financial rubber band pretty tautly and while it wasn't about to snap, I needed to rein it in.

I received an offer to buy Polaris. I didn't want to sell because I had put myself through the mill to acquire her, however the offer was pretty good and so, with family in mind, I agreed to sell. The new owner took her under his care in January 1995.

It was now time to be a more dedicated husband and devoted father. It was time to walk away from the idea of sailing around the world my own. Or so I thought.

CHAPTER 5
Dream, Think, Talk, Commit, Act

At the Mowbray household, things went back to being as close to normal as they might be.

Holly turned 3 years old in January 1995 and Jordan rolled 2 years of age in August that year.

In June 1994, just after the around Oz adventure, I had started working for Doug at his core business, wholesale distribution of TV aerials, cabling and associated components taking on the role of national sales manager. Through 1995 I was earning reasonable income, working hard to try and balance the ledger financially and as a family.

Always thinking of the next project, I conceived and organised "Sail for Canteen '96". CanTeen assists 12-25 year olds whose lives have been turned upside by cancer which may have struck a sibling, parent, friend or themselves.

In February 1996 Keir, Vince Bezzina and myself, aboard Vince's 42 ft yacht, "Struth" sailed non-stop for seven days and nights around Lake Macquarie as a fundraiser for this worthy cause. It was sort of like the aquatic equivalent of sitting in a small cubby house atop a telegraph pole in a shopping centre car park that had been a popular marketing strategy decades prior. The trip was easy stuff and we had a fantastic time. Through the course of the week we welcomed members of CanTeen on board for a few hours at a time to have some fun. We generated a lot of media exposure for them and raised $20,000 for their coffers. It was great result all round.

In 1996, I stopped working for Doug and went to work for a great mate, Craig "Flano" Flanagan, who had been a successful sailmaker but had steered his business into the emerging market of eye-catching fabric shade structures catering to a national and international market.

It was an exciting, innovative and stimulating product. Flano's business was growing exponentially so I joined, to look after sales.

1997 rolled around and I purchased a low cost, older 30 ft yacht, "Seaforth". I wanted us to have some fun on the lake and Seaforth was an economical fuss free way to do that. I believe that many of Holly and Jordan's fondest boat memories were created on Seaforth. I have a beautiful photograph of them standing at the stern, beaming as they hold a freshly caught small fish. It is one of my all-time favourite photographs.

Life was pretty good.

Since mid 1994, I had shut down any thought of a solo world attempt but as 1997 dawned I found myself, like an addict, broaching the subject yet again with those close to me and Lorraine, whose attitude never faltered. She would support me in whatever I decided.

Back 'n forth, back 'n forth swung the pendulum in my mind.

Will I or won't I?

Will I or won't I?

Back 'n forth, back 'n forth.

WORDS

There are five words that I began to notice everywhere in the 1990's. If I spoke or thought one of these words, or read one in a book or a newspaper, then independently of the others, each word had a certain strength or extra character.

As a result of some events in my life, these five words now go together in my mind, in what is for me a clear and logical sequence. They mesh together like a piece of finally dovetailed furniture, or a hand into a glove and when I look at the five words as one entity, for me, they take on a very powerful meaning.

I didn't make these words up. It's only the order in which I've placed them, that is my doing.

DREAM

Aren't they wonderful things? I absolutely love them. At high school, I had stared out the window, transfixed by the ocean and lake, dreaming but not being able to give the dream definition.

There is no time limit for dreams. They may stay a dream forever, however, sometimes either voluntarily or involuntarily, a dream might move to the next realm, where you actually start to think about it.

THINK

Maybe I can actually do it? Maybe I can get my golf handicap down, or lose weight or, gain a mature age qualification at university and earn more money with which I can better help my kids?

There is no time limit for thinking. You may think about it forever and say nothing.

TALK

One day, you might choose to sit with the person or persons whose opinion you really value. It could be your wife, husband, mum, dad, brother, sister, a peer, work mate, your boss or a close friend. You then talk about the thing you've been dreaming of and thinking about.

What do you think about us starting our own business?

If I go on a diet, will you stop bringing chocolates into the house?

If I stood for parliament (why would you?) would you support me?

And so on.

Talk, talk, talk.

There's been oodles of times in my life when I've been wide awake at 4 am, lying in bed, staring at the familiar black void of the bedroom ceiling and a moment of clarity hits. "You know Tony, you've been talking about this thing for sooooooooooo long that you are boring yourself, let alone those around you"

At that point, it is definitely time to shut up and stop talking about it. Or what?

Do it!

COMMIT

Commit to that which you have dreamt, thought and talked about. This step is brief for a reason. Are you in or are you out?

ACT

It's an old adage but so true. Just like Mum and Dad taught me, your ideas will not work unless you do. You have to do it for yourself.

At the forefront of my thinking, is the word COMMIT.

Over the years, I've come to understand a heck of a lot about commitment. I know that when you are fully 100% boots and all committed to a course of action in your life, a challenge, a task, or a goal it is amazing what some people around you will do to help you.

100% commitment is extremely powerful.

But how do people know if you are 100% committed?

It doesn't matter what you say, it's how you say it.

It's not what you promise, it's what you do.

It's how you shake a person's hand.

It's the way you look them in the eye, the way you engage, the way you carry yourself.

It is impossible to hide 100% commitment. It oozes from every pore and by osmosis is transferred to others. It is infectious.

Others want to be around someone that is 100% having a go.

Conversely, it is also impossible to hide 90% commitment as it oozes from you as well. People just know if you are only 90% of the way there..

Let's say you want to buy a new television. You've researched the Internet, spoken to your friends, checked out the letterbox brochures, scanned newspaper ads and finally the big day arrives where you think your credit card might actually work. Off you go to the local electrical retail store where you find rows of televisions.

A salesperson swoops and hurriedly says something like, "Hi, I see you looking at the televisions, the one on the end is on special for $1,999, check it out" before rushing off to the whitegoods section, spending 10 fleeting seconds with a lady looking at refrigerators. Next, off to spend another 10 seconds with someone in the computer section before doubling back to you, still in a hurry, "Have you made a decision yet?" before rushing off yet again.

As opposed to:

"Good morning sir, my name is Jarrod and thank you for coming in this morning. May I ask your name?" As I tell him my name, he extends his hand for a nice firm hand shake. He looks me in the eye and says something like, "I see you're looking at televisions Tony. I don't know if you will purchase a television or not here today but what I really would not like is for you to purchase the wrong television for your needs, if indeed you do purchase one."

"Would you mind if I asked you a few questions about your intended use of a new television, your expectations, budget, that sort of thing?" All the while focused on me and me alone. "I want give you the best advice I can so that you don't make a mistake. Would that be okay Tony?"

It's taken just 30 seconds for him to demonstrate his 100% commitment to me. The chance of me purchasing a television has skyrocketed.

It is mindbogglingly unbelievable how often we experience some iteration of the former example and walk out of the store dissatisfied without buying anything or worse still, with the wrong product?

100% Commitment is amazingly powerful.

In June 1997, Lorraine and I sat in in the lounge room of our modest family home. After my dreaming, thinking, and talking about my idea, Lorraine and I committed ourselves 100% to my attempting to sail solo, non-stop and unassisted around the world.

It was now time to act on that commitment.

CHAPTER 6
It's like climbing Mount Everest in Thongs

It was not a race.
It was a personal challenge, simply, to see if I could do it.

Solo, non-stop and unassisted around the world. What do those words mean?

SOLO

Just me.

NON-STOP

Sail out of Newcastle Harbour, go all the way around the world without stopping. Don't stop anywhere. Just sail, sail, sail, sail, sail until one day, if I were lucky enough and good enough, sail back into Newcastle Harbour. How crazy is that little idea?

UNASSISTED

This is the backbone. I could receive no physical assistance whatsoever.

When I crossed the start line, I had to have everything on board to sustain me for however long it took. I thought it would take about 6 months but I factored in a 3 months safety buffer. So, I needed 9 months of food, water, spare parts, tools, spare sails, clothing, navigation equipment etc.

The right physical capabilities (An Olympic athlete I am not) had to be on board. The right mental attitude had to be on board. In so many ways it would be a test of my mind, not my physical ability. The mind can be your greatest asset but at times, unfortunately, it can be your greatest enemy.

At the time that I committed, only 3 Australians had ever achieved the feat. Between my commitment and getting to the start line, 2 more Aussies did it.

1 Jon Sanders
2 Kay Cottee (1st women in the world as well)
3 Dave Dicks
4 Jesse Martin
5 Vinny Lauwers

I read once that approximately 700 people had been into outer space and only about 200 had completed a world trip the likes of which I had set myself. I don't know how accurate the numbers were but to me, 700 V 200 is a pretty bloody crazy ratio.

Renowned Australian sailor, David Adams, compares the feat to climbing Mount Everest in thongs (flip flops). It was an onerous task that I had set myself.

How do you get out of the lounge chair in June 1997 and make it happen?

Breaking the big challenge down into a series of smaller challenges, goal setting, leadership, teamwork, visualisation, self-belief, focus and much more went into the equation.

People asked me: "Why?"

Why did I want to do it?

What did I want out of it?

I actually didn't have a succinct answer, and I used to blather on with a long winded, philosophical reply, like "mountains are put there to climb, oceans are put there to sail across…" Blah blah blah. Keir reckoned that I wouldn't know the answer until I got back, and even then, I might not know.

One day I decided that I needed to try and find an answer.

Why am I doing this?

What is it that I want?

What am I trying to achieve here?

I used the **KISS** method. **K**eep It Simple Stupid and it works extremely well for me (being stupid, that is).

After a lot of thought, I decided that all I wanted for me (I desperately wanted other things for Loraine, Holly and Jordan) was to one day round the end of Nobbys breakwater, at the entrance to Newcastle Harbour, look up the Hunter River and sail my boat to the finish line in concluding the around the world trip.

If I could achieve that, then I'd be a happy man.

Next question: How would I go about finding that breakwater?

Embedded in this huge challenge were a series of smaller challenges. I decided that I needed to clearly identify as many of these smaller challenges as I could and make a list. I realised that, just like in life, from time to time various unexpected challenges would confront me. I had no way of knowing what the "sleeper" challenges would be, but I did know that when they arose, no matter how unpalatable they might be, I had to look them in the eye and embrace them. Just like in life, you cannot sweep things under the carpet as they will more than likely come back to haunt you.

I made a comprehensive list of the tests/challenges/goals which in part included:

THE FINANCIAL CHALLENGE

How to pay for it? I still haven't got a clue!

THE SAFETY CHALLENGE

My adventurous spirit needed to be satisfied, but I wanted to do it as safely as I could. I wanted to get back home and hang out with my kids.

THE EMOTIONAL CHALLENGE

This has always been by far the most gut wrenching challenge of them all, particularly when Holly and Jordan were very young. In June 1997 Holly was 5 years old and Jordan was 3 years old. How could I embrace and accept what I regard by far as the most unpalatable challenge of all? They had no say in what was about to happen to them and their mother, over however many years it took for me to find that breakwater. If indeed, I ever found it. Gut wrenching is a vast understatement.

So, what did I do then?

I wrote a "to do" list which would be the first of many (read as a fucking lot) that I composed over a number of years.

I needed to restructure financially for the life of the project. Most of us do the financial "add ups and subtractions" from time to time.

Hopefully our net worth increases with each check. I joke about it, but it's a fact, that I embarked upon an asset reduction program and it worked magnificently. For a number of years, whenever I did a financial check, our net worth reduced.

We had two residential investment properties that we had borrowed to acquire. We had some equity in each, however servicing the loans over the period of the project was an unrealistic expectation. We took the decision to sell, and the net proceeds were put into the project and a swimming pool.

A swimming pool? Yep, a swimming pool.

When I committed in June '97 I knew it was going to be a long, tough road and that Lorraine and the kids would have a difficult time of it. The very first thing I did was install a swimming pool. My rationale, which turned out to be correct, was that whilst I was off sailing my kids would get a truckload of fun from a pool. In November 1997, it was swum in for the first time. The kids and their friends had wonderful times in it over many years and it was worth every cent. Some weekends Lorraine would churn through a couple of loaves of bread making sandwiches for all the local kids that turned up to join in the fun. We loved it, and so did the all the kids.

1998 rolled around with the consolidation process continuing, including the sale of our beloved yacht, Seaforth. It was now time to find a suitable boat for the world attempt. The search was on in earnest as I had set departure for September or October 1999. My budget purchase price was capped at $120,000, which was a reasonable amount of money back then, but I had trouble finding the "right" boat.

Originally, I discounted a Cole 43 like Polaris.

Structurally, a Cole 43 is an absolute battleship, but I thought I wouldn't be able to modify the deck layout properly to set one up for efficient solo work. Despite looking long and hard at other designs, I could not find a suitable boat. I revisited the Cole 43 option and eventually worked out that I actually could rejig the layout to suit, plus a Cole would most likely fit within my budget.

"Rangatira" (a Māori chief of either gender) was launched in 1984 and was one of the latter, of approx. thirty Cole 43s to hit the water. I had been aware of her for a few years. Also, we had raced against her in the 50th Hobart and I had been impressed. She was for sale in Melbourne, with a price tag of $120,000. On Friday, 15th May 1998, after working all week for Flano I left Newcastle late that afternoon and drove to Melbourne to check her out. Would this be the one?

At 7 am Saturday, I arrived at St Kilda Pier where Rangatira was berthed in a small marina shrouded by an eerie blanket of white fog. I nervously trod the length of the pier until she finally emerged from her white cocoon, nestled quietly in a corner. It was like she was sitting there, waiting for me. Standing on the dock gazing down at her, I had no inkling whatsoever as to how much this boat would come to mean to me, and others, in coming years.

I went over her with a fine-tooth comb assessing her viability for the task.

Taped Diary:
Sunday 17th May 1998
1.40 pm

I am on the freeway heading home from Melbourne. I have just come from Kevin Williams and am overly excited to record that I have agreed to buy the boat for $109,000 and have given him a $5,000 deposit.

It is coming out of the water this week for a final inspection by me next weekend.

I am excited. What does it all mean? It's very interesting emotionally. I haven't rung Lorraine yet but she will be pretty excited. It's good value for money I believe. It's a really good boat and will do the job admirably.

I actually feel a bit lost for words.

Taped Diary:
Friday 22nd May 1998.

Kevin rang to let me know the boat is out of the water ready to inspect.

Here I go again, full of anticipation, off to Melbourne. I'm not looking forward to another 21 hrs of driving but am happy to do it as it's another piece of the jigsaw. If all is okay we'll sign a contract.

After that the next step will be to sail her home which most likely will happen around the June long weekend.

In my canoe, Belmont Baths 1959.

Prophetic words from Mum.

Dad and I in 1974.

Mum and I in 1975.

Bob Snape. The old man and the sea.

Preparing for 1974 Sydney to Hobart, aged 19 yrs. I had hair once!

Running a marathon is about pain. The hair is on the way out!

Crew of *OzFire*, 1991 Sydney to Hobart, me back right. A further receding hairline!

Morrie Morgan and I. Around Australia, 1994.

Holly, Jordan, Lorraine and I. Around Australia, 1994.

The pool with their friends, Jordan on chair (left), Holly 2nd on right at front.

One of our favourite photos on yacht, "Seaforth".

"Rangatira" (Solo Globe Challenger) in Melbourne. She was waiting for me.

17 metre mast on 6 ft x 4 ft box trailer hitched to Flano's car.

CHAPTER 7

The Bass Strait Eight locked and loaded

Dream
Think
Talk
Commit
Act

It was time for full on ACTION - on so many fronts.
After purchasing Rangatira, the sail from Melbourne to home had not revealed any unforeseen problems. However, I did have a huge list of modifications that were needed to convert her, a boat designed to be operated by a crew of 8, to a vessel suitable for solo sailing.

We needed a succinct project name and *"Solo Globe Challenge 2000"* was decided upon, pretty much saying it all. No one knew what Rangatira meant and whilst some would say that to change the name of a boat is bad luck, and subsequent events may have proved them correct, I chose to rechristen her *"Solo Globe Challenger"* (*Solo Globe*) which also, in my opinion, pretty much said it all.

One of our first major tasks was to crane the 18 metre long aluminium mast out of the boat and transport it home. We did this with the mid-section of the mast lashed atop a 2m × 1.5m box trailer and one end lashed to the tow ball of Flano's car. It was heart in mouth stuff, but bloody hilarious when I look back on it. With great difficulty and a lot of swearing, 12 of us finally got it to home, down the driveway and set up on supports in the carport with a long length of mast sticking out either end.

I ploughed all of my available cash of around $15,000 into the boat over the later part of 1998 and a large chunk of that went on the mast. We poured what was most likely hundreds (but seemed like thousands) of man hours into stripping the mast back to bare aluminium, checking every fitting for wear and tear, cracking, or fatigue, and making good as necessary. We replaced all of the stainless steel rigging, rope halyards, and electrics. No stone was left unturned.

I was getting up close and personal with my mast (that sounds a bit weird I will admit) but I wanted to know it intimately as I felt that intimacy would stand me in good stead. Standing on a pitching deck, looking aloft, I would know exactly what was up there and I'd have a mental picture of what it might or might not withstand.

David "Dave" Marshall is a champion bloke. 10 years younger than me, he has always had a fresh faced, youthful appearance that belies his age. At times, he has been known by those of us close to him as "The baby faced assassin". I first met and sailed with Dave in the mid 90's on some long ocean races, and connected with him quickly as Dave also spent time under the tutelage of Jack Morgan. I was struck by Dave's sailing skills, his enthusiasm and down to earth approach. He is an all-round fantastic guy.

Dave became the youngest member of the Bass Strait Eight.

David "Cookie" Cook is one of the funniest guys I know and always has a great joke to crack. Cookie is about three years younger than I and has been a part of the fabric of Belmont and its sailing community for as long as I can remember. I had not sailed with Cookie previously, however I was well aware of his sailing prowess plus he is a fun loving, easy to get along with character. Every boat should have a Cookie on board.

Cookie, along with Cyril, Keith, Keir, Dave and myself, made up six of the Bass Strait Eight.

Taped diary:
Have I been a busy boy or what?

I have worked some very, very long hours on the mast with a lot of help from Dave, Biggles, Snapey and many others. I don't like asking too much for help but if I don't, it will take forever. I can't believe the hours I, we, have put into it. It's bullshit.

I work all day for Flano, come home and start again in the carport on the mast. Christ, the mosquitoes are phenomenal after sunset. Evenings are very humid but I have to wear tracksuit pants and long sleeves to try and keep them at bay. I swat the bastards all evening, finding them full to the gills with my blood.

With effort comes reward and after all the graft and toil the refurb was complete. The mast was a thing of beauty.

As work on the mast and other elements of the project continued at pace, on top of that I sadly had a proper grown up's job to go to during the day. When Lorraine and I had committed 100% to me having a crack the very first person I told was Flano.

Flano was, and is to this day, a bloody great mate but back then he was also my employer and I had responsibilities to fulfil if I wanted to pick up my pay packet at the end of each week. Responsibilities, like actually going there five days a week. It's amazing how a proper, grown up's job can really get in the way of your passion, however that's not unique to me, is it?

I was really worried that Flano, being a sailor and having a better understanding than most as to what I was getting myself into, may, quite rightly have wished to sever my employment. It was a genuine option for him and one I thought likely. I nervously outlined my plans and instead of being apprehensive, he immediately dived into the deep end. "I'm 100% in. What can I do to help?" was his attitude.

I was so relieved. Craig Flanagan has a heart the size of Phar Lap and the spirit of a lion. He is one of my favourite people and I am forever in debt to him for his support and understanding. Flano's support over the years was massive.

Overall, my financial situation was definitely NOT a beautiful thing.

Taped diary:
15th July 1998

I am as broke as buggery. How broke? I have 80 cents in my pocket, nothing in my cheque account, I owe $1000 on Bankcard. Lorraine asked me for $20 this morning so she could buy some sausages for dinner and I didn't have it. That is how broke we are. That will change but right now I don't have any cash. I don't want anyone to feel sorry for me. This is the situation that I have put us in and I fully expected it to be like this from time to time. Like I've said many times. If it was easy, everyone would do it.

Lorraine is remarkably patient and I don't give her enough credit. Wandering around all day with no money in her purse is not what the average wife should have to do. I have to make sure that she is rewarded for her patience with me and that she understands how much I appreciate her.

If I write a book one day she will hopefully realise how much I value her trust in me.

It's school holidays and Lorraine was very sick in the first week and couldn't do much with the kids. I would like to have had some time off but that was not possible. I currently have two weeks holidays owing and if I don't have any time off before Christmas, we can have a good time together then. The weather has been bloody cold. I get home from work, light the fire, spend a short time with Lorraine and the kids, wolf my dinner down and head to the garage and carport to sand, file and bang away, getting covered in itchy dust. Around 9.30 pm it's shower time, then a brief bit of TV then collapse into bed exhausted.

The next day I do it all again.

Around August 1998, my so-called mates asked if I would be interested in entering Solo Globe in the 1998 Sydney to Hobart yacht race. My immediate reaction was an emphatic no.

My rationale was thus: Firstly, I was far too busy to take time out to compete in a race that I had previously sailed in 13 times. It no longer held its original allure. Secondly, I seriously needed to focus on the around the world attempt with departure only a year or so away. Thirdly, there was no way I could afford it.

Those so-called mates had another chat amongst themselves and came back a couple of weeks later offering to help with the entry fee and other costs if I would like to reconsider. When they first raised the subject, the seed had been subconsciously planted in my mind.

The human mind can rationalise anything if it tries hard enough.

Now, with some of the costs covered, my rationale changed a bit (read: a lot) and switched to: Firstly, it would be a great opportunity to test out the mast refurbishment and new systems. Secondly, at conclusion I would have a more concise job list to attend to prior to departure 10 months hence. Thirdly, "All work and no play makes Tony a dull boy." (I actually said that).

I thought to myself, "I don't want to be in a rocking chair saying if only. Let's do it!" On that day, in October 1998, the decision was made to race south. It was the first piece of an amazing real-life jigsaw that continues to unfold to this day.

One day, prior to the 1994 Sydney to Hobart, I had seen a "crew available" message on the noticeboard at the Lake Macquarie Yacht Club. At that time, I wasn't able to fit Tony "Biggles" Purkiss into our crew, but I liked his style and made sure I made room for him later. I have described Tony (tongue in cheek) as physically imposing at about 6 ft 6inches tall, 3 pick handles across the shoulders, and when he has had a drink I'm bloody glad he's on my side.

Some older readers may remember the adventures of Biggles, a fictional daredevil pilot and adventurer in novels written from the 1920's onwards. Books about Biggles and his adventures were eagerly read by young boys of that era. When Tony started to sail with us, having two Tony's was a problem, so in the inimitable style of sailors it was decided that I would answer to Tony but Tony Purkiss would become "Biggles" because he actually had a pilot's licence. The catch cry amongst us became (and still is) "Biggles air, if you dare!"

Biggles became the 7th member of the Bass Strait Height.

Earlier on I wrote about Snapey and the astonishing influence he had on my life since I first sat at his dining table. When asked to pen some words about me as I celebrated my 60th birthday, in part, this is what he wrote.

How long have you known Tony?

Answer: Almost 50 years

How has he influenced/ruined/made a difference in your life?

Answer: I consider him my eldest son.

What three words do you think he would use to describe himself?

Answer: Handsome, Debonair, Irresistible.

Snapey was 66 years old and became the elder statesman of a rough and unruly mob. He chafed at the bit and was excited to be going to Hobart as he hadn't been for a couple of years. I was looking forward to having a good sail with him and a quiet drink together once we got there. We had covered a lot of miles together, both on water and (metaphorically speaking) on land. It was going to be special to join forces with him again.

Snapey became the final member of the Bass Strait Eight, which was now locked and loaded.

Glen "Cyril" Picasso, 41 years
Keith Molloy, 46 years
Keir Enderby, 45 years
Tony "Biggles", Purkiss 38 years
David "Dave" Marshall, 33 years
David "Cookie" Cook, 40 years
Bob "Snapey" Snape, 66 years
Me, 43 years

The experience of the above bunch of ratbags was varied. Snapey was lining up for his 23rd race whilst I could put my name to 13. Cyril could lay claim to 3 and Biggles knew his way there with 5 under his belt. Keir and Keith had done the '94 race with me. Dave and Cookie while both very experienced, had never been anywhere near Bass Strait.

I considered the crew to be like any well-balanced footy team. A blend of youth, maturity and experience.

We became an official entrant in what was to become the horrific and ultimately fatal 1998 Sydney to Hobart yacht race, and our gang would henceforth be referred to by me, as "The Bass Strait Eight". At the outset, our goals were to enjoy the race and have fun, while assessing the worth of the work already done and compile a concise job list to be attended to for the around the world attempt.

Taped diary:

I went to Simple Slimmers a couple of months ago, lost some weight and started feeling good about myself. Then I stopped going and put the weight back on again. My pants and shirts are tight again and I am disgusted with myself. It has been a rollercoaster ride all of my life with my weight. I love eating the wrong things and too much of them, particularly sweet things. I love drinking beer too.

I might try Hypnosis [I never did]

I am such a strong willed person and it pisses me off that I am so strong but on the other hand I am so weak and can't control my eating.

I had decided to start the world trip in October 1999 and when September 1998 arrived I started to mildly panic, realising that

I had just 13 months left and so much still to do. It was a tad overwhelming at times.

The World Speed Record Sailing Association in England advised that they had received my request for clarification of the course that I needed to sail. They also advised that at that point approximately only 80 people had ever completed the task which I found extraordinary.

In October, Lorraine, Holly, Jordan and I took Solo Globe away for a few days. We sailed 30 nm on the open ocean to Port Stephens on a Saturday, returning on Monday. On the sail back, we had a following breeze that was pretty fresh. I didn't have a self-steering system fitted and I darted around madly correcting course and the trimming sails until I got her humming. Once I had her on track at speed, I had a massive adrenalin rush and exclaimed a huge "YES!", punching the air at the same time. We had a great time together and the kids loved it. Jordan was jumping around helping me, chattering away like his old man. I was then, and still, am, so very chest burstingly proud of them.

On the 9th October 1998, we officially launched the project, *Solo Globe Challenge 2000*, in front of 200 attendees.

Throughout 1998 I felt strongly that our financial position would improve but that it may take a while to get traction. The lack of money was stressful, and I am sure I'll never fully appreciate the difficult position that I placed Lorraine in. She put up with it but every now and again we would have a terse (read: very terse) "conversation".

When you distilled it all down, we had a comfortable suburban home with a swimming pool in the backyard, two beautiful healthy kids, a boat to go sailing on, and were all getting three feeds a day (albeit sausages most of the time) so we weren't doing too badly.

When I go back through my transcribed taped diaries from the latter 6 months of 1998, I am agog and completely taken aback. Only now do I realise how much of my time and energy I dedicated to trying to work out how to pay for the project. I spent an inordinate amount of time talking to potential sponsors or putting my case forward to equipment suppliers in the hunt for goods or services. I reckon 60% of my taping is dedicated to the almost unsolvable financial riddle of how to pay for it.

In 1993/94 I'd had a pretty easy entrée into the world of sponsorship via Endeavour Credit Union. When they came on board for the around Australia sail I thought it was easy. What are those other people whingeing about that are unsuccessfully looking for sponsorship? I had thought I had the magic touch, the knack and secret to unlocking sponsorship funds.

What a lot of bullshit that thinking turned out to be.

Apart from the emotional challenge, the question of sponsorship, and the financial challenge associated with the around the world project, was by far the most gut wrenching and soul-destroying exercise that I've ever put myself through.

Christmas Day 1998 rolled around as it inevitably does every year, and I was determined to take some time off, albeit just a micro break from the grind. Relaxing around the pool, as a family, I had time to reflect.

Originally, when we decided to enter the '98 Hobart, my idea was to simply front up at the start line having fulfilled the basic requirements. However, the pressure of passing safety inspections, getting the boat into some sort of race mode, getting it to Sydney etc. had added substantially to the overall workload, and I needed a second wind.

Work, work, work, and more bloody work. The harder I went, the more work there was to do. In the week prior to Christmas, I worked until midnight one night, 10 pm the next and on the third walked in the door at 11 pm. It went on and on, as if there would never be an end to it.

As I sat by the pool, for a variety of reasons, none of them significant, our financial position had improved a little. We were pretty well debt free apart from the loan to buy the boat. I didn't have a lot of ready cash in the proverbial tin, however we would be able to regroup and move to the next phase after getting back from Hobart in January.

Taped diary:
Christmas day

We took the boat to Sydney last Sunday in readiness for the race. We are berthed close to some of the big guns. Sayonara, Brindabella, Wild Thing which are pretty impressive weapons, each crewed by 20 or more.

Lorraine's mum Noelene (Nanny), and other family have arrived for Christmas lunch. The kids were up early this morning to open their presents. I am sitting by the pool and it's a beautiful day. About to go for a swim and might have a couple of beers but I won't get too carried away.

We are going to spend the evening with Mum, Marina, Tom (her husband) *and nephew, Callan and niece, Mikala. The older I get the more I appreciate my family, my origins and roots.*

The forecast for the race is not all that encouraging but of course, it is still a little way off. Looks like we are going to get the inevitable front come through in the early afternoon or evening on Boxing Day. Then another front as we enter Bass Strait. The standard arrangement so often is that you get a front on the 1st night, then it settles for a while before getting your arse smacked at least once more and maybe twice more before the finish. I reckon it will take us about 3.5 to 4 days to complete the course.

Hopefully it will be okay?

CHAPTER 8
At 4.03 pm it happened

115 yachts crossed the start line of the 1998 Sydney to Hobart yacht race on Saturday 26th December, Boxing Day, the day that so many Australians and others around the world tune in to watch the start of "The Hobart", whether they are sailors or not.

Our story is just one of many.

There was a huge domino effect that lead to the catastrophic events that took place and if one were to remove one of the key elements then the outcome would have been so very different.

When Biggles, Bob, Cyril, Cookie, Dave, Keir, Keith and I crossed the start line, not for a millisecond did any of us understand or appreciate that in just a little over 24 hours, we would all have to reach further within ourselves than we had ever had cause to reach before. In my case, I can place my hand over my heart and assure you that I went to the very core of my soul.

I found out what the hell makes Tony Mowbray tick.

When I revisited the experience, trying to make sense of it all, I realised that the 8 of us had participated in a prime example of the ultimate team challenge. Very simply, in so far as the result was concerned, or the outcome that we were seeking or whatever jargon you want to use it was really simple.

To win was to live.

To lose was to die.

As far as I'm concerned, the stakes don't get any higher.

Start day was a beautiful, warm, glorious summers day complete with a powderpuff blue sky and a gentle sea breeze. The type of summers day that many Australians know and love. We got a reasonable start, made our way to the harbour entrance, turned right and headed toward open ocean before turning the bow south to Hobart, 630 nm (1165km) away.

The first domino then came into play.

There is a south flowing current of warm water that originates at the Equator and when it reaches southern Queensland it kisses and brushes the coast as it streams south, generally paralleling the coast of NSW and SE Victoria before entering southern waters and dissipating. This current (we sailors call it "set") is officially called the East Australian Current and runs at varying speed at different times of the year. The temperature of the ocean is directly related to the speed at which the set is running. If the ocean temperature off the coast of NSW or Victoria is warm to hot, it means that the current is flowing quickly, not having time to cool. If the temperature is lower, it generally means that the current is slower, having cooled since departing its equatorial origins.

If a boat is moving at 6 knots and has 2 knots of favourable set from behind, then the boat is actually achieving 8 knots toward its goal. Conversely, if a boat is moving at 6 knots and has 2 knots of unfavourable set from ahead then the boat is only achieving 4 knots toward its goal so it's easy to see why in the world of yacht racing, set can play a pivotal role.

The water temperature off the coast of NSW in December is usually around 22-24 degrees Celsius with the set running at anywhere from bugger all to around 1.5 knots. What we didn't know prior to the start was that the water temperature was almost bathwater hot at 27 degrees Celsius and the set was hurtling south at an almost unheard of 4 knots.

The fleet were collectively catapulted toward Bass Strait, as if fired from a slingshot.

To understand the impact that this so called, "favourable" (it hurt much more then it helped in the end) set had, it is remarkable to note that the entire fleet were ahead of the race record 7 hours after the start. 14 hours after the start, the entire fleet were still ahead of the race record. That was absolutely unheard of.

Incredibly, 25 hours after the start, 75% of the fleet were ahead of the race record. That was completely and utterly unheard of.

The set had picked up the entire fleet as one, and marched it south at never before seen collective speeds. It was a phenomenon.

When ocean racing overnight or longer the crew are divided into "watches". We ran two watches with one headed by Cyril as watch leader and principal helmsperson along with Keir as co-helmsperson plus Keith and Biggles (someone had to put up with those two). The other watch was led by me, with Dave as co-helmsperson plus Cookie. Snapey, the 4th member of our watch, would spend a fair bit of time below deck navigating, carrying out radio ops, gathering weather forecasts and generally keeping things ticking over.

The 1st afternoon saw a strengthening, following ENE to NE breeze that allowed boats to carry their multi coloured spinnakers in a "hands 'n heels" bolt down the coast. We didn't start the watch system that afternoon, as adrenaline had our competitive juices flowing and we wanted to try and cement a good position with a full team effort early on. As afternoon gave way to early evening, the wind increased and we ripped the arse clean out of one of our spinnakers, but we had the bit between our teeth and after hoisting another, kept pushing reasonably hard.

Prior to the start, the weather forecast had been for a SW 50 knot (90km/h) breeze to hammer us in the very early part of Sunday morning. I was not uncomfortable with a forecast of 50 knots. Having covered truckloads of sea miles including crossing Bass Strait around 30 times I was not phased. 50 knots is reasonably standard issue for that part of the world.

Under us, we had a time proven sturdy yacht. We had just completed a massive rebuild of the mast and had some new sails in the wardrobe. With all the work we had put in I felt that we were in good shape and would be okay.

How wrong I would be.

Once the new weather system rolled in and built to the forecast strength, my strategy was to take the foot off the throttle, snug her down and not do anything too flash. As darkness settled and midnight came and went, the wind progressively swung around the compass. What had been NE all afternoon swung progressively to NNE, N, NNW, NW and WNW. This "clocking" of the wind was a sure sign of the imminent arrival of the new weather system.

All the while we, and the rest of the fleet were hurtling south, compliments of the strong following wind and the unbelievably fast flowing set.

The approach of the new weather system was accompanied by rain squalls and the night sky was brilliantly illuminated by blinding, and at times, very close at hand, lightning bolts discharging their deadly voltage into the ocean all around, in a truly memorable and powerful display by mother nature.

In the pre-dawn, the wind settled for a while from the WSW and increased in strength progressively. The sun rose, and the breeze inched its way around to the SW and settled in for the long haul. It was blowing 40 - 50 knots (70 - 90km/h) at this time.

We progressively reduced sail in concert with the deteriorating conditions and by 9 am we were down to just the micro-sized Storm Jib but as the morning wore on the conditions continued to deteriorate further.

On reflection, I realised that the deterioration happened incrementally, and you could almost set your watch by it. Every hour or so, the wind would ratchet up to the next level of intensity and the associated confused seas would go to the next level. Conditions would plateau for a while, and then an hour or so later it would intensify further, escalating to a new level, clawing its way up to the next rung of the ladder.

The morning wore on. We had now entered Bass Strait.

Claw, claw, claw.

Ratchet, ratchet, ratchet.

By midday the conditions had deteriorated further. The wind had risen to 60 knots and the seas were starting to get concerning, but we were not overawed or overly concerned.

The second domino now comes into play.

The island state of Tasmania used to be a part of the mainland of Australia, however, eons ago when some big geological meltdown occurred, Tasmania was created and the body of water that ended up separating the two chunks of land is now Bass Strait. The strait is relatively shallow compared to the surrounding ocean.

On the 27th December, the East Australian Current was a deep angry torrent of water belting south at breakneck speed and had to physically heave itself up and over relatively shallow Bass Strait. The result was similar to a giant washing machine on full blown agitate.

Now for the third domino.

It is not commonly understood that the opposing forces of wind against current generates disproportionately higher and confused wave patterns, as opposed to those generated by wind only. When the waves generated by 60 knots of wind clashed headlong with 4 knots of set moving in the near opposite direction – set that additionally, was very busy trying to heave itself up over the shallower waters of the Strait – a massive collision of nature took place. The mass of rapidly flowing water exploded like a bomb had gone off, driving it upwards, multiplying the height of the waves and distorting their shape so that they became vertical cliff faces with the tops tripping over themselves, leading to cresting, dangerously breaking sections.

At midday, we still had the storm jib up, but the situation had deteriorated further and while still racing we had certainly backed way off, primarily concerned about working our way through the conditions waiting for an abatement.

Abatement would not come until it was too late.

At midday, two factors were combining to make life complicated. As the boat rose to the top of some waves, the powerful momentum of the wave as it passed through would try to fling the boat down onto her side. In addition, as we crested each wave, we were exposed to the full ferocity of the wind which lent us over as well. The cumulative effect of these factors saw us, at times, being flung so far over that the top of the mast was nearly in the water.

It was not a good look. Something had to change.

As skipper and leader of the team, I had to make a decision.

I'm an absolute believer that whether you are a leader in business, your family, on the sporting field, or leading a team competing in and trying to survive the 1998 Sydney to Hobart yacht race, the rules and principles are the same. No one respects a leader that won't make a decision. A leader that sits on their hands procrastinating, scared to choose, is not a leader and others will recognise that quickly.

My advice? Just make a decision. If it proves to be wrong, then change it around a bit until you get the right solution BUT you need to make a choice, and get on with it.

At midday, after consultation with some of the senior members of the crew, I took the ultimate decision to lower the Storm Jib as even with this tiny sail up, we were overpowered. With the "SJ" down we proceeded under "Bare Poles". Just the bare mast and rigging exposed to the wind and the elements. "Bare Poles" doesn't sound, pretty does it?

Let me wholeheartedly assure you that being under Bare Poles in Bass Strait is definitely not pretty. In this scenario, there is nowhere to run and hide.

I mean absolutely nowhere.

Our collective destiny was in the palm of our hands. As a leader, if I were to make a wrong call it could have meant death, for one or more or all.

Snapey, Cookie, Dave and I were on watch from 10 am until 2 pm. As I steered the boat, I was particularly interested in two things:

1) How was she performing in the new mode i.e. no sails, and was that the safest option?
2) How might the still deteriorating weather, impact us.

Through to 2 pm I was able to reasonably safely guide Solo Globe up, over, through and around the waves at an angle of approx. 60 degrees to the oncoming waves. We were still, as mystifying as it might sound, making some speed forward, albeit not directly where we want to go but not too far off course.

I was very wary, but not acutely concerned for our welfare. As the clock ticked toward 2 pm, the wind was a steady and ferocious 60 knots and the sea state was getting "very average".

For those of you that have ever swum in the surf at a beach or watched waves break in the shallow water close to the shore you may know that waves will quite often break on the shoreline in "sets". Each set might consist of 3, 4 or 5 or more waves, some of which may be bigger than others in the set. Each set is separated by smaller than average waves.

From Midday to 2 pm, I managed to discern that amidst the seemingly disorganised chaos and mountainous waves bearing down on us, that there was actually some sort of structure.

I realised that at times the waves were coming through in sets of four and the third one in the set was what I call "the kicker". "The kicker" was significantly bigger than the other three and it was the one that we needed to be super careful of. It was the one that had a bigger chance of taking us out.

At 2 pm Keith, Keir and Biggles came on deck with their trusty watch leader, Cyril. Before handing the helm to Cyril, I had him stand by me for 10 minutes to observe the waves' characteristics, plus I gave him the heads up on the boat, the way it was handling, and the best course to steer. After passing the helm to him I stood by him for a while longer to make 100% sure that he had it sorted, which he did. Good man, that Cyril.

At 2:05 pm a pre-planned compulsory radio schedule (Sked) began. At designated times throughout the race, all boats were required to report their position. Skeds are fairly staid, conservative affairs and communications are succinct. Since first venturing on the ocean around 30 years prior, I had listened to and participated in a lot of skeds.

As I felt comfortable that Cyril and the guys had it under control, I went below decks at around 2.30 pm to listen in on the back end of the Sked.

Snapey, the radio operator was seated at the navigation station near the radios. I wormed my way into my bunk, immediately behind him, and lay there, eyes closed listening to the various communiqués.

It was through that Sked that afternoon that what eventually became the tragedy, the trauma, the chaos and ultimately the death that pervaded the 1998 Sydney to Hobart yacht race began to leak out to the outside world. It appeared on television screens around the world, the front page of newspapers globally, and it began to etch its place in Australia's history.

As I lay there, I could hear the fear in people's voices. It was tangible.

I felt that I could almost reach out and touch the fear as it resonated out of the speaker of the radio. As long as I live, I NEVER want to hear fear like that again in a human voice.

During the Sked, I decided to cease racing and focus entirely on getting safely through the storm that was obviously starting to impact many of the fleet badly, including "Winston Churchill", who were in lot of trouble.

Around 3:30 pm I stuck my head up to check how the on-watch mob were travelling. In the hour or so that I had been below, conditions had rapidly deteriorated. Cyril, Keith, Keir and Biggles told me that they were amazed at how quickly things were going downhill but they were still quietly confident to keep us all safe. In the 60-minute window that I was below, the wind had increased exponentially in raw power every 15 minutes by about 5 knots on each occasion.

Our situation had gone from "not so good" to "are you fucking kidding me?"

The wind had now clawed its way up to a shrieking 75 - 80 knots (140 – 150 km/h). The waves had increased significantly in that short space of time to around 60 ft (18 metres). Conditions were now close to horrific.

Cyril and the guys all echoed my sentiments regarding forgetting the race, agreeing that we needed to focus entirely on getting through it in one piece. Confident that Cyril and the boys had it under control as best could be, I went back to my bunk to continue to monitor the desperate radio communications that were becoming more common.

On Sunday afternoon 27th December 1998 at 4.03 pm a wave came along that changed my life forever.

I do not wish to be melodramatic, however, I can assure you that this wave kicked off a process of change in me that continues to this day and I believe will continue until I draw my last breath on this planet. If you drop a small pebble onto the silky smooth surface of a pond, it creates a reaction. It will create small concentric wavelets which if left unimpeded by land will radiate and radiate forever outwards.

In my mind (as crazy as it is) this wave was a pebble dropped into my pond of life, and I am perched upon one of those small wavelets being taken for a journey.

I don't know where I'm going.

I don't know if I'll ever get anywhere.

I know that I need to go.

It's not a problem.

I'm hanging on.

It has been one heck of a ride thus far.

Cyril, Keir, Biggles and Keith were on deck. Snapey, Cookie, Dave and I were below.

At 4:03 pm it happened.

CHAPTER 9
20 seconds can be an eternity

For a hairs breadth of a second, Solo Globe reeled and lurched to her starboard (right) side as she was sucked into the vortex. She was then smashed broadside by a vertical wall of water with an impact similar to what I imagine it might be like to be taken out by a runaway locomotive.

We were then driven over viciously on to our port (left) side. At 90 degrees, the mast entered the water and as we were thrust obscenely to an almost completely upside down position the mast snapped.

The noise of the breaking mast reverberated through the boat like a blast from a cannon.

Kaboom!

Solo Globe was inverted to an angle of about 150 deg and we were then surfed and smashed down the face of a 60 ft wave, in that upside down position, for what we later estimated to be 20 seconds.

20 seconds can be an eternity.

One half of my brain was scrambling to make sense of my now upside down world, where what used to be the floor is now the ceiling. The other half of my brain was saying "FUCK! You are in a lot of trouble."

A lot of serious "stuff" happened in that 20 seconds.

Directly above my bunk, in which I was laying, a 6mm thick piece of clear Perspex, 1 metre × 400mm had been fibreglassed in at construction to create waterproof skylight. Unfortunately, and unknowingly over the years, Ultra Violet rays had degraded the Perspex, as I was to find out, regrettably. When catapulted over and driven downwards the raw power of the water pressure on the skylight caused it to implode. It shattered, allowing what seemed like, and probably was, tons of water to flood into the boat.

My 100 kg body was flung around like a rag doll as a wall of water wholly picked me up and blew me out of my cocoon. I cannoned into Snapey in a jumble of arms and legs as we both grappled desperately searching for hand holds. The avalanche of water exploded in the navigation area, wiping out all communications and electrical equipment in one fell swoop. All radios, mobile phones, satellite navigation system, laptop, satellite email system etc. were completely obliterated.

After what seemed like an eternity she finally slid off the back end of the wave and we flipped the right way up.

Much later Cyril told us what happened.

The second wave in a set of four was very steep, and as the boat climbed the face of it, she struggled to get over the apex and was sat back on her haunches. As a result, the boat's speed was washed off and without speed he lost steerage. Simultaneously, the second wave slewed us around so that we were side on to the next one. With no meaningful speed, Cyril could not steer the boat back to the favoured 60 deg course.

We were now a sitting duck. The next wave was the "kicker", much bigger than the others, and it took us out broadside.

Once the boat righted itself, I struggled through knee deep water in the cabin to the sliding hatch and threw it open. In the cockpit, I was greeted by what looked like a war zone. I guess from that point on it was a war?

Biggles was dazed, his face streaming blood from a head wound that later required 18 stitches. We didn't know it at the time but he had also broken his left leg just below the kneecap.

Keith had smashed his lower back and was in agony.

Keir had been knocked unconscious and was laying half in and half out of the boat with his legs straddling the taught stainless steel wire of the life lines. The broken mast was laying in the water beside the boat and had pinned his legs so that as the boat and mast heaved up and down, the weight of the mast threatened to snap his legs at the knees, like two carrots. He regained consciousness and starting screaming frantically, "Get it off me, get it off me, get it off me". Later, we discovered that Keir had also fractured ribs.

A safety harness is a must have piece of equipment for anyone that goes to sea, regardless of whether they be there to race or cruise. The rules of the race dictated that each sailor had to have a harness, but regardless of the rules you would be an idiot to venture out there without one. Often constructed from seat belt webbing type material, a harness fits around the upper torso and over the shoulders, clipping together below the sternum where a stainless steel ring is incorporated.

A tether is usually a 1.8 m long piece of webbing with a heavy duty stainless steel clip attached at each end. A well found boat will have strategically located stainless steel U bolts bolted in various locations to create "strong points". One end of a tether is attached to a strong point and the other end is attached to the harness keeping the boat and the sailor attached (hopefully) to each other at all times, similar to an umbilical cord.

All four guys had their harnesses on and were attached to strong points when we were knocked down.

Thank fuck.

Due to the volume of water that flooded into the boat through the imploded skylight and other openings, we had a massive gutful of water down below. The aft end of the boat was dangerously low in the water with the deck virtually flush with the ocean. Standing at the hatch looking aft, taking stock of the situation, my gaze locked onto Cyril who was in the ocean at the stern, dazed, with blood flowing from a head wound plus a broken wrist.

Later Cyril shared what happened.

When the boat rolled, he had been flung over the back into the ocean. As the boat thundered down the wave upside down he was dragged along, completely submerged by his harness and tether like a fishing lure. The pressure of his harness compressed his rib cage, snapping a number of ribs. He knew that if his harness or tether broke he would probably be a dead man as the chance of getting back to the boat would be bugger all.

As he was dragged relentlessly underwater he repeated over and over, in his mind.

"Don't break, don't break, don't break, please don't break."

Then, the load went off the tether and he thought that one of two things had happened. Either the tether or harness had given way and he was a goner, or, maybe, the boat had slid off the back of the wave and stopped. He was still under water and raised his arm, feeling and grabbing hold of the boat as if his life depended on it.

It actually did.

At the time my gaze locked onto Cyril's, it was probably only 30 seconds since the boat had righted itself. I shouted, "Cyril, for Christ's sake stop fucking around and get on back on board will ya?"

The boat was so low in the water at the aft end that he simply floated back on.

We were in a lot of trouble. If one more monstrous bastard broke on us at that point, we would have gone straight to the bottom. Another distinct possibility was that the broken, jagged mast would spear a hole in the hull and it would be "goodnight, she wrote."

My mind snapped into gear, immediately prioritising what we needed to do. I could have sat in the cockpit, consoling the injured guys, but they would have to wait as there were bigger fish to fry. We needed to stabilise the situation immediately.

It was time for action.

Keith had managed to get mobile and so he, Cookie, Dave and Biggles (with a bloody broken leg) and me crawled along the deck progressively releasing various attachments that connected the mast, boom, rigging, ropes and sails to the boat.

As I crawled along the deck, I thought, "Fuck! We are in a lot of trouble."

An indelible recollection is of Keith (not as experienced as some) crawling beside me screaming in my ear: "Tell me what to do, tell me what to do! Tony, tell me what to do!" The urgency and desperation in his voice is as clear all these years later, as it was in that moment.

We scrambled around the deck, harnessed on, hanging on for grim life, progressively disconnecting each attachment. I remember like it was an hour ago, when all that remained was a 10 mm thick piece of blue rope to be cut, to free us of the crumpled, twisted mess that used to be a statuesque thing of beauty. Kneeling with knife in hand I cut it and as I was doing that my eyes locked with Keir's and we both gave an almost imperceptible shake of our heads.

When the last thread of the rope gave way, I watched briefly as the tangled mess that I had spent $15,000 on over the preceding months and that I and others had poured countless hours into, sank to the bottom of Bass Strait, where it sits to this day.

We had been sailing in company with the yacht, "Pippin", who was a little ahead. They saw what happened and eventually managed to turn around and head back to see if they could help. Whilst in the midst of detaching the mast they came within 50 metres or so. By now, conditions were way off the dial. As I pondered whether or not Pippin might be able to assist us, she herself took a wave that very nearly turned her upside down and went close to dumping her crew into the ocean.

I raised both arms in the air, palms outstretched and upwards in a resigned manner, to indicate, what the hell can you or anyone do to help us? My next lot of arm signals said, "Get out of here, go save yourself, you need to look after yourselves, go now". It would have been suicidal for them to do anything but focus on their welfare.

A month or so later, Keir wrote, in part:

"This was the most significant afternoon and night of my life. I've had my share of crazy adventures due mainly to my impulsive nature but with no regrets. I've been in places, where on reflection, I should not have been.

I've confronted bigger people, smarter people and my fears. My life has been full, I've no complaints and wouldn't change it for anything.

It's now about 4.30 pm on Sunday afternoon. The mast, complete with brand new main, rigging, new halyards, boom, and everything that could punch a hole in "Solo Globe Challenger" is gone.

Thank Christ.

Tony apologised later for initially focusing solely on just getting rid of it and for not attending to the "wounded". If a fly could have hung on in those conditions it would have seen all hands go into survival mode.

It would have seen Biggles with a broken leg at the mast with Tony, Dave and Cookie with Keith ordering tools from below. It would have seen Bob calmly finding everything and passing it up "daisy chain" via Glen and myself to where they were doing the dismantling.

The fly by the way would have been shitting itself hoping the next wave didn't come down on us while we were doing it.

That fly was probably saying "There's blood over there but stuff it, I'm outta here!"

The seas at that time were really huge. I remember looking behind, and looking up almost mesmerised by the constantly breaking top of them.

What about the noise? The noise was intense."

A violent ocean is not silent. It is angry and loud.

Now that above deck was reasonably sorted, I went below to assess the situation there.

Snapey had triggered both of our Emergency Position Indicating Radio Beacons (EPIRB) which, as the name implies, should only be activated in an emergency. If ever there was an emergency, this was it, so let 'em rip!

Snapey and others were manning bilge pumps and anything else at their disposal, madly bailing the water out and I jumped in to help. There is a saying that the best bilge pump is a scared man with a big bucket. I now know that to be 100% true. I remember scooping up water with a very large saucepan and frenziedly heaving it out the hatch thinking to myself, "This water does not belong in here. This water needs to be back outside."

I figured that we could have a very long night ahead of us. I was wet through and thought that me getting hypothermia would not help the situation so I took 10 mins and rummaged around in a couple of the guy's gear bags, found some dry clothes and donned them, as most of my gear had been in the bunk where I had been and was sodden.

I kitted up again with wet weather jacket, pants, sea boots and safety harness and climbed into the cockpit at around 5.30 pm for what would be a very long haul. Once we had jettisoned the mast and rigging, Cyril had, even though he was in a lot of pain, resumed steering the boat and was now guiding her on a course with the wind and the waves directly behind us, which was by far, the safest option now.

I resumed steering the boat.

Cyril and Keir were in a terrible pain with their fractured rib cages and we managed to get them below to lay on some sails. Later on, when some humour was able to be resurrected, we decided they were twins and christened them "Ooh Ooh" and "Agh Agh". Snapey stayed below as well, caring for the injured guys and running the show down there. Biggles, with his broken leg, wanted to stay in the cockpit.

Cookie, Dave and Keith set up a rotating watch with 2 out of the 3 on deck to complement Biggles and I at any given time.

So off we went.

On a 15 hour fight for our lives.

I'm asked lots of questions about the '98 catastrophe, but there are two common ones that standout.

"How strong was the wind?"

Later we unanimously agreed that the average wind strength for a core 15 hour period, from around 4 pm Sunday until 7 am Monday was 80 knots (150 km/h). If you were to drive your motor vehicle along the freeway at 110 km/h and put your arm out the window you would feel a certain force, energy and power. If you increased speed to 120 km/h, 130 km/h, 140 km/h and then wound it out to 150 km/h you would be able feel the raw power and energy on your arm that we did for 15 hours. It's exactly the same result, just created in a different way.

"How big were the waves?"

Make your way to the roof of a 6 or 7 story building, walk to the edge of roof and peer down at the ground 6 or 7 floors below. Then stand there for 15 hours whilst getting belted with 150 km/h of wind and you might begin to understand how the 8 of us felt perched at the top of those monstrous waves.

We unanimously agreed that the average wave height for the 15 hour core period was 60 to 70 ft The coronial findings, for which I was interviewed, as were many people, are public of course. Within the findings are the records of interview with the rescue chopper pilots, who are NOT prone to exaggeration.

In their interviews, they routinely report that they would have their chopper in hover mode trying to render assistance to a stricken yacht with the altimeter set for the chopper to hover at 110 ft above average sea level. They said that regularly waves came through where the altimeter would rise to 10 ft and then drop back down to 110 ft.

100 ft waves. Only in the movies you say?

No.

I'll never forget the involuntary shiver that went through me when I read (I read the findings from cover to cover) a record of interview with pilot, Darryl Jones, who has very sadly passed away. He said, in part and slightly edited:

"I noted on the altimeter that it would go from 100 ft and drop right down to 10 ft at times as waves were going underneath us so I was in awe that we had 90 ft waves passing underneath us. At one stage Barry advised

me that he had to winch out a lot of winch cable, into the water because Dave was going up and down these waves and there was no way we could keep a little bit of slack on the cable. You just had to give him all the cable and leave him to his own devices basically. I don't know how long, a couple of minutes or a couple of seconds, but I could sense something building, I could see something building, I wasn't particularly, didn't see a wall of water but I, I said to Barry, how much cable have you got paid out, and he said I've got heaps you know I said, all right, I've got to climb. I pulled the machine up to about 160 ft on the altimeter and there was just like this wall of water went under us, the altimeter came up to 10 ft and it stayed there for probably 200 or 300 metres of water and then just dropped back down to 160 ft again"

A 150 ft wall of water!

I am often asked about the movie "Perfect Storm" starring George Clooney, whom a lot of people confuse me with (if you believe that, you will believe anything) and how it compares to our real life perfect storm?

Take the Hollywood bullshit out of it and it is very close to the mark except, for our production there was no director to call "cut" when we were cold, wet and scared.

I've watched the movie once, struggling through it. I've had a few attempts to watch it since but have never been able to watch it in its entirety again. It's too close to the bone.

In the years since, I have been asked many times by journalists and members of the public about the inaccurate weather forecast. In this increasingly litigious world, many people look to blame others for their inadequacies or shortcomings and many look to me to apportion blame and are visibly disappointed when I don't set out to blame anyone, including the weather forecasters.

Over the years, I have strung three words together that in my opinion can be applied to many aspects of life including that of imperfect weather forecasting.

Flexibility, Understanding, Acceptance.

Weather forecasting is not a perfect art or science. The quality of forecasts has and continues to improve but mother nature will always have her way, at times defying predictions. You only have to watch the weather segment on the evening TV news where they predict the next day to be sunny and warm but it ends up cold and raining. It is not a perfect art. So be it.

We were told to expect 50 knots and we received 80 knots plus. So be it.

Too many people in this world are not prepared to take responsibility for their decisions. The way I see it, is that if you stick your head in the lion's mouth often enough, one day he is gonna snap his jaws shut tight.

Other questions that are quite often asked go something along the lines of, "Why didn't the race organisers call off the race?", or, "Why didn't you retire and head for land when the conditions got too bad?"

There is a long held tradition/rule/expectation that "It is the individual skipper's decision to start and/or continue to race". It is as simple as that. It was my decision to cross the start line, and it was my decision to continue to race up until the point that things got out of control. I accept that, as did Cookie, Dave, Keir, Keith, Snapey, Biggles and Cyril.

As for the returning to land part of the equation, I understand perfectly the reasoning behind the question but it's not always that simple. It is a fact that some of the yachts (not all) that retired and headed to land inadvertently positioned themselves side on to the oncoming waves and it was then that they got themselves into a lot of trouble, including some knockdowns.

When conditions deteriorate to the point that survival is the priority, land can be the enemy and trying to get back there may well be your undoing. Forget land. Steer the safest course.

On the compass, the wind was blowing from 240 deg (WSW) so to run with the wind directly behind us meant steering 060 deg (ENE), which took us roughly toward the top of the North Island of NZ about 1400 nm away. Bugger getting to Australia.

Whilst I was below getting kitted up, Cyril had decided that the safest course to steer was straight downwind at 060 deg. I am a great believer in assessing your options in life, determining the best one and going for it. When I came back on deck around about 5.30 pm, I took time to assess any other vaguely possible options that may have been a safer bet.

There were only two options.

One was turn the boat into the wind and waves and hold her there by deploying a makeshift sea anchor consisting of sails, ropes and other sundry equipment lashed together and thrown into the ocean and attached to the bow with a bloody strong rope. I floated (excuse the pun) this option amongst the crew and the feedback essentially was, "You are fucking kidding me, aren't you? You are a fucking lunatic".

They were absolutely right. It was not a viable option unless it was your only option. Also, they quite correctly identified that I am a lunatic.

Cyril's favoured option of running with the wind and the waves directly behind us was by far the best option (by a bloody mile), so off we went.

For the rest of that afternoon and all through the night, we were hammered mercilessly by the wind from an unwavering 240 deg. It NEVER varied. Not 1 degree either way.

I had to stand up to steer and it was easy to know if I was on course because apart from using the compass as a guide, the very second the boat deviated I would be belted by a cyclonic blast on the right or left side of my face. When on course, I was relentlessly bombarded on the back of my head.

Biggles took up station near me, sitting on a cockpit seat, looking astern. He was constantly focused on the approaching waves, telling me if I needed to steer right, left or straight ahead as we tried to pick our way through it all. It was common for the top 25 feet of a wave to be tumultuously tripping over itself and breaking in an explosion of white seething tumultuous water.

The breaking section was not constant. One part of the wave would break then stop, then another section would start to explode so it was a constant challenge to avoid the "white bits". When a breaking section was about to engulf us, Biggles would fearfully yell "right, right, right, right!", however, as some waves were on final approach the breaking section might melt away, but simultaneously fire up in the spot right behind us. When this happened, Biggles would yell, "Oh fuck no. Left, left, left, left, LEFT."

For fuck sake Biggles, make up your mind.

I have a large number of indelibly etched images in my mind. One of which is that the waves existed for one reason, and one reason only.

To kill us.

They were vertical walls of water moving through the ocean, hunting and seeking their prey, and if one had your name on it, you were a "goner".

As daylight faded toward night, I remember taking a moment to look back over my right shoulder at the sea state. I could not believe what I was seeing. I murmured to myself, "Have a look at this. You will probably never see anything like this again in your lifetime". I could not see how any sort of a rescue "vehicle" whether it be ship, helicopter, or yacht could possibly render assistance. Trying to transfer off the boat, I felt, would almost guarantee death.

I told the crew that if indeed some sort of a rescue craft did actually appear, that I felt strongly that it would be each individual's decision to stay or go. I should not, and would not, be making that decision for them. From my own personal point of view, I decided that I would see what developed and make a decision at that time. That night I was clear in my mind that if we could be rescued safely, I would have abandoned my yacht without hesitation. No problems at all.

We speared off towards the horizon and spent the whole night thinking that the next wave could be the one that would finish us off.

Keith has a couple of nicknames. To a very select few, he acknowledges "Two", because, we say he is as thick as "two" short planks. (We are terrible mates aren't we.) Another moniker is "The Senator", because of previous political aspirations. At one point, he was infatuated by Senator Amanda Vanstone, an Australian federal politician.

In true Aussie spirit, moments of comic relief bubbled to the surface at times, relieving the pressure and giving us a laugh.

Early evening, Keith, seated in the cockpit, poked his nose over the hatch slides and told Snapey, down below, that he badly needed a piss. Snapey, forever the practical one, suggested to Keith that because he was completely wet through under his wet weather jacket and pants then why not just piss in his pants? Keith reflected on this sage advice from Snapey and decided he was right. Keith reckoned the 20 seconds of warmth down his legs was glorious.

As I stood at the wheel that night, there were many times that I pissed my pants as well. You have to do what you have to do. Keith and I weren't the only ones.

Keith was a smoker at that time and being a tight arse tried to save money by rolling his own cigarettes. He was huddled in a corner of the cockpit, soaked through and a bit on edge (read: crapping his pants). He decided, in his very limited wisdom, that what would fix all this for him would be a ciggie. He rooted around inside his wet weather jacket and fished out a small plastic bag complete with tobacco, papers and matches which were unbelievably still dry. Who says there is too much plastic in the world?

In a miraculous performance, somehow or other he managed to dry his hands then roll a nice big fat cigarette using just about all of the tobacco in the bag. I think he thought that if it was going to be his last one, then why waste tobacco? Plus, he could then say that he had quit smoking before he died. In the fetal position, to keep the wind at bay, he struck a match in 150kmh of wind and got that baby fired up, sucking on it like he was trying to suck a golf ball through a garden hose.

I am crying tears of laughter as I recall this.

CHAPTER 10
Which one will I think of last?

Later, Keir wrote (lightly edited):

Due to injuries, the only option we had was for Tony to steer and this became an all-night, quite superhuman stand for 15 hours without relief. Biggles never came below with his seriously broken leg.

From my point of view, (hear would be more apt) This stand will go down in my memory as one of the most inspiring things I've witnessed. Not because of Tony alone (taking nothing away either) who was at the helm for over 15 hours in the most horrendous seas any of us will ever encounter, but because of the character that came to the fore from Keith, Dave, Biggles and Cookie.

Those guys never gave Tony a break, realising that this could indeed be it. He became our lifeline and they never let him lose sight of that fact. Their torment was relentless and it saved our lives.

"Here comes another one Tony, concentrate"

"Come on, you can do it!"

"Focus Tony, think of Holly and Jordan"

It went on all night, determination from all on deck, clinging, hanging on and not giving up. There is nothing heroic about it, nothing eloquent or clever one can say. We were at the mercy of those seas and I don't have any hesitation saying the power of the sea was in total control.

My contribution was just one of eight in a massive team effort that had the goals of keeping that 13.33m long piece of fibreglass afloat and sustaining life.

Around 1 am I was exhausted. I hadn't slept for over 40 hours, plus had used a hell of a lot of adrenaline as well as nervous and physical energy. Even though the guys were urging me on, keeping me focused, I could not keep exhaustion at bay. I started to hallucinate. At one point, I saw a monkey perched on the broken stump of the mast about 1.8m above deck level. I shared this encouraging piece of news with the crew and the collective opinion was that I was a dead set dickhead and a nutcase.

In general, I resist swallowing chemical based tablets or taking prescription medication unless I absolutely have to. However, desperate people can do desperate things, so I asked if we had any tablets that might help keep me awake. "No", was the answer.

However, if through the course of the night, I was to suddenly develop constipation, erectile dysfunction, athletes foot, arthritis, gout, high blood pressure, diabetes, heart problems, shingles, enlarged prostate or high cholesterol, then these blokes had me covered with their various medications.

Fuck. What to do?

I had given up tea and coffee years before. I think it was Snapey that came up with the idea of a strong coffee. He managed to get a burner going on the stove and made me a mug of coffee so thick that you could stand the bloody spoon up in it. It was like drinking black tar, however it did the trick. For about 30 minutes or so I would have an energy boost before sagging again. From roughly 1 am - 5 am, Café de Snape cranked out 3 mugs of black goo. Later, when I asked him how much coffee he put in each one he said, "Let's put it this way, Tones, I didn't use a spoon."

It was not possible to sit and steer effectively in those conditions so I had to stand all of the time. All other helmspersons were injured. For others that weren't injured, taking the helm was not an option. For example, Dave said, "Tony, I'll take the wheel but I'll probably kill us all."

Snapey was 66 yrs of age, a seasoned veteran, and wanted to have a steer but there were two main things stopping me from giving him a run. Recently, he'd had knee replacements and I was really worried that one or both knees would give way on him at a critical moment. The pressure on my younger (by 25 years) knees and legs was intense. The other reason that I was reluctant to put him on the wheel was that he was like a father to me, and there was no way that I wanted to put my 'father' in the firing line in these absolute bastard conditions.

Biggles is a formidable man, an imposing figure physically and mentally and ever so tough. All night, he sat in the cockpit close by me, guiding, supporting, urging and cajoling me. Despite having a broken leg, the silly big bastard did not complain once.

As I battled fatigue, Biggles employed various tactics to keep me on the pace. On one occasion, as I reached a new low, the following exchange took place between he and I as another ploy to keep me going.

Biggles: *"What's your name?"*
Me: *"You know my name"*

Biggles: *"What's your name"*
Me: *"Tony"*

Biggles: *"What's your name?"*
Me: *"For fucks sake Biggles, you know my name."*

Biggles: *"What's your name?"*
Me: *"Tony Mowbray"*

Biggles: *"Where do you live?"*
Me: *"Belmont"*

Biggles: *"Are you married?"*
Me: *"You know I'm married."*

Biggles: *"What is your wife's name?"*
Me: *"Lorraine"*

Biggles: *"Do you have any kids?"*
Me: *"You know I've got kids"*

Biggles: *"How many kids have you got?"*
Me: *"I've got two"*

Biggles: *"What's their names?"*
Me: *"You know their names"*

Biggles: *"What's their names?"*
Me: *"Holly and Jordan"*

Biggles: *"How old are they?"*
Me: *"7 and 5"*

Biggles: *"Do you love 'em?"*
Me: *"Are you fucking kidding me? Of course, I love 'em"*

Then, a long pause and then out of the darkness:
Biggles: *"Do you want to get out of here alive and get home to see them?"*

Sometimes in life, that inbuilt intuition that we all have kicks in and you sense that you should be a bit more careful in a particular situation. You know the gut feeling that alerts you? That sixth sense that gnaws away at you, warning you, saying "beware, beware, beware".

However, at other times "stuff" just happens doesn't it. With no inbuilt warning, no sixth sense or intuition, it's KABOOM and there it is.

At sea, in storm conditions the same principles apply. Sometimes a wave, bigger and uglier than average, may announce its arrival. You might hear the hiss in the dark. Maybe you feel the boat lurch backwards into the void of the preceding wave for a split second before you are catapulted upside down. You might stare, head angled, unblinkingly into the gloom of the night and finally you bring into focus the white breaking top section of a massive wave as it crests and is about to thunder down on you.

However sometimes a really bad bastard of a wave will lob with no warning. No sixth sense. No intuition. You are smashed without any warning whatsoever.

The following monster gave no warning.

It was pitch black, and I mean absolutely pitch black.

Biggles, Cookie and Keith were in the cockpit.

Snapey, Cyril, Keir and Dave were below.

Completely unannounced, out of the darkness roared a wave that completely engulfed us. The wave had COMPLETE and utter disregard for us and the bit of fibreglass we were perched on and in.

In the wave's mind, we did not exist.

In the wave's mind, we were irrelevant.

It overwhelmed us and I have never felt a force of water like it. I was hurled forward, pinned to the steering wheel at my sternum by a wall of water that felt like a hydraulic ram jammed into my back. I could not move.

When the initial force passed, I managed to struggle back to a standing position, gripping the now bent and twisted steering wheel. I realised that from my chest down, I was standing under tumultuous white seething water. I was almost wholly submerged under the broken body of the wave. Biggles, Cookie and Keith were completely underwater.

The whole 8.5 tons and 43 ft. of boat was completely submerged as it hurtled down the face of the wave at an obscene angle of about 45 degrees. As she thundered along at an incredible warp speed that she was never designed to achieve, I involuntarily started yelling at the top of my voice.

"This is it, this is the one!"

"This is it, this is the one!"

"This is it, this is the one!"

I truly felt that this wave would be the final nail in our coffin.

As we plummeted towards the trough of the wave, which I call the "pit", I knew that at the very bottom one of two things was probably going to happen. One distinct possibility was that the bow would bury further to a point of no return and the boat would then "Pitch Pole" meaning that it would cartwheel end over end. Imagine an 8.5 ton yacht, cart wheeling across the ocean like a child's toy on a pitch black, cold, friendless night and its 8 crew being cast adrift to their death. It would not have been a pretty sight.

Not fucking pretty at all.

The second possibility was that when we got to the "pit", that the positive buoyancy might kick in, the bow might rise up and we might survive that one.

As we charged headlong down the face of the wave, I realised that the only part of the boat that I could actually see was the shiny stainless steel curved bow rail at the very front of the boat. In my crazy mind I thought, "that piece of stainless steel is connected to the bow and when we get to the pit, if that piece of stainless steel lifts and rises, it means that the bow is coming up as well and if that happens then we might just get through this bastard".

I stopped yelling and I started focusing on the stainless steel rail. If you want to know anything about how to focus you can ask me because I've now got focus 100% covered.

As we got closer and closer to the point of no return, through gritted teeth and clenched jaw I chanted aloud.

"Get up!"
"Get up!"
"Get up!"
"You've got to get up!"
"Get up!"

Have you ever been in a swimming pool? Have you been in a swimming pool, and thrown an inflatable beach ball around? Have you ever been in a swimming pool throwing a beach ball around and thought, "I'll push it under water and see how far down I can get it?" Most people have had a crack at it. I know I have.

Initially, the beach ball doesn't resist too much but as you push more, the resistance increases. As you push and push, it becomes more of a challenge, because of the positive buoyancy increasing and it starts to take on a mind of its own. You push, and push, until suddenly, the beach ball gets to a point where it decides that no matter what you do, it's coming to the surface. In a lightning fast move, it escapes your grasp and erupts to the surface.

The rules and the principles are the same, it's just a different example.

As we got to the "pit", the bow continued to drive down and the angle of incline increased. I could feel the back end of the boat starting to rise further. The speed dropped off and she started getting sluggish. We were now extremely close to the trip point.

"Get up!"
"Get up!"
"Get up!"
"You've got to get up!"
"GET UP!"

Then all of a sudden, the positive buoyancy in the bow kicked in (just like the beach ball) and KABOOM, 8.5 tons of lead, smashed up fibreglass, busted bodies, and injured men gasping for air, erupted out of the ocean like a missile fired from a submarine.

An indelibly etched image from that moment is looking up and seeing crystal clear seawater ribboning off either side of the hull as she launched upwards, prior to pancaking back down on the surface of the ocean.

A question was then yelled into the darkness, as it was many times that night:

"Are we all still here?"

The answer was "Yes". We were all still there.

What do you reckon you get by surviving that wave? You simply get the opportunity to go for the next one. You bloody beauty.

Your life is the next wave.

Forget about what you might have this evening for dinner, who you may meet for drinks after work tomorrow, where you may go for Christmas vacation or celebrating your child's birthday.

All of that is gone. It's out the door. It does not exist. Your life is the next wave and if you survive that one, then you get to go for the next one.

Seven out of the eight of us were married with young children and thoughts of our children were at the forefront of our thinking when conditions allowed.

Snapey has six children (Someone should have told him what causes it?) On 27th December 1984 (14 years prior, to the exact day), his youngest son, Andrew was born and I am his co-godparent.

Later, Bob shared with us that he had been thinking about his children amidst all the chaos and that when he had heard me yelling at the top of my voice, "This is it, this is the one" he was hoping like hell that the fibreglass tube he was in (Solo Globe) would not end up being his coffin.

As Andrew celebrated his birthday every year hence, Bob desperately did not want him to do so on the anniversary of day that his father died on that bleak ocean.

Cookie has attempted to emulate Snapey with regards to procreation, running second with 5 great kids (Stop it Cookie). He and Michelle's two youngest daughters, Tiff and Mel and were just 5 and 4. Mel had a tiny plastic dolphin in her toy collection and on the morning of the race gave it to Cookie telling him that it would look after him and guide him back home. Through the night, Cookie had the tiny dolphin in a pocket of his wet weather trousers and when thoughts of his children came to mind, he would caress the plastic dolphin in his pocket all the while thinking of his kids.

Dave observed Cookie with his hand in his pocket a bit more often than normal and asked him what he was doing. Cookie shared the story of the dolphin and how he felt that he and his kids were connecting through the small piece of plastic.

We jointly reflected somberly and quietly on this. A few minutes later, out of the darkness, came Dave's voice, "For fucks sake Cookie, give me a go at that dolphin will ya?"

He wasn't joking.

On our relentless march to sea through the night, I kept hoping and wishing for stars to appear. When I could, I would look upwards to the overcast grey sullen night sky wishing and hoping.

"PLEASE! Let me see some stars."

I thought that if a clutch of stars would pop out and stay visible for a while, then that might be a sign of improvement. Fleetingly, my spirits would be lifted very occasionally as a star or two would peep out ever so briefly and I would think "YES!". But as quickly as they appeared, they would close over, and my hopes were dashed.

There was another wave that night that burns bright in my memory, however it seems so unbelievable, as if it is part of my imagination as against actually happening. I stopped talking about this wave long ago, as one element of it just doesn't seem possible. Seasoned sailors could be forgiven for classifying part of the following as "Bullshit".

The problem is that it's not bullshit.

I've been back through my taped diary from early January 1999 and there it is. I've still got the audio tape. Believe it or not, this is what happened.

A huge wave picked us up, slewing and broaching us to port (left) and we took off like an arrow out of a crossbow, across the face of the wave like a surf board on steroids. The boat hurtled across the face at what seemed like 20 knots (40km/h), an incredible speed for her. It thumped across the face like a high performance, sailing dinghy.

Thump, thump, thump, thump.

The guys on deck dropped low to the bottom of the cockpit and covered up, waiting for the worst. I got as low as I could into a kneeling, balled up crouch, tightly gripping the steering wheel. My mind raced, needing to make a split second decision.

Do I try to pull the boat away down the face to try to get back on course, knowing that pulling her away could wipe us out?

Do I try to steer her up the face and attempt to have punch her way through the back of the wave like a surfboard rider pulling off a wave?

Do I steady her on the course she was on, banging and crashing along. Let her have her head and she might negotiate the wave in her own way and look after us?

There is a saying, look after your boat and your boat will look after you. I decided to let her have her head and hope that she would look after us.

Crouched behind the wheel with the boat crashing along at 20 knots, I had my mouth and eyes closed waiting for the inevitable wall of water to engulf us. After some time, I realised that we were not underwater. What's happening?

I opened my eyes, looked up and unbelievably the wave was curling over the top of us and enveloping us. We were in the tube. It was curling over us, and we were smoking along at warp speed staying out of the broken section. As unbelievable as it sounds, that's what happened.

No Bullshit. We were in the tube.

Shortly after that we were taken out by the body of the wave, flung down the face, underwater and pummeled yet again.

After that wave that I made some promises to myself. Amongst them, to abandon my attempt to sail solo around the world.

Throughout that night, I felt that I could see and smell death in the water.

I am not religious, however one way I look at what happened to us is that all of a sudden, with no warning whatsoever, the devil came along, took me and my seven mates by the hand and lead us to the edge of a huge precipice. He made the eight of us stand there on tippy toe, balancing for 15 hours, clinging by a gossamer thread to life.

After 15 hours, he allowed us to relax and step back from the brink but devastatingly, he sent six men from other yachts to their deaths.

For 15 hours, I thought that I had found out how I was going to die. Drowning huh?

So, it's not going to be old age, nursing home, cancer, stroke or a heart attack.

So, it's drowning?

Well now that I know I'll think about that for a while.

Mentally, I was still fighting, kicking and screaming, doing my bit to try to keep the boat afloat and sustain life but in the back of my mind I was thinking.

"Drowning, huh? Wow. Now I know"

I remembered hearing that at the very end of the drowning process, as you lose consciousness, that it actually becomes quite pleasant. I thought, "I wonder if that is the case? It looks like I'm going to find out."

Later still, when we would get a slight reprieve from the really huge waves, I thought some more.

"I wonder what it is going to be like when the boat has sunk, my 7 mates have disappeared, and I'm in the water on my own. I wonder what that's going to be like?"

Then, with my mind getting the better of me, I thought,

"What about when the boat has sunk, my mates are gone and I'm in the water on my own drifting toward death. I wonder what my last thoughts will be?"

Then, a little while later.

"I really, really, really hope that I think of my children last."

The kicker that blows my mind is.

If I think of my children last?

Which one will I think of last?

CHAPTER 11
I made promises to myself that night.

I believe that a human being cannot survive an experience like that and not be changed forever, and so it is for me. My life is so different in so many ways. My attitude towards life is so different in so many ways.

I made promises to myself that night.

I promised that if I got out of there alive, there were things I was going to do immediately and others that I would for the rest of my life. I've kept every one of those promises and will continue to do so. Those promises will become apparent throughout the course of this book.

The wind continued to shriek like a banshee. Vertical walls of water 60 -100 ft high continued to bear down on us. We continued unerringly on a compass course of 060 degrees. Finally, the eastern sky started to lighten, ever so minutely at first, heralding the dawn of the new day. Jet black faded to black, giving way to dark grey, then light grey until eventually we could see more clearly the wrath and fury in which we were embroiled.

The arrival of some light on the subject gave me a "second wind" mentally and with renewed vigour I continued to do my bit so that maybe, just maybe, we could escape this living hell alive. Around 7 am, change started to take place, slowly and almost imperceptibly at first.

For very short periods, I needed to steer 055 deg to keep the wind directly behind us before having to revert to 060 deg. Then I noticed the first "soggy" patch, as I call them. Ever so briefly, the wind dropped from 80 + knots to 70 knots then back up to 80 knots. A while later, down to 60 knots but only climbing back up to 70 knots. At times, I could steer 050 deg or even 045 deg for longer bursts before reverting back to 055 deg, rarely having to go back to good old 060 deg.

The viciousness and height of the waves started to reduce in concert with the reduction in wind strength and slight change of direction. The wind dropped off to a consistent 60 knots and waves were now down to around 40 ft and I was easily maintaining 045 deg to 050 deg. Suddenly, we were no longer in fear of our lives.

"It has spent its penny" is a saying that I have used many times over the years when a destructive slow moving weather system has finally decided to move on and it now appeared that this system had indeed, "spent its penny". It couldn't blow that hard for fucking ever, could it?

I had started to think that it might.

The previous afternoon Snapey had triggered our 2 EPIRBS, however, to the distress of family and friends, we later found out that only one was working. More on that later.

Throughout the night, our only tenuous link to the outside world had been via an invisible signal from an EPIRB to a satellite, bounced back to earth and received by the Australian Maritime Safety Authority (AMSA) in Canberra. This signal provided AMSA with the EPIRB's position within a general area and was only an indication that the boat may be afloat.

When all hell broke loose on the Sunday afternoon we were approximately 30 nm from land, and by the Monday morning we had been swept out to approximately 125 nm from land. That was a pretty good average speed of over 6 knots without mast or sails.

At 8 am we heard it.

The unmistakable sound that can conjure up feelings of fear and loathing by some who have been to war, was heard by us. On this occasion the whup, whup, whup, whup of a Victorian Air Ambulance helicopter was sweet music to our ears. We could hear and see them in the distance as the crew strained their eyes, peering at a vast expanse of boiling ocean, trying to pinpoint us.

Searching, searching, searching.

Whup, whup, whup.

One at a time, we set off three smoke flares, trying to attract their attention, worried that they would not see us and move away.

The 1st went unseen.

The 2nd went unseen.

The 3rd one did its job when suddenly the chopper reared on its axis (I cry as I type) and headed straight for us.

Whup, whup, whup, whup.

The pilot manoeuvred the chopper deftly, taking up a position ahead of and facing back at us, slightly to my right and low down. He was so close that when he flicked up his visor, our eyes locked unwaveringly. Very deliberately he pointed at me and then the ocean, repeating the action three times. The message was clear and simple.

You guys are going to get off that boat and we're taking you all with us. You're going to abandon the boat.

Whup, whup, whup, whup.

Hurry up.

After a dangerous, complicated and time consuming procedure, an emergency radio was dropped to us and passed below to Snapey.

After speaking with the chopper, Snapey told us that we had been instructed to all jump in the ocean one at a time, to be retrieved by them.

How the hell are we going to do this thing?

Whup, whup, whup, whup.

It was still blowing 60 knots and 40 ft waves were still rolling through.

Fuck.

Let's do it.

Hurry up.

Cookie was the crash test dummy, being first to go. He jumped in the ocean, Solo Globe surfed away and then an absolute hero of a man resplendent in a frogman's outfit, descended on the chopper's winch cable. In one swift action, he hooked Cookie and they were winched to the belly of the chopper.

One down, seven to go.

Whup, whup, whup, whup.

Come on, hurry up. Come on, let's go.

Now another message from Snapey.

The procedure has taken longer than hoped for and they cannot take us all. Shit happens.

Okay. Who's next?

Biggles then had a go. Overboard he went, we drift away, the chopper swooped and now there were two in the "bird".

Whup, whup, whup, whup.

Come on, hurry up, it's low on fuel. Let's get moving.

Keir decided that he didn't want to risk puncturing a lung or further damaging his already fractured rib cage so decided to stay.

Cyril appeared in the hatch ready to go. Our gazes locked for what seemed like an eternity. In a moment of unsurpassed poignancy, he shook his head a little and went back below. Someone else could take Cyril's place. He wasn't leaving.

As long as I live, I will never ever forget staring into Cyril's eyes at that moment.

Come on, hurry up, let's go.

Whup, whup, whup, whup.

From Snapey, another message. The chopper has enough fuel for one more lift. Snapey and Keith declined the "invitation".

I wasn't going anywhere.

Let's send the young buck? Dave, you're up.

He was reluctant to go but I insisted that he do so. As the chopper was setting up for Dave's plunge, he was perched close to me. I told him that with all of my heart I wanted him to go. I wanted him to get back to his family. If didn't make it out of there alive, I didn't want him to carry that around as baggage for the rest of his life. He quietly thanked me and then over the side he went, to be safely retrieved and lifted by the hero on the end of the wire to join the other two boys.

Some outsiders looking in, might not understand.

But outsiders weren't there, were they?

With its precious cargo on board the chopper wheeled and headed for land. On their way out to us they had covered 125 nm in 40 minutes as the cyclonic tailwind gave them a massive bonus. The return journey was very, very different as they ground out each mile painstakingly, finally touching down at Mallacoota, Victoria, 1 hour 40 minutes after leaving us.

They had three minutes of fuel left. 180 seconds!

How fortunate they didn't go for a 4th lift.

That afternoon Biggles was airlifted to John Hunter Hospital in Newcastle where he was operated on and had a plate inserted in his broken leg to knock him into shape again. Cookie and Dave had a big day out, kicking off with, a 125 nm helicopter ride, then a fixed wing flight with Biggles, followed up by a stint riding shot gun for him in the back of the ambulance. They weren't leaving our mate. Go boys.

That night, Biggles, Cookie and Dave were in the arms of their loved ones.

Meanwhile, on board, there were 5.

As the whup, whup, whup, whup of the chopper faded to a memory the mood on board became sombre. What now? Well, nothing for it, we have to get ourselves out of here. We have to get ourselves back to land.

As the weather system moved further away to wreak havoc elsewhere, our conditions became far more manageable. If you were going out for a pleasure sail you would be absolutely crazy to head out into the conditions that we still had, but for us, relatively speaking, it was now almost a stroll in the park. Maybe we were, or are, crazy?

Cyril managed to get up into the cockpit and took over steering. I remember saying, "Cyril, people died out here last night. I just know it. People died out here".

We pondered that for a while.

Looking around forlornly, we contemplated the condition of the boat and I said, "Look at the boat Cyril, it's fucked"

Cyril: "It will be okay mate, you've got insurance, haven't you?"

Me: "Well, I'm not sure about that".

Before I share my "insurance story" I would like you to understand that my attitude throughout the night was that I would have happily handed over whatever assets I possessed, that I would have signed away the opportunity to ever create another asset in my life, no matter how long I live. I would have gladly given up the opportunity to earn any income ever again, if the powers that be could have just done one thing for me.

Get me back to my children.

When perched right out there on the edge, the view is crystal clear. What is important jumps straight out. Money and assets are not on the list any fucking where. If my yacht sank, and I managed to survive and get back to land, then it would be a wonderful, fantastic day because I would be alive.

I had previously pondered the question of boat insurance.

I had come to the following conclusions.

1) What insurer would be silly enough to cover me for such a dangerous escapade as sailing around the world?
2) If I did find a lunatic insurance company to cover me, I probably would not be able to afford the massive premium, which of course is the time that you most need the insurance. I had decided to embark on the world trip with no boat insurance although I did have some life insurance.

Greg Gilkison (Gilko) is a bloody good bloke and was a few years ahead of me at school in Belmont. Gilko was an insurance broker and we had spoken about insurance for the world trip before I gave up on the idea.

When we committed to the Hobart race I spoke to him again about the cost of cover for the race only. I was super strapped for cash, and the premium that Gilko sourced was very close to prohibitive.

In deciding not to insure the boat for the race, I rationalised my thinking telling myself that if I were prepared to set off on a 22,000 nm journey solo without insurance, then what could possibly go wrong on a short 630 nm race that I had competed in on 13 previous occasions? Plus, I would have seven others on board to help keep me out of trouble.

Trying to decide if I should try to rake together the money to pay for the cover was like a pendulum swinging back 'n forth, but favouring a no. Gilko, always looking out for my interests, gently tried on a number of occasions to guide me towards taking out the cover. I kept resisting.

Late on Christmas Eve afternoon, he phoned, in one last attempt to get me to insure the boat. The conversation swung back 'n forth until finally I blurted out "Mate, I appreciate you thinking of me but I'm not going to take out the cover". Gilko's words: "I hear you Tone. Okay"

The conversation ended and I drove off. Then, it hit me like a ton of bricks. What if we were on the start line and I ran into a multimillion dollar Maxi yacht sinking it and it was my fucking fault? What if someone died or was disabled due to my negligence? That might be millions and millions in damages.

I rang him back and told him that I had reversed my decision. I was a fair way from his office and we both had truckloads of other "stuff" to do, so we decided it was impractical for us to meet for me to give him a cheque (electronic transfers weren't around then).

Gilko: "Don't worry about it Tone, give me the cheque when you get back after the race".

So, the answer to Cyril's question as to whether I had insurance cover or not was "I think so, but I'm not real sure". Whatever would be, would be.

It was time to devise a plan to get us back home.

CHAPTER 12
Well and truly fucking rooted

The engine was rooted (read: destroyed) for what turned to be a number of reasons, so motoring at that point was out of the question. We weren't about to drift aimlessly, so we had to get the boat sailing somehow.

We built a "jury" rig.

We still had our 2 × 4.5m aluminium spinnaker poles, so using them we constructed an "A" frame to which we attached sails and try to get the boat headed to land. Even though conditions were progressively easing, it was still dangerous, and demanded respect, but was nothing like what we had just come out of.

Moving around on deck was difficult because of the sea state, but further complicated because my thought processes, movements and ability to communicate were significantly impaired. I felt as if I were operating at about 10% of my normal physical and mental capabilities. In simple terms, I was rooted.

Well and truly fucking rooted.

As Keith, Snapey, Cyril and I (Keir was in too much pain and needed to stay below) built the makeshift mast, I realised I was bilious. I don't suffer from seasickness and so I couldn't pin down the reason for my upset stomach. Too much adrenaline maybe? It became almost intolerable so I stuck my fingers down my throat and threw up over the side. A gusher of black tar like bile liquid spewed forth. Snapey's jet black, super industrial strength, coffee had done its job.

We erected, and lashed in place, the A frame and attached a couple of small sails, one of which we tied a knot in to get it to fit. The setup may not have pretty to some but to us it was pure perfection. Off we went.

We weren't about to break any speed records and we still had a little bit of "golf to play" to get to safety, but that was okay cos we were alive.

The weather continued to abate throughout the morning and afternoon, however it was very slow going for a number of reasons including the bloody set that had contributed to our grief and was now slowing us up as we tried to head back into it. Additionally, the waves were still quite large, not allowing a course directly to land.

Cyril and Keir were the two most mechanically minded of us five and took it upon themselves, with painfully busted rib cages, broken wrists and a treasure trove of other injuries, to take the bit between their teeth and try to get the engine going. They worked tirelessly that afternoon, painstakingly identifying and fixing a host of problems. Saltwater was in the starter motor plus had invaded a multitude of electrical connections and the fuel lines as well. The concentrated sludge at the bottom of the fuel filters had become dislodged when the boat was upside down, further screwing up the fuel supply.

Just your average day out really.

Late that afternoon we heard the unmistakable roar of an Orion RAAF search aircraft coming in hot, sweeping straight over us. He made number of passes before flying off. Unfortunately, we could not communicate with him because the emergency radio that the chopper had dropped now had a flat battery.

Snapey managed to dry out an AM/FM radio and through news broadcasts we started to learn how big a catastrophe the race had been. News of sunk or missing boats, as well as dead and missing sailors, echoed into the cabin. We all felt absolutely terrible that we could not communicate with our families to tell them that we were okay and were confident of getting out of it in one piece. It was terribly upsetting for us, but nowhere near as upsetting for loved ones on land waiting for news.

Race rules required each boat to have one EPIRB but we had two. Snapey had triggered both on the Sunday afternoon and they had been transmitting in parallel ever since, or so we thought. We didn't know how long the batteries would last or how long it was going to take us to get to land or be located again. Thinking that it would be silly for both batteries to expire prior to being located we decided, as evening approached, to turn one beacon off to preserve its remaining power.

What we didn't know was that the unit we had left on was broken and not transmitting, so our flickering beep, beep, beep on the screen at AMSA suddenly evaporated with the flick of a switch by us. We had decided to alternate beacons by turning one off and the other on at 12 hour intervals to hedge our bets. Turning off the working beacon meant that we unknowingly went into the night with no link to the outside world.

That simple flick of a switch caused great distress for many people, not the least of which were our families. The next day, the front page of the Newcastle Herald newspaper was dominated by the heading "LOCAL YACHT LOST".

When Lorraine was shown this headline, she buckled at the knees and sank to the floor, sobbing uncontrollably in front of Holly and Jordan.

As sunset morphed into evening, we now had beautiful gentle conditions. Keir and Cyril suspended work on the engine for the night as they did not want to drain the batteries by using power for lighting. We ran a "dead" ship that night using ABSOLUTELY no battery power whatsoever for any purpose. We preserved what we had so that in the event the boys got to a point where they wanted to try and start the engine, we would hopefully be able to crank it over.

As the night progressed, it became more pleasant on the ocean as we drifted along. Snapey dug around and managed to find some beers so we enjoyed a couple each, rejoicing at simply being alive.

By Tuesday morning it was not quite three days since we had set out from Sydney Harbour. Just after daylight we alternated the EPIRBS, turning the crook one off and the good one on, completely unaware that with the flick of a switch the beep, beep, beep kicked in again on the screen in Canberra and once again we were on their radar.

Keir and Cyril resumed their battle with the engine.

Then, bugger me, there it was again.

The distinctive throaty roar of 4 Orion search aircraft engines. The plane blasted over us after being given the heads up by Canberra of our freshly transmitted position. After several roaring low level passes, they dropped a package into the ocean which we retrieved. Inside were sachets of fresh water which we didn't need as our fresh water tanks were still intact. More importantly it contained another emergency VHF radio.

We spoke with the pilot, Paul Carpenter, who told us that the warship HMAS Newcastle was 36 nm from our position and had been directed to us.

As the Orion flew long lazy loops above us, an ABC news helicopter piloted by Gary Ticehurst arrived, taking up station nearby as the warship Newcastle lumbered over the horizon.

I remember thinking that we had an Orion search aircraft, a news helicopter and a warship so if weren't saved then we never fucking would be.

As the Newcastle closed in, Cyril and Keir worked feverishly to bring the engine to life. We had discussed the possibility of being forced to abandon the boat if eventually found and had all agreed that it would be a heck of a shame to leave her, as we all thought the boat was "saveable" and could be got back to land by us given some time and reasonable weather. We felt that if the engine was running when found it would demonstrate some independence and perhaps authorities might not be quite as forceful. Cyril got seriously fired up, declaring, "Fuck it, I AM going to get this motor going before the Navy gets here".

After the hours of hard painful work by Keir and Cyril and their frantic last ditch effort, 20 minutes before the navy arrived the engine roared to life.

You fucking beauty.

Keir's words:

It had occurred to us that they could order us off the boat and after what we'd been through and with it now pretty much under control the last thing we wanted was to abandon Solo Globe. So, we had another go at the engine. One last bleeding of the complete system, some Aerostart into the air intake and it fired. The motor was running like a Swiss clock. We didn't know for how long for but it was running.

The emergency radio crackled, "Solo Globe Challenger, this is the War Ship Newcastle"

Talk about shivers and goose bumps.

I cry (again) as I type.

At this point we had blue sky, calm, settled weather, an engine ticking over and a jury rig allowing us to sail the boat in a fashion. We were 95 nm off the coast and given reasonable conditions it would be fair to assume that in around about 48 hours or less we would have made landfall at either Bermagui, Ulladulla, or a bit further north, to Sydney.

The Newcastle took up a position nearby and deployed a large inflatable dinghy which scarpered over to us pulling to a halt about 5 metres off our stern. A young male officer spoke first and I remember the conversation as if it were one minute ago.

Him: "Good morning Sir."

Me: "Good morning to you too, old mate"

Him: "Sir, we are instructed to remove all personnel from the vessel."

Me: "Old mate, thanks very much for coming, but I really don't want to abandon my boat"

Being used to taking orders, I could see he was a little taken aback. By now you may have deduced that I'm neither in the navy nor used to taking orders.

"Old mate" backed the rescue boat away a tad and had a chit chat with the warship on radio, I guess telling them about this recalcitrant guy who was knocking back such a good offer in the middle of the ocean.

I then spoke via radio with Commander Steve Hamilton, who was a pleasure to speak with and so very helpful. It was a really comforting chat with such a fine ambassador for the navy. He asked what we would like.

I told him that we were in reasonable shape, that I thought we could get the boat back to land, but I wanted to get a weather forecast to ensure that we weren't going to get belted again over the next couple of days which might require rescuers to be called out again. I also asked if Cyril and Keir could be transferred to the ship for medical assistance.

The weather forecast for the next few days was good, so I made the decision, as did Snapey and Keith, to stick with Solo Globe but that Cyril and Keir would leave.

"Old mate" manoeuvred the inflatable alongside us, and Keir and Cyril were dispatched in a fairly ungainly manner (Keir says I pushed him but I reckon I was steadying him) into the rescue boat and they were whisked away.

Keir later wrote:

It was decided that Glen and I would go, leaving Keith, Tony and Bob. The rubber duck came alongside and I was pushed into it, (thanks Tony) and Glen and I were taken aboard. A medical check, hot showers, and four bowls of hot soup later things were looking up at last. We then found out the HMAS Newcastle had been looking all night for us, with no signal from our EPIRB and the word that night to family and media was that they had lost us. I can only imagine how they felt hearing that news.

They had been searching, allowing for drift only, unaware of our jury rig pushing us away from their search area. Still, a happy ending and I thank the Commander and crew from the bottom of my heart.

They put the hammer down and we were back in Sydney 6 hours later covering 180 nm at a top speed of thirty knots.

We arrived to a media frenzy.

As you may have deduced by now, I can be a very determined individual. With the weather looking benign, an engine ticking over and a jury rig, I came up with an option that I had not previously thought feasible.

Was it possible to sail Solo Globe the 210 nm to the entrance of Lake Macquarie, up the Swansea Channel, into the Lake and moor her to the wharf at Lake Macquarie Yacht Club?

I had started to think about this as a distinct possibility and for reasons that may elude many, I decided that if things unfolded favourably I would love to give that option a crack. However, the first priority was to get Snapey, Keith and I close to land before we pursued that option. I floated my idea to them and they were up for it.

Okay then, let's see what happens and the more I thought about it, the more I wanted to do it, BUT I would not jeopardise our safety for what some may perceive as an egotistical exercise.

A radio message from Commander Hamilton scuttled my Lake Macquarie option.

He advised that a large fishing trawler from Eden was closing on our position as it had been retained by our "insurers" (So maybe I did have insurance after all?) to try to find and/or tow us to land. We rendezvoused around midday to find a not very personable trawler skipper. He was downright fucking impatient actually. It had me intrigued as to why he was not more affable. Later, I found out that he was paid $20,000 by our insurers to help us and was to receive another $20,000 to try and locate another yacht after us.

For some it's about the money. Fair enough I guess.

We secured a tow line and at around 12.30 pm he took off like a scalded cat almost skull dragging us along behind. 15 hrs later, at around 4.30 am the engine of the burgundy hulled trawler throttled back as we glided into the harbour of the NSW coastal town of Eden. We ghosted up to the wharf in darkness, casting mooring lines to eager recipients. We were greeted by so many people that it ended up being a bit of a blur, HOWEVER I do remember being bloody glad to be there.

Amidst the throng on the wharf were numerous television and print journalists, photographers and representatives of a multitude of news outlets. This was an international event and news of it occupied front pages of newspapers around the world and prime time TV for a time.

As I write, it is 27 years later and I have just watched footage of Snapey, Keith and I being interviewed on the wharf. The vision shows three very worn, weathered, wind and salt burned faces illuminated by TV camera lights, sombrely describing their feelings in the pre-dawn darkness. I find it incredibly ironic that the three of us are framed with a background of harbour waters which are incredibly still, silky smooth and calm, completely contrasting the hell on the high seas from which we had just escaped.

As I watched the footage a watershed moment in my interview occurs.

On national and international television, I declared that I was abandoning my attempt to sail solo, non-stop and unassisted around the world.

What I can also see is my raw state emotionally. The analogy has been used by others but I'll use it again. If you progressively peel away the layers of an onion, peeling each layer until all you have left is the tiny little nodule at the centre, then in your hand, you hold the soul of the onion.

Over a 15 hour period, all of my protective layers were peeled away, just like peeling away the layers of an onion. The protective layers that had been built up over my life were all gone, exposing the tiny little nodule at the centre. As I stood on the wharf at Eden, the soul of Tony Mowbray was there to see for anyone that was interested to look. Ever so sadly, I needed to almost immediately re-build those protective layers to insulate and protect me in part, from so much of the bullshit that surrounds us.

For a while I was completely cleansed.

Bob Snape "Snapey"
Glen Picasso "Cyril"
Dave Marshall "Dave"
Keith Molloy "Two" or "Senator"
Keir Enderby
Tony Purkiss "Biggles"
David Cook "Cookie"

You are men of truly outstanding character and courage, and I am honoured to call each of you a true mate, which in my mind is the highest accolade I can give. True mates always have each other's backs. You all had my back in Bass Strait and continue to do so to this day. I am forever in awe of you all. I love you all and will do so until I no longer walk this earth.

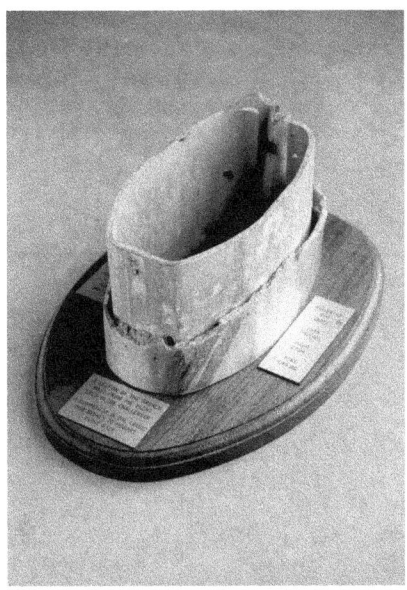

The jagged edge of the mast where it broke in Bass Strait. Snapped at internal strengthening sleeve.

Remnant of sail cloth and mast slide as cut away in Bass Strait.

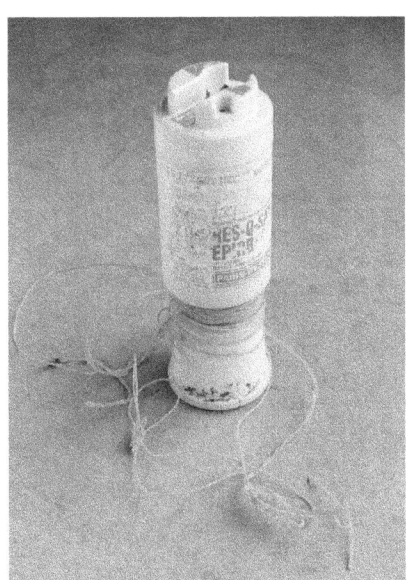

One of two EPIRBS from 1998 Sydney to Hobart.

My tether (umbilical cord) from '98 Hobart.

Cookie's plastic toy dolphin that gave him, and us, great comfort.

Cookie (nearest) and Dave in the Chopper after airlift.

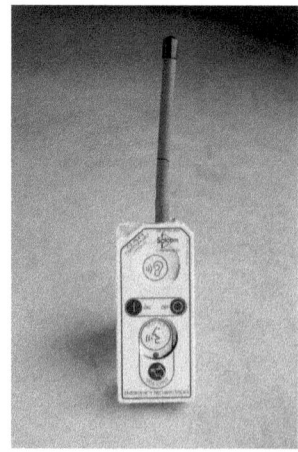

Emergency handheld radio dropped from Orion search aircraft.

Found by the HMAS Newcastle. Snapey at wheel, me standing. Note, A frame jury rig and stump of mast.

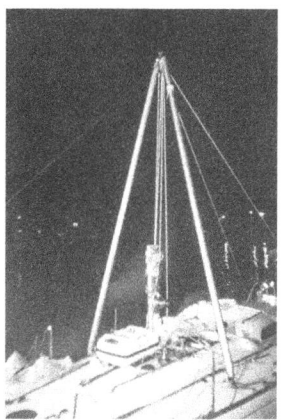

In Eden, close up of A frame and all that remained of the mast.

Snapey and I in Eden embracing. I am holding an EPIRB.

Snapey, Keith and I. Bloody glad to be alive.

Solo Globe arriving home via road transport.

HMAS Newcastle, Australia Day 1999 with Commander Steve Hamilton. From left, Cookie, Keir, Cyril with broken wrist, Biggles on crutches, me, Keith, Dave, Snapey.

Crew and families on HMAS Newcastle. Imagine the flow on effect if one of us didn't make it back.

CHAPTER 13
Catastrophic or Phenomenal

The inaugural Sydney to Hobart yacht race was first held in 1945 and was conceived of, as a "cruise in company", but evolved into a race in which just nine yachts competed. In the early days of the race, carrier pigeons were released from some yachts with messages attached providing updated positions.

Each year, from 1945 to 1998, many thousands of men, women and children competed. In some races prior to 1998, crews were tested at times by seriously bad weather.

In my humble opinion, the 54th edition of the race in 1998 was the granddaddy of all the bad weather "tests". When interviewed by Mark Rothfield for Rob Mundle's excellent book, "Fatal Storm", I concluded by saying: *"Before this I thought I knew where the top rung of the ladder was. I was wrong. I now know it's about 50% higher"*.

For any reader wishing to gain a more detailed overview of what happened to other boats I strongly recommend "Fatal Storm".

Some Facts:

115 yachts started.
71 yachts retired.
44 finished.
5 yachts sank.
7 yachts abandoned.
55 sailors rescued.
6 men lost their lives.

The knock-on effect on competitors, family and friends was, and continues to be, dramatic for some. There are a number of sailors who have never ventured on the open ocean again. I completely and utterly understand and accept why they made that choice.

Larry Ellison, the US computer mogul was aboard his maxi "Sayonara" and is credited with having said that if he lives to be 1000 years old he will never do the race again.

In my opinion, no winners came out of the 1998 Sydney to Hobart yacht race, and for me it is not important to record the name of the boat that crossed the finish line 1st or those awarded a trophy. All boats and crews have my respect.

On Australia Day, 26th January 1999 HMAS Newcastle visited Newcastle. Commander Steve Hamilton invited us and our families aboard to meet some of the crew that were involved in helping us. I have a photograph of the eight of us surrounded by wives, parents and children taken on the foredeck of the Newcastle. Every time I look at that photograph, the one resounding thought that comes to mind immediately is how so many people's lives would have been adversely affected for a generation or more if just one of us had not survived.

If the weather "bomb" had exploded further away from land than it did, many rescue vehicles would have been stretched to beyond their capabilities and the list of fatalities and associated carnage would have been significantly greater. We were lucky that it happened where it did geographically.

We were extremely fortunate to have at hand those people from government, professional and volunteer organisations who came to the fore in exemplary fashion, aiding in the search and rescue. Their performance was world class. Hero is an overused word today and I do not use it lightly. Make no mistake though, the people involved in those rescues are true heroes and we should be forever grateful.

The race is jointly organised by the Cruising Yacht Club of Australia (CYCA) in Sydney and the Royal Yacht Club of Tasmania (RYCT).

My impression, rightly or wrongly, is that the CYCA take the major responsibility for the race whilst the RYCT supplements it at the back end.

There were various inquiries conducted after the race including those by the CYCA, the Australian Bureau of Meteorology (BOM) and a coroner's inquest charged with finding the cause of death of six sailors and making recommendations to minimise risk in the future.

In the BOM internal review of their own performance they, in part, found "*Our performance was world class*"

I strongly beg to differ.

The following diatribe has nothing to do with their weather forecasting skills. It is more to do with ingrained practice that would appear to be almost immovable. When weather forecasts are issued by BOM, they include a word association, as well as a numeric wind strength, so that mug punters like myself can get a more complete picture as to what to expect.

For example, they may say that the forecast for the next 12 hour period is for "Light Winds at 10 knots or less" or "Moderate winds at 11 to 16 knots" etc.

The actual scales and associated words are:

Calm: nil breeze
Light: 10 knots or less
Moderate: 11-16 knots
Fresh: 17 - 21 knots
Strong: 22 - 33 knots
Gale: 34 - 47 knots
Storm: 48 - 63 knots
Hurricane: 64 knots or more **ONLY USED FOR TROPICAL WATERS**

The problem is that a massive percentage of Australian waters is not in the tropics, so when a weather forecast is issued for non-tropical waters, the word Hurricane cannot, and is not, used. The word used for the **ABSOLUTE WORST** conditions to be expected in a non-tropical area is "**Storm**". To my mind the word "Storm" does not take me to a state of ultimate alert. Does it do so for you?

By far the vast majority of us seasoned sailors did not know that "Storm" was (and still is) the top rung of the ladder and I am prepared to bet that many today still are not aware. I spoke to many experienced sailors after the race and asked them what they thought the associated word was that BOM used to indicate the highest wind strength in their forecasts for the Hobart race area? Everyone I spoke to thought that there would have to be a word to paint a higher alert than "Storm" but did not know what it was. That is because one does not exist.

If BOM used a word like "Catastrophic" or "Phenomenal" as word association for expected wind strengths in excess of 63 knots, then it stands to reason that many seafarers would be far more guarded and make more prudent decisions. To my mind, it's a simple fix and I still shake my head in wonderment that it hasn't changed.

The coroner's inquest, for which I was interviewed along with many others, was as you would expect, a most comprehensive and far reaching objective analysis and without doubt Mr. John Abernathy's findings are the best reference as to what happened. His report set out many valuable recommendations and resulted in changes both for future Sydney to Hobart races and other yachting events internationally.

I understand that the youngest crew member in the '98 race was 12 years old. There were a number of other young, inexperienced crew, including one or more that had won a school competition and were rewarded with a berth on the race. Some prize.

New regulations have largely outlawed that and 18 years of age is now the minimum to be able to compete. More stringent requirements are in place requiring crew to have achieved "safety at sea" qualifications. The list is extensive and warranted. What worries me a little is that we can all be "fast forgetters".

I've heard people say that it won't happen again.

That's bullshit. It is entirely possible that generations to come will look at some of the requirements as being too restrictive and think about relaxing them. It's not a matter of if those conditions will ever reoccur, it's a matter of when.

For those that may be caught in "Catastrophic" or "Phenomenal" conditions you need to be as well prepared as possible.

Six men from three yachts paid the ultimate price in pursuit of their sport.
"Sword of Orion": Glyn Charles
"Business Post Naiad": Bruce Guy and Phillip Skeggs
"Winston Churchill": John Dean, Jim Lawler and Michael Bannister
Gentlemen, I salute you.

I must go down to the seas again, to the lonely sea and the sky,
And all I ask is a tall ship and a star to steer her by;
And the wheel's kick and the wind's song and the white sail's shaking,
And a grey mist on the sea's face, and a grey dawn breaking.

NEVER, EVER GIVE IN!

I must go down to the seas again, for the call of the running tide
Is a wild call and a clear call that may not be denied;
And all I ask is a windy day with the white clouds flying,
And the flung spray and the blown spume, and the sea-gulls crying.

I must go down to the seas again, to the vagrant gypsy life,
To the gull's way and the whale's way where the wind's like a whetted knife;
And all I ask is a merry yarn from a laughing fellow-rover,
And quiet sleep and a sweet dream when the long trick's over.

John Masefield

CHAPTER 14
We can all be slow learners and fast "forgetters"

Snapey, Keith and I set about tidying the boat up. As we did, we took initial inventory of the major damage with the list including the mast, boom, some sails, laptop, electronic navigation systems, rigging and electrics. The cost would amount to tens of thousands of dollars. To add to our woes, the engine had failed again.

The structural integrity of the hull and deck appeared to me to be okay, which is a huge rap for Peter Cole, the designer, and Bruce Fairlie, the builder.

Keith's wife Jane, had driven 8 hours through the night and was standing on the wharf when we arrived for a very emotional reunion. Late morning, I urged Keith and Jane to leave Snapey and I to it, as we had found out that Cookie and Dave had lost no time in hiring a large enclosed trailer in Newcastle and were part way into the 8 hour drive to come help. We were now safe, and it was important to me that Jane and Keith have some time together to start their emotional recovery.

The cavalry, disguised as Cookie and Dave, arrived mid-afternoon and we four got to it, loading the trailer with sodden sails, computers, trashed bunk cushions, saturated pillows and bedding, wet weather clothing, sea boots, dripping navigation charts plus a thousand and one other items all got heaved into the trailer for sorting later.

Gilko (of "Do I actually have insurance cover?" fame) arranged for Solo Globe to be craned from the water and trucked home, however, some had negotiation was needed to convince me to abandon the idea of getting her back home under her own steam. I am a stubborn bastard.

The boys managed, unbelievably, to wangle a room at the pub. The town was bursting at the seams and getting a room was like winning lotto. With the trailer loaded to the hilt, we headed there for a, luxurious hot shower and dry clothes. The room was basic and just big enough for two double bunks and not much else, but for me it equated to the best six-star resort you could nominate and I was not complaining. At the bar, I knocked back three beers and a glorious steak. By 10 pm I was totally rooted, falling asleep in my chair so I gave in to exhaustion and went to bed.

I don't think I have ever slept so soundly.

The next day we were up early, doing more interviews and attending to the boat. As we four drove away from Eden Harbour that morning, I looked wistfully out of the window at my beloved boat. I felt like I was deserting her.

Lorraine and I had organised for her and the kids to stay at a caravan park, a couple of hours drive from home, for a week whilst I was away.

When I had stepped ashore in Eden my first request went something like:

"I NEED a mobile phone please!"

"I NEED to speak with Lorraine and the kids!"

A very emotional conversation ensued that was chockful of tears all round, supercharged with deep emotion. She wanted to come home but I urged her to stay put and enjoy their remaining days. I had a lot of "stuff" to attend to (read: a totally rooted boat with me not far behind it), so we decided that I would focus on the "stuff" and when reunited we could concentrate on family.

Also, I wanted to "protect" Lorraine, Holly and Jordan from the media scrum. Lorraine would have been trampled in the frenzy plus I didn't want to subject my 6 and 5 year old children to more anguish. I wanted to keep them cocooned for the time being and so it was convenient that they were out of town.

The boys dropped me off at home and as I walked through the door at 6 pm on New Year's Eve the phone was ringing. It was Craig Hamilton, a longstanding ABC radio broadcaster. Craig is a top shelf human being for whom I have a lot of time.

His opening words were, "Tony, tell me to piss off if you want to?"

"Nah Craig, you have always been very good to me. How can I help mate?"

He asked if I would like to come to the studio on the morning of 2nd January for a live interview, to which I agreed. I spent two hours live on air with Craig. I am an emotional person and make no apology for wearing my heart on my sleeve. What you see is what you get. Tears flowed in torrents from both Craig and I as raw emotion filled the studio and airwaves. In the years since, I have met a lot of people who listened to that interview and comment on how deeply affected they were. One lady, driving to Sydney with her husband, told me they both had tears streaming continuously down their cheeks.

Lorraine, Holly and Jordan arrived home that afternoon and as they got out of the car we collectively embraced in the driveway for what seemed like an eternity. There were lots of muffled, "I love you", through sobs of unadulterated joy that we were together as one.

Talk about bring me undone again all these years later.

Bloody hell! The tears!

I caught up (as a priority) with Gilko, taking my cheque book. I'm not sure if the insurance company ever knew about the deferred payment plan but my file was marked, "paid".

I was insured! You bloody beauty.

My insurers first task was to determine if they would accept a claim and as January ticked over, facts were gathered and reviewed. The claim was accepted. YES!

Gilko was a shining light and exemplary in his attitude over the ensuing months as we worked together with the shared goal of getting Solo Globe back together in one piece. I could not have asked for better support than that from Gilko and his team in such a sensitive and caring manner. They were brilliant. I was glad to be alive and would not have worried if a claim had been rejected, but it was comforting to know that the financial side of things was going to be okay.

Solo Globe was craned out of the water onto a low loader and delivered back to my care within a few days. Once back home, Snapey, Keith (haven't they got a home to go to?) and I did some work on the underwater hull, repairing deep scarring caused by the jagged broken mast. We relaunched her and using Dave's (another person who seemingly didn't have a home to go to) Dad's yacht, Dave, Lorraine, Holly, Jordan and I towed Solo Globe to a marina berth at LMYC as the engine was still buggered.

Taped diary:

The world trip is off. I have cancelled it. It's now 2 weeks since Hobart and the brain starts to say that maybe it wasn't that bad etc. but its off.

I've been pushing the envelope fairly hard for the last 18 months and doing it on a shoestring. I decided out there that with the cost of and the amount of damage and the time it would require to get back on track that it is unfair on my family. I would have to push myself to a new high, time wise and financially to leave in October '99.

I came so close to dying out there. I ask myself why am I doing this? Why do I need it? I cannot find a satisfactory answer. If I did leave for the world trip I would not be here for Holly's 8th birthday (her 7th was just days prior to this taping) *It all gets a bit tedious and monotonous and starts to become pretty selfish so I decided to cancel it. It would require a minimum of 6 months away from my children and wife. What do I need to prove? It all sounds wonderful and romantic sometimes but I thought stuff it, I don't need that anymore. When you have a near death experience it changes your attitude in a lot of ways. I'm going to try to get the boat back in one piece slowly and progressively, not rushing and without too much pressure. I'll then just toodle around the lake, mow the lawn, swim in our pool, drink some beer and try to have a reasonably relaxed life. I'll work hard for Flano and try to repay him for the support he has given me. I won't give up sailing. I'll sail until the day I die but I will be more selective as to when and where I sail in future.*

The next day, Sunday, we had a reunion at our home, strictly limited to crew and families. It was a wonderful day. I had been looking forward to it with great anticipation and knew the others were as well. Cookie gave each of the crew a gift that represented a poignant moment relative to them. He gave me a toy monkey as a reminder of the monkey that I saw perched on the stump of the broken mast when hallucinating. The thought he put into each gift was extremely touching. We swam, drank beer, barbecued steaks and devoured cheesecakes. It was great to have just the inner circle there, rejoicing in each other's company, thrilled to be alive.

I was shell shocked by the events of Bass Strait, and some might use the phrase, "Post-Traumatic Stress". They might well be correct. Bass Strait blew me out of the water physically, emotionally and mentally and any other "ally" you can think of.

I remember going down to the boat one Saturday morning, intent on getting stuck into my job list as I wasn't getting traction on my tasks. I went below and sat in Snapey's navigator's seat to start working my way through the mess there. As I pondered what to do first, I found a piece of the shattered clear Perspex that had imploded above my bunk. Immediately my thoughts went back to that moment and the ensuing 15 hours. I became transfixed, sitting there, not moving, doing absolutely nothing but think, for 5 hours.

After 5 hours of sitting and thinking, I closed the boat up and went home.

Eventually, with the help of the crew and many others, the Solo Globe rebuild took shape, albeit not at a frantic pace, as time was on my side having abandoned the world attempt.

In 1993, I had my first crack at public speaking when I spoke at a charity fundraiser. I really enjoyed the experience and wanted to do it again, not realising at the time that I would become thoroughly hooked. From 1993 through to late 1998 I had volunteered my time to speak at numerous charity fundraisers and for many community service groups about our fundraising efforts that we had piggybacked onto our sailing adventures thus far. In early 1999, with a suddenly increased public profile, invitations flowed thick and fast for me to speak and I always tried to assist where possible.

New York's Vanity Fair Magazine featured me in an article. It's a long way from being an apprentice in an underground coal mine to Vanity Fair magazine, but I was happy to go along for the ride. The boys gave me plenty.

Over the years, I had read many "I survived" or "I achieved" books and learned that many of the authors had gravitated towards corporate speaking to earn income, whether they be the short-term flavour of the month or, if they were good at it, became a long-standing and successful speaker. I thought that as a way to earn income this sounded right up my alley. You mean I can get paid to talk? Give me a hard job! How long has this been going on? I'd been flapping my gums for years for no charge.

Which came first? The chicken or the egg?

I met with Steve Potter who ran a large speaker's bureau, booking paid professional speakers for conferences, dinners, product launches etc.

Steve, rightly so, was not keen to place me with his corporate clients until he was confident that I could cut it in the big league of corporate speaking as against free charity work. Fair enough.

One day, he rang to tell me that he had an enquiry from Goodyear Tyres, but that their budget was too lean for it to be commercially viable for him. He offered me the opportunity to liaise direct with Goodyear to maybe earn a few dollars. Let me at it!

In 1999, Peter Smith from Goodyear booked me for my first professional speaking engagement. I earned $500, which was a very welcome supplement to my pay packet. Trying to sound humble, but not succeeding, I delivered the goods and Peter was thrilled with my presentation. He immediately booked me for another function a few weeks hence. I absolutely loved it and was now seriously thinking about being a professional speaker one day.

I had managed to get the boat back in some semblance of order and with a working engine, but no mast, we had many enjoyable family escapades on the lake.

If the Sydney to Hobart race was held every six months I'm pretty sure no one would compete, because it takes at least 6 months for the not so good memories to fade.

We can all be slow learners and fast forgetters. I am definitely a slow learner sometimes, and a bloody fast forgetter a lot of the time. I've said it before - the human brain can rationalise out most things if it tries hard enough. Unbelievable as it may seem, it was not quite two weeks after we escaped Bass Strait with our lives intact, that my brain started rationalising and whispering to my sub conscious.

Maybe it wasn't quite that bad?

Whisper, whisper, whisper.

This is evident when reading the opening lines of the following tapings.

Taped Diary:
9th January

My world trip is off. I have cancelled that. It's now nearly 2 weeks since Hobart and the **brain starts to say maybe it wasn't that bad** *etc. but its off.*

Whisper, whisper, whisper

Taped Diary: *(in part, verbatim)*
24th February

The world trip? I don't know what is going on there. I decided out there it was off. It didn't take long after I got back, about 2 weeks or so at the most, where I started having doubts about that decision. I have since thought about it but haven't applied myself deeply, as I need a bit more time. At this stage, my thinking is that I am definitely not going to go this year. I am trying to make up my mind whether to do it at all. If I am going to do it I will look at leaving next year in October 2000. A number of people have asked me if the trip is off? I say yes, it is. They respond saying they believe that is the right decision.

Just lately I have said to people that I am thinking of maybe doing it and you can see they are a bit taken aback. Haven't you had enough you idiot? I was genuinely scared out there that night. I have thought about it a bit and I know the human mind can rationalise out anything if you try hard enough.

This is a tough period.

I look at it and say the conditions were pretty bad. I look at all the experienced yachtsman that were there as well and to a man they concur as to how bad it was. I think, I might strike such bad conditions again but the chances of it must be fairly slim. In all the years I have been out there it was the worst I have ever had it so hopefully it won't happen like that again. If I do get clobbered like that again I would like to think that I would be a better prepared. I have learnt.

You don't commit yourself to a project like Solo Globe Challenge 2000 on a whim. I have put myself through a fair bit over the last 9 months. You don't walk away from that too easily. I set myself a goal and I am the sort of person that once I have set a goal I like to achieve it. If I delay it a year it will be easier to sneak up on it. I need to see what develops. Let it take its own course. I don't know how long it will take, a week, a month or two months. We will just have to see.

I have to talk to Lorraine once I get it straight in my own mind. I will need to see how she feels.

So, there it is, the sub conscious whisper had now morphed into a full-blown discussion in the conscious part of my crazy mind just 58 days after escaping the horrors of Bass Strait.

February rolled into March and work continued on the boat.

John Denton owns a yacht mast manufacturing and rigging company, Whalespar, a 1 hour drive from home. John was the rigger for Kay Cottee when she became the first woman in the world, and 2nd Australian ever, to go around the world solo, non-stop and unassisted in 1988. John is an extremely experienced and accomplished mast maker and it would be a foolish person that ignored John's always sage advice.

I had asked him to prepare a quotation for a new mast, telling him that one essential criteria was that when, not if, the boat went upside down again, I wanted there to be a good chance that the mast would be standing when the boat righted itself. I also shared that I didn't know where I was at with the world trip but that the quote should be prepared assuming I was doing it.

In March, at a secondhand bookshop I paid $4 for "The Longest Walk" by George Meegan. The book chronicles George's longest unbroken walk in the Western Hemisphere, when from 1977 to 1983 he walked 19,000 miles from the southern tip of South America to the northern tip of Alaska. It's a fascinating read and I recommend it. After reading just the foreword, I felt that it was four bucks well spent, but continued on to devour the remainder of the book. The foreword reproduced, in part, is from a speech delivered by President Theodore Roosevelt at the dedication of The Panama Canal. Since reading it that first time I have come across variations and, with respect, I have modified it as well.

It is not the critic who counts, nor the man or the woman who points out how the strong man or woman stumbles, or where the doer of deeds could have done better. The credit belongs to the man or the woman who is actually in the arena, whose face is marred by dust and sweat and blood, who knows great enthusiasm, great devotion, and the triumph of achievement, and who at the worst, if he or she fails, at least fails while doing greatly, so that his or her place shall never ever, ever, ever be with those cold and timid souls who neither know victory nor defeat.

For me it translates to, "You just have to have a go".

George's book was incredibly inspirational. He endured 7 years of suffering deep lows and embracing the highs. He slept in pig sheds, gutters, under tables and dossed in flop houses. Sometimes he ate nothing for days, or foraged from rubbish bins. He froze, was hot, was sad or was uplifted. It is unbelievable what he went through. I would have given up for sure.

But then again, would I have?

On a Saturday evening in late March, 300 people gathered at the Cruising Yacht Club of Australia for a very emotional evening to pay homage to the many heroes that came to the fore in December. Snapey and wife, Alana, Biggles and wife, Mary Anne, and Cookie, Lorraine and I represented our team. I shook hands with John Winning, the skipper of Winston Churchill from which three crew perished. What can you say?

Nothing really.

Business Post Naiad lost Bruce Guy, the owner, along with crew member, Phil Skeggs. Bruce and Phil's widows had flown in from Tasmania. I wanted to connect with them in some small way and made my way to them waiting for a quiet moment. I managed, in a highly emotional state, to tell them from which boat I was and expressed my deepest sympathies to them. I gave both women a hug. Mrs. Skeggs could not speak. As I hugged Mrs. Guy, she leaned into my ear and whispered faintly "You must have gone to hell and back". All I could manage was a muffled, "Yes, we did".

I then moved to a quiet part of the auditorium and gazed through wall to ceiling glass, at the yachts bobbing sedately in their Marina berths.

Tears streamed uncontrollably down my cheeks.

From my voice diary, not quite 2 weeks after escaping Bass Strait, where I said, *"the brain starts to say maybe it wasn't that bad"*, the discussion in my head had ramped up and was now raging.

I had not broached the subject with Lorraine and the day after the CYCA function, as we drove home I pulled to the side of the road. I turned to her and asked, "If I said I wanted to go back, what would you say?" Without hesitation, she replied "If you want to go back, then go back". For the rest of the journey we talked, and it turned out that she knew all along that I'd been struggling with the question and had decided she would back me.

Taped diary:

On the way home from Sydney yesterday morning Lorraine and I had a good chat in the car about my world aspirations. I have been mulling the whole thing over since mid-January and I am now thinking seriously about trying to get it up and running again. We spoke about the pros and cons of it all. If Kay Cottee can do it and the current young Aussie guy having a go, Jessie Martin, can do it, then, why can't I? If they can, I can. Additionally, the boat has proved itself to be brick shithouse and the new mast, when built, will take a huge beating if need be.

I am thinking of leaving in October 2000. If I do decide to go ahead I will just chip away at it quietly and make an announcement later. My major concern is leaving the kids for 6 months. We have decided to not say anything to them at this point. Holly worries a lot.

I had read about and learnt a hell of a lot about what happened in Bass Strait and why. I had spoken to many sailors who had been there as well, whose abilities I greatly respected and I took on board their observations. I revisited key parts of the experience.

I did a lot, and I mean a fucking lot, of thinking.

The rationalisation process continued. The ferocious conditions we experienced were so abnormal that the chance of me getting that combination of wind and wave action again in my life would be fairly minimal (I told myself). Sure, it could happen again, but the chances would have to be fairly slender? If it did happen again, I reckon I would be better equipped in a lot of ways.

Thinking, thinking, thinking.

Sometimes, when trying to solve a problem, the brain goes around and around, like a merry go round, stopping at a possible answer. But perhaps there is another answer?

More thinking happens, and off goes the merry go round again, but it stops again in the same spot.

Then another ride, only to arrive back at the same answer.

Finally, the realisation hits, THAT, must be the answer.

Around and around and around went my brain, always coming back to the one answer.

The answer was the word, COMMITMENT.

I could not escape the fact that in June 1997, I had 100% committed to having a crack and whilst I didn't have much of a shot left in the locker, I knew I had to go back. In April 1999 I recommitted.

I have never seemed to be able to accurately convey in mere words the mental turmoil and anguish that I put myself through from early January to April 1999. As I sit at the keyboard in 2025 reflecting on that time, it is like looking from the outside in, through a very different set of lenses. I struggle to come to terms with what I put myself, and much more importantly, others through. I could construct pages and pages of monologue, but I don't think I ever would be able to explain to you, or to me, the true essence of what drove me.

I knew I was a long way from being right psychologically, but I just knew I had to give it another go.

In so many ways it was a need to "get back on the horse".

DREAM
THINK
TALK
COMMIT
ACT

Taped Diary:
19th April

I have decided that the around the world trip is on but it's difficult to say it out aloud. I did tell John Denton this morning, so it's all systems go with him. I am going to put things in motion fairly quickly. I have delayed departure until October 2000. I am pretty relaxed about it but am also very hesitant, which I suppose is only natural and should pass with time. I am not going to make a lot of noise about my decision. I will just talk about it progressively. I just want to coast along with it as I'm getting a bit tired of talking about it so much. It's time for some action and work. All talk and no work is a bit of bullshit really.

Actions speak louder than words.

The boat was now back on its mooring at the yacht club, necessitating a 300 metre row back and forth in my small fibreglass dinghy. It was a lovely autumn Sunday in early May, complete with blue sky and tranquil waters, and sunset was imminent. I was heading back to shore after working for the day, standing up, paddling the dinghy with one oar on alternating sides, "Indian style". Without warning I experienced one of those never to be forgotten moments of poignancy when a massive burst of raw energy suddenly gushed up from within. I let out a huge shout, yelling at the top of my lungs, "Yeeeeeeeees!" pumping the air with closed fist.

I was a long way from being 100% right, but I was back.

CHAPTER 15
A Nudie run with Cookie

I was both energised and motivated, but hesitant, and not fully convinced, however, I knew it had to happen. I hoped that as each day went by, I would become more focused on the job at hand and less focused on what had happened in the past. I remember thinking, we have to keep looking forward, while keeping an eye on where we have been, to learn.

I was haltingly comfortable that it would work out somehow, even though I didn't have all the answers. I reminded myself that it wasn't the first time I'd been in a position of scrambling to get a project completed, and it would not be the last. I now had 17 months to get my act together. I didn't want to run out of prep time at the back end and get caught.

When I acquired Solo Globe, air vents were fitted to the deck. They were supposedly designed to allow air in or out but not water. When upside down in Bass Strait, submerged under tons of water, it was VERY clear that the design intent did not match the outcome. Water fucking pissed in. I removed all of the air vents and filled in the holes, so that the only openings left in the boat were the forward and aft hatches through which I could access below decks. I would much rather be hot and sweaty in the tropics rather than wet, freezing and drowning in the Southern Ocean.

The aft hatch to below deck was a sliding one and impossible to completely waterproof. In Bass Strait, a huge amount of water had flooded in around the perimeter and I knew I had to do something to minimise future ingress. I am "hands on", far preferring to do my own work where possible, for a number of reasons including keeping cost down. Plus, if it fails, I only have myself to blame. In the marine industry, there are very few people that understand the rigours of the Southern Ocean and extended ocean sailing. People that haven't been there do not get it when it comes to understanding how important it is to have the spot on, right piece of equipment, installed correctly, to cope in that environment.

I designed and built a moulded permanent cover from fibreglass with a foam core that I fixed permanently over the sliding hatch, almost like a hat. Cookie's "Belmont Smash Repairs" team spray painted it gloss white and it looked bloody fantastic.

To help build a template for the cover, I climbed into the industrial garbage bin at the yacht club and rooted around, eventually digging out a discarded rectangular foam tomato box. I cut segments from it, sticking them together to form a featherweight mould of the desired shape. Whilst shaping the mould I had an "expert" watching me from the wharf. After 10 minutes, this unknown expert observer couldn't help himself, blurting out, "That won't work!"

I asked why he thought that.

He replied that he "just knew it wouldn't work".

I asked if he knew the purpose of it, which he didn't, but he still insisted that it wouldn't work.

Many are critical. Many think they are an expert. Many rush to tell you why it won't work. Many think they have a better way. That hatch cover ended up sailing approximately 40,000 nm to various corners of the globe, saving my arse on more than one occasion.

Sorry old mate, but it did work.

As previously mentioned, Solo Globe was designed to be raced by 8 crew. To prepare her for solo sailing, I invested a huge amount of time redesigning the deck layout, sail handling systems, sail configuration, and cockpit layout, including new updated winches. I dovetailed those changes in with the new mast so that she could be sailed efficiently and safely solo. She ended up seamlessly integrated and, in many ways, a new boat, as technology advances allowed me to set her up in a way not possible when originally launched in 1984.

I knew that each time I got out of the cockpit to move around on the deck, I would consume fiercely coveted energy. Clambering around the deck would also increase the chance of getting wet and cold, injured or falling over the side, so I wanted to minimise leaving the relative safety and comfort of the cockpit. I started at the bow and worked my way aft to the stern, leaving no stone unturned in my quest for efficiency. By the time, I had finished, I knew every nut and bolt that held that boat together.

"You cannot make a silk purse out of a sow's ear" goes the expression, and in so far as the old shattered mast was concerned, that saying was, in part, true.

The old mast was designed in a bygone era and certainly not with solo sailing in mind. On reflection, the work that we had done on it in preparation for the Sydney to Hobart was in some ways, trying to bring it to "silk purse" status, which was never going to happen due to its core design. It was a great bit of kit but losing it over the side was a good thing at the end of the day, as it enabled me to purchase a more fit for purpose piece of equipment.

The interest in the Bass Strait catastrophe was overwhelming and the public thirsted for more information. I organised three functions in July 1999 allowing the community to meet the crew and hear more of our story. The evenings were held in the auditoriums of three licensed clubs and were a roaring success. Each event ran for 2.5 hours and we raised $7000 for the charity, John Hunter Children's Hospital Kids Club.

The functions required a lot of organising and at completion, I took stock realising that I was seriously burning the candle at both ends and the rubber band was stretched taut. I can be my own worst enemy a lot of the time, stepping forward to be involved when often, it is not in my best interests to do so. I guess I'm not the only one afflicted in that way.

Public profile can be self-perpetuating. A newspaper story can feed a TV report, which might generate radio interviews. Speaking voluntarily for a community service group (which I love doing) generates more requests as word spreads that, "Tony will help out". I had a lot on my plate and decided that I badly needed to prioritise. I was a husband and a father to 2 young children, and still, somehow, working full time. Those commitments alone are enough to keep many fully occupied.

If I wasn't busy enough, I also had to source a serious amount of sponsorship money. I had to finish repairing the boat, prepare and provision her for the journey, get to the start line, and keep the fires burning at home including throughout the 6 plus months I planned to be at sea.

Throw in speaking requests from community groups, fundraising activities, plus trying to lay the foundations for a possible future as a professional speaker, and it is easy to see why some of these things were not being done well.

I realised that if I didn't focus on the preparation and execution of the trip first and foremost, then at the end of the day I would not have a real hook to hang my hat on. I decided to scale back community involvement for the time being, knowing that the opportunity to help would always be there.

I also put on the back burner my aspirations to be a professional speaker, and pivoted to a reactive, rather than proactive approach. If an income earning opportunity presented itself before departure, I would grab it with both hands. However, I would not divert my energies by proactively trying to build that business for the time being. I needed to make the world trip as successful as possible and then I would be able to focus on being a paid speaker.

In July 1999 I was interviewed by Seargent Dave Upston of Sydney Water Police for the coroner. He was a lovely guy with a very empathetic approach as he guided me down memory lane. It was a huge "trip" for me as I delved into emotion charged memories. He was also keen for me to provide any suggestions that might help create a safer environment for future seafarers. I have always remembered Dave with great fondness.

In mid 1999 I attended the launch of Rob Mundle's fantastic book, "Fatal Storm", which documented the 1998 Hobart race. Commander Hamilton launched the book on board the warship Newcastle in Sydney, and it was wonderful to see him and some of the crew again.

At the launch, a pivotal moment occurred when I met Roger "Clouds" Badham. Clouds is a world-renowned meteorologist and weather forecaster for international ocean going yachts, providing marine forecasting and weather routing. Over the years, he has guided many top class boats around the planet, dovetailing them perfectly into weather systems to enhance their chance of victory, or shepherding cruising sailors away from the nasty bits. The long list that have relied on his shrewd weather forecasting, includes Kay Cottee and Jesse Martin.

He has an extremely dry sense of humour and minimises the use of the spoken word. I say this with fondness and total respect! I like his style.

I emailed Clouds an outline of my project as I truly wanted him on our team if I could be so lucky. We spoke on the phone later and after the usual fact finding and preamble, the conversation distilled down to:

Me: "Roger, would you be able to tell me roughly how much it will cost?"

Roger: "How much money have you got?"

Me: "Somewhere between fuck all and not much."

Roger: "That will do. I'm in."

I was ecstatic. I told him that I seriously had bugger all money, but promised him that one day I would pay him. I just didn't know when or how much. He didn't care and said he would help regardless of financial outcome. To say that I was thrilled to have Clouds as part of the team would be a vast understatement. I was going to source and analyse my own weather information but to have Clouds' professional assessment would be the icing on the cake!

He would be a true comfort to me on many occasions.

Mark Schroder had committed to help, yet again, by having his company create a website for me. In 1999, the world of the internet, cyberspace and websites was very different to today. Building a website was complicated and time-consuming, however we finally launched it in 1999. I "archived" the site in 2001 to preserve the content. www.sailsolo.com is still worth a look.

Over the next 22 months, we posted 98 updates.

Update #1
28th June 1999
Our website is on air!

Mark Schroder has dragged me, kicking and screaming, into the 20th Century world of Cyberspace and what a fascinating trip it has been. I am deeply appreciative of, and indebted to him.

Update #2
19th July 1999

Yesterday I spent the day working on the boat fitting the two new forestay fittings to the deck that will take the 2nd furler and the forestay for the storm jib so I now have a couple more jigsaw pieces in place.

Holly and Jordan have been on school holidays for the last 2 weeks but their run comes to an end tomorrow when they return to the "salt mine".

I haven't sold the old winches yet but have been eyeing off some new ones and dreaming. I had a couple of stickers made up to advertise the website and put them on the hull last weekend.

Taped Diary:
26th July 1999

Have just left Whalespar after checking the mast progress. It looks really nice and I have so much confidence in what they are doing. It is so good to have someone else worry about the design, structural integrity etc. I get excited when I think about it standing in the boat. It will be a while but that's okay as I have many other things to do.

Jordan's 6th birthday was in August and sadly I couldn't be there as I had to go to Queensland to speak and earn some money to try and keep bank manager happy. He was never happy!

A few days later, Lorraine and I took Holly and Jordan snow skiing for the first time and they loved it. It was an expensive exercise, churning through the dollars, but well worth every cent, providing enduring memories.

Update #3
10th August 1999. (in part)

Money! Money! Money! I'm about to embark upon a concerted effort to secure some sponsorship as self-funding can go just so far.

I stumbled across a book by Pete Goss, a British yachtsman, and ripped through it in record time, totally absorbed by his story. "Close to the Wind" chronicles Pete's participation in a solo, non-stop around the world race in raw detail, including his battle to fund his campaign. The budget was £500,000 and the lengths he went to get to the starting line was scary. It included selling their home. What was particularly eye-opening to me was how closely aligned Pete's philosophies, experiences and approach were with mine.

A couple of significant differences was that I needed nowhere near £500,000 and I would NEVER sell or risk our family home in pursuit of my dreams.

Taped diary:
24th September 1999

Some money came in the other day which I had intended to use to pay off some of the $60,000 loan on the boat but I have used it for daily expenditure and am back to zero available cash again hitting another financial brick wall.

Taped diary:
30th September 1999.

I am quite excited that the new mast and boom are in the boat. John Denton and Whalespar "went the extra mile" and I am so pleased. Everything is so precise and so well thought out.

Lorraine and Snapey were there helping to stand the mast and it all went stunningly well. It is a work of art and a big step forward. We are not far off going for a sail.

The day after stepping the mast I celebrated my 44th birthday, noting in my taped diary how crazy it was that if I were still kicking in only 16 years more, I would be 60 years of age. If I thought it scary to be turning 44 years old, then let me assure you that having racked up 69 years, as I have done so now in 2025, is much greater cause for concern.

I spent a lot of time identifying the individual pieces of equipment that I needed to acquire and install, focused absolutely on quality and suitability to the task. It was not easy at times, as many are quick to spruik the real or imagined benefits of their product with the short-term goal of a quick dollar. The old Aussie saying, "She'll be right mate", wouldn't apply on this occasion. If a piece of equipment failed in the Great Southern Ocean, I couldn't go back to the shop and have it repaired or replaced. It needed to be right to start with.

Once I had identified the correct bit of kit, I then had to work out how to pay for it, which was a whole different challenge.

When contacting someone who I thought may have a suitable product, my approach often went something like, "My name is Tony Mowbray and I am going to attempt to sail solo, non-stop and unassisted around the world. I think you may have a piece of equipment suitable to the task, but I've got no money, so can we talk about that?" If you say it with a smile and a laugh in your voice, it's amazing the positive responses that can be forthcoming. My negotiations did not always turn out positively, but up front they knew I was on a limited budget and people would so often help as best they could.

A frequently asked question, then and now, is: "How do you steer the boat when asleep (or awake)?"

Broadly speaking, self-steering systems perform with or without the aid of battery power i.e. electronic or mechanical. There are other significant differences between the two options and each has its merits. To cover most bases, I chose one of each.

An electronic pilot, once engaged, will steer the boat on a straight course to a nominated point regardless of changes in wind direction. If the wind veers, the sails require trimming, which can mean regular attention. I chose an Australian made, world class, Coursemaster Autopilot as my electronic pilot. Their autopilots are brilliant and have been designed, built and exported around the world for decades. I cannot rate Coursemaster highly enough.

A mechanical self-steering wind vane will steer the boat on a course relative to a wind angle. If the unit is engaged with the wind hitting the vessel at 90 degrees, then the boat will constantly steer at that angle to the wind. If the wind veers, then so too will the course of the boat. I chose a Monitor self-steering mechanical wind vane manufactured by Scanmar International, from California USA. The vane was installed over 25 years ago. It is an incredible piece of kit, still performing at optimum levels today.

An omnipresent problem was working out how to pay for the thousand and one things I needed. I had not been able to raise any significant sponsorship and was funding the project from my earnings and small amounts of financial support.

Snapey and Alana kindly organised a fundraising night to help me pay for the Coursemaster. It was a bloody great evening, and we managed to raise most of the purchase price. Flano stepped into the breech and bought the Monitor. I am, humbled by people like Snapey, Alana and Flano.

In late October, we took the boat and new mast for a sail. Lorraine, the kids and I stayed overnight on the lake. Hoisting sail for the first time was a HUGE milestone and step forward, and was all the more special as it was done with just us four on board. As November rolled around, I was blatantly aware that my start date, 15th October, was now less than 12 months away.

The Shorthanded Sailing Association of Australia (SSAA) conveniently scheduled a two-handed race from Sydney to Auckland, NZ for March 2000. I decided that participating in the race would be an excellent "shakedown" for the new mast and the remedial work, plus give me a more finite job list. It would also get me back on the ocean allowing me to assess my head space, which was still pretty fucked up.

Entering the race would put us under the pump but would give a clear line in the sand to work to. It would have been relatively easy to drop off the pace, thinking that October 2000 was a fair way off.

As a really serious test of my head space, I decided to return from NZ solo. I knew that if couldn't cope emotionally sailing home solo for 1200 nm, then I was wasting my time (and others') contemplating 22,000 nm around the world. As soon as I mentioned the race to Keir he jumped in as crew, making it two crazies together.

As Christmas approached, I was super busy on all fronts but determined for us to enjoy some quality family time over the holiday period. I decided to isolate myself for the week between Christmas and New Year, focused solely on family. I allocated the first 2 weeks of January to work on the boat.

As 1999 drew to a close, my financial situation was getting grimmer by the day and something had to change.

Taped diary:
20th Dec 1999

I am out of money again as I have been spending up large lately. I haven't done enough work on getting sponsorship. Desperate people do desperate things and in the New Year when I am super desperate I will go out and beat the bushes again. Maybe when it's closer to October 2000 people might see the light and jump on board in a meaningful way. I know the trip is going to happen somehow for sure. Lack of money won't stop me.

The 1999 Sydney to Hobart race saw just 79 yachts compete, way down on the previous year's 115. In the weeks leading to start day, I was agog when reading some of the macho, gung ho comments made by some uninformed people who said things like "It could never happen again."

Are you serious?

Fuck me.

Would I miss going to Hobart that year?

No way.

I felt that I would probably do another race sometime, but I had much bigger fish to fry.

None of my seven blood brothers from '98 were competing either.

The new millennium was ushered in at midnight on 31st December 1999 and Lorraine, the kids and I rejoiced in the company of Cookie and Michelle at their home along with others. A standout memory is Cookie and I doing a "nudie run" up the street. It was probably not a pretty sight. I also remember drinking copious amounts of beer and playing darts with Cookie and Jordan, then just 7 years old, until 3.30 am. At that time, I walked (I use the term loosely) home with "Jordo" as my wingman and guardian.

I woke on New Year's Day with an animal of a hangover.

The new century was here.

2000 had arrived.

CHAPTER 16
Proving ground - Race to New Zealand

On the 2nd January 2000, Snapey and I delivered a yacht from Sydney to the Lake. It was a paid job for him and I gave a hand. Neither of us had been on the open ocean since the '98 race. It was supposed to be a nice, easy, relaxed day sail. The weather was benign, and we alternated between easy sailing and motoring. Parallelling the coast, we stayed close to shore and as we snuck around a rocky headland, just .5 nm off, disaster struck. In the gentlest of conditions, a rigging wire broke, and the mast crumpled into three pieces and fell over the side.

Fuck me. Our first time back at sea and we lost another mast. Our form wasn't looking too good.

We tried to retrieve the broken, twisted and tangled remnants, but decided to jettison it all. As I cut through some rope using a serrated bread knife, I cut my thigh deeply, bleeding profusely. As we were heaving the fucked mast over the side my back gave way. Earlier on, I had snagged my watch band and my $300 watch bounced off the deck and straight over the side. It was an adventurous day out, to say the least.

Does anyone sense a common thread here? I think it was all Snapey's fault.

At 9 pm that night I hobbled through the back door totally rooted - doubled over with severe back pain, a significant leg wound, hungry and having just thrown $30,000 worth of mast, rigging and sails into the ocean, not to mention my fucking watch. You would never believe it but the insurance broker for the boat was our good mate, Greg "Gilko" Gilkison. Tongue in cheek, he reckoned that any boat that I was on in the future that he had insured, was going to have the premium tripled.

Ya gotta laugh. Haven't ya?

Update #8
30ᵗʰ January 2000
SPONSORS BADLY NEEDED

I am out of money and have embarked upon a serious campaign to sign up sponsors. Be they big or small it does not matter as there is plenty of room for everyone. Ha Ha.

*This project is absolutely "ripe" and ready to be "picked" so if you can help in any way then **NOW** is the time to talk to me as I would like to get the kids back up to three feeds a day.*

Lorraine (Lucky) my wife keeps asking me how she is going to cope financially whilst I am away and I have told her that she shouldn't have to work much more than 60 hours per week and can have Sundays off.

I urge you to contact me if you are interested or perhaps you can introduce me to a decision maker who can sign a cheque. Sponsors will definitely get value for money.

Work is progressing at a hectic rate with major things happening. The new cabin windows are now in and leak proof but we'll see what happens when we put them to a real test. We have removed all the steering components and have either, replaced or refurbished everything. Generally speaking, it was in reasonable shape considering it had been doing its job for 16 years but with what it is to be subjected to, it had to have a massive birthday.

This weekend sees the preliminary fitting of the solar panel frame

We are slowly but surely getting there. I am really looking forward to some serious sea trials to see how the "jigsaw" is coming together.

It's late at night with everyone in the house tucked up in bed. Tomorrow is another day closer to "that" Sunday in October.

Barry Rae was in his mid 60's and I had known him for a couple of years, when, in 1999, he offered to work on the boat with me. I accepted and it soon became obvious that he had a great deal to offer. He is an absolute gem.

On an incalculable number of days, Barry would drive an hour from his home to the boat, arriving before me. He would work all day uncomplaining, making innumerable cups of tea for me and put up with my bullshit and tantrums, never once losing his cool. Plus, he was extremely thorough and did a top quality job.

Very few people were as interested in the project as Barry was. At day's end, when I'd had an absolute gutful, ready to down tools and go home, Barry would say, "Come on mate, let's do another hour?" On top of all of that, he would bring my morning and afternoon tea as well as my bloody lunch. The man is a legend. Barry is now nearly 90 years old and still going strong and "up for it" whenever I need a hand with anything.

Like a lot of Aussies, I have a habit of giving some people a nick name as an indication of my affection for them, "Baz" is stock standard issue for Barry, but one of my more imaginative for him is "Barry Stud Muffin Rae of Boat Harbour", (where he lives), or just plain old "Bazzarooney".

Earlier, I wrote about one of my older mates, John "Stanno" Stanton. He was an absolute champion and his character is typified by a comment I made as I delivered his eulogy.

"No one **ever** heard Stanno speak badly of another, or be critical of someone else."

Stanno was a special person, a valued friend and would never let a mate down. A particular forte of his was electrical work on boats and he was bloody good at it. Stanno was living in Sydney in 2000, and I coerced him into coming to my aid, to take charge of the electrical refurb.

Through February, he "gutted" the boat and rewired her, plus installed a huge amount of new electrical "stuff" including the Coursemaster, solar panels, wind generator, VHF and HF radios, GPS, new banks of batteries, switchboards and circuit breakers, electric bilge pumps, cabin and navigation lights and a high output alternator on the motor.

Lorraine continued to be deserving of a medal for putting up with me. It was common for me to leave home at 6 am, fit in a couple of hours on the boat before going to my "grown ups" job with Flano, and not get home until 8 pm after spending more time at the boat. I then might splice ropes on the lounge room floor, or work on the computer until 11 pm or later. My dinner was always cooked, my clothes were always washed and ironed, and Holly and Jordan were cared for, all the while with a smile on her face. I was racking up a fair sized debt to her.

The Neo Natal Intensive Care unit (NICU) at John Hunter Children's Hospital is an incredible place charged with caring for premature and term babies as well as babies with surgical conditions. If you visit the unit for any reason, you will leave a changed person and so it was with me. In March 2000, I was shown through the unit and instantly decided to help however we could. They specialise in giving tiny babies a crack at life. At that time their smallest surviving "miracle baby" had weighed a tiny 500 grams (1.1 lb.) at birth. Photographs lined the wall of the reception area and I will never forget one of a micro premmie baby's wrist encircled by her father's wedding ring worn as a bangle. How can one not help?

They needed money to purchase ten new "Vital Sign Systems Monitors", costing $18,000 each. The machines monitor the vital signs of babies to alert nursing staff in the event there is a problem. Their current machines would reach their "use by date" in 2001 and so I decided we would use the world project as the catalyst to raise money to buy as many machines as we could.

That same month, Baz and I discovered that a vital section of the engine cooling system had corroded through and the only way to repair it was to take the engine out of the boat. I had planned on pulling the engine out for a general overhaul after returning from New Zealand, but now the job had to be brought forward, crammed into an already packed job program.

The race to New Zealand was postponed until mid-May, which suited me in many respects but did mean that I would be sailing back to Australia solo in June, the 1st month of winter, which would be much colder with a higher risk of bad weather. I was keen to get out there because by the time May rolled around, it would be not quite one year and five months since our Bass Strait escapade, and I seriously needed to test the boat and myself. Arriving back in June meant that there would be just four months to departure. Time stands still for no-one, and the ticking of the clock was resonating in my head like the clanging of a church bell.

The date change meant Keir couldn't make it, so I approached Hugh Brodie. I met Hugh in 1985 and we have been firm friends ever since, sharing a similar (some would say perverse and twisted, but what would they know?) view on many aspects of life. He is a fantastic guy to be around and have as a friend, plus is a world class sailor.

By the time I spoke with Hugh, the reality of getting back to sea soon had me extremely nervous and jittery. I shared my emotional state with him asking him to "hold my hand" on the trip, taking the lead where necessary and I would follow. I knew it was to be a huge psychological mountain for me to scale and Hugh was the ideal guy to help me.

Taped Diary:
18th April 2000

I have not taped since 5th January as there has been too much on my plate. I have been keeping track a bit, writing updates for the website in the event that I write a book.

The work has been bloody relentless. The time I have spent on the boat is unbelievable. The project is all encompassing. I am absolutely stony broke and I keep spending money as if I have it and am racking up debt. Lately, I have been spending a fair amount of time trying to generate sponsorship. I am at a critical point where I can't go further without something major happening financially.

I MUST SAY IT AGAIN. THE WORK HAS BEEN RELENTLESS.

My mate Wally, at the marina, says to approach it as if I'm eating an elephant. Just one bite at a time

As an example of how broke I was and the lengths I went to:

Mum was 77 years of age and living with my sister Marina and brother-in-law, Tom. In desperation, I went to Mum, completely strapped for cash and asked her if she had any money that I could borrow, to help me keep funding the "beast". Her total wealth was $4700 in her funeral fund account.

I borrowed $3800 of it.

Jokingly, but half seriously, she asked "What if I die while you are going around the world?"

"Mum, it will be okay, just hang on"

Taped Diary:
18th April 2000

The last 3.5 months have been a series of highs and lows. Generally, I don't let it get on top of me but there are times when you wonder what it all means. I can ring 10 people, leave messages to call me back and sometimes I am flat out getting even one of the bastards to call. What do you do? You have to weed them out as you go. When you are tired and broke with not enough money to pay your bills, when your Mrs. wants some money, when you see the kids with bugger all and you don't have any money whatsoever to give them treats.

I have to make sure that at the end of all of this that there is a payback for them. I don't know what form the payback will take, absolutely fucked if I know, but it has to be something good for them, as this is bloody hard work for all of us.

Around this time, I was honoured to be appointed the Honourary Ambassador for Lake Macquarie City as lake Bicentenary celebrations took place. I was also invited to be the Master of Ceremonies at an outdoor function in August as the Olympic Torch passed through on its way to the opening of the Sydney Olympics. I was told to expect a 20,000 strong crowd. That would be a BIG day out for little Tony.

The increased public profile brought about by both the Hobart race and the imminent world trip paved the way to being invited to fulfil these very important roles.

I was on a knife's edge, balancing work, family, boat preparation, and hunting sponsorship. However, the opportunity to participate in these activities was inviting and enjoyed by my family as well. I also hoped that the increased public exposure might lead to potential sponsors recognising the project as a value proposition.

I came up with an idea around this time that went nowhere. I explored it vigorously and ran into brick walls but I'm still convinced that the concept has merit.

In Australia, there are radio networks with multiple affiliated stations around the country. I offered myself, free of charge (except for the cost of a satellite phone call) to the networks proposing they interview me regularly, possibly weekly throughout the trip, and syndicate the interviews across each station. Trying to be humble, but not succeeding, I knew I would attract regular listeners.

Each station could sell advertising to their local clients, plus the network could capitalise as well with their national client base collectively generating a lot of sustained advertising income. The only thing I wanted in return was the opportunity to surreptitiously mention from time to time, my major or supporting sponsors, should I ever find one! It would allow me to demonstrate to potential sponsors that their name would be heard regularly over a minimum of 6 months on possibly 30 or 40 radio stations weekly.

No matter how I tried, I couldn't get the concept off the ground.

Similarly, I met the Group Promotions Manager of a newspaper group with a weekly readership of one million. I offered to write a syndicated column free of charge for a year, hoping that I could get some value as a knock-on effect, but it went nowhere.

No matter how well prepared you think you are, there are always last-minute hiccups and roadblocks trying to prevent you getting to the start line. It goes with the territory and as the 13th May loomed the pressure increased.

Update #11
11th May 2000

The stress of it all. It is some time since my last update. I have been so busy with preparation for the Trans-Tasman Race and all the other various bits and pieces that I have to do that I have not had time to sit at the keyboard. I am in Sydney with the race starting in two days and we still have a myriad of tasks to complete.

For the last 4 weeks or so I have had myself under a huge physical and mental workload and stress is at an all-time high but somehow it is coming together. I have a nervous anticipation as start time draws near, as this will be my first major hit out since the 1998 Sydney Hobart.

Sponsorship discussions have been continuing as time permits. I am surprised by the lack of creativeness and appreciation of the opportunities from some people who are regarded as marketing professionals.

As we crossed the start line heading to New Zealand, I couldn't shake a sense of foreboding and déjà vu. I knew I had to get on top of my fears.

If I could not help sail this boat successfully to New Zealand and bring her back on my own, then I was kidding myself and everyone else by going any further.

Now was the hour!

I had a re-baptism of fire on the 1st night when we had a pretty wild ride caused by very strong winds and big confused breaking seas allowing the demons from December 1998 to give me a fucking hard time in my head. Hugh took charge as I was very apprehensive. The next day we were further tossed around violently on a real bitch of a sea that caused the boat to roll gunwale to gunwale, on a day that gave both of us the shits big time.

The weather eventually settled down, as did I.

Each day rolled into the next, as we pushed the boat hard. Eventually, the outline of the North Island of New Zealand appeared on the horizon. Each evening, the moon would rise a little later than the previous day. The period of darkness from sunset to moon rise increased each night, and for that period we were cloaked in a jet black shroud of darkness. We sailed onwards, into a black void. Under normal circumstances that can be off putting, but for me it was causing much more angst than normal.

The last night of the race we were relatively close to the coast. It was pitch black, plus it was pissing down rain and blowing strongly. Hugh was below navigating, and I was on deck. I would dart below to get a quick update on our position, then bound back up to the cockpit, all the while anxious and on edge because of the average weather and close by land. I nervously did this a number of times.

On about the 5th occasion as I climbed back on deck, I saw a glint of light reflect off the stainless steel solar panel frame. This immediately alerted me to the fact that someone or something, possibly a lighthouse or a flashing beacon, was shining light on us. I turned to see a fishing trawler no more than 50 metres away with his spotlight ablaze and I freaked out. He hadn't been there 2 minutes prior. I panicked, yelling for Hugh to take control because I couldn't get my shit together. Hugh steered us around him safely.

At the end of the race I was very happy and pleased with the performance of the boat. As it had progressed, I regained some of my confidence and got rid of some, not all, of the gremlins that had been living inside my head - although the fishing trawler incident had sat me on my arse. I hoped that as time progressed my fears would further subside. They needed to!

There were times during the race when the boat was powered up, galloping along, and I would stand in the cockpit, gripping the spray dodger stainless frame looking forward, mesmerised by the grace and beauty of the bow slicing through the waves. The power that it generated was awesome and made me feel so good for having got to that point.

The 1260 nm race took us 9.5 days to complete, finishing 2nd from a disappointing fleet of 5. Hugh did a wonderful job and I will be forever grateful for his looking after me.

NOW, to get her home. On my own.

CHAPTER 17

It's definitely not hot, dry or dusty out here.

The return journey marked the first time that Clouds would be "on board", metaphorically speaking.

In the late 1990's a new cutting edge form of maritime communications, allowing satellite email, came to be.

I had acquired a "Satcom C", and planned on it being the cornerstone of my contact with the outside world including receiving Clouds' forecasts.

I would also obtain other weather information from various countries as I circled the globe but more importantly, it would provide me ready access to any email in the world INCLUDING my family!

It would be an invaluable tool!

The first 130 nm required paralleling the coast north before turning left at the tip of New Zealand to head towards Australia. The forecast for the Tasman Sea had me feeling very uneasy and my suspicions were confirmed.

Email from Clouds: *"You are heading off into a shit fight. The whole situation does not relax until later in the week. There is no neat way through this."*

The more I analysed the weather forecasts the more nervous I became, eventually deciding it would be foolhardy to knowingly sail into such a major crap shoot. I entered Whangaroa Harbour to wait it out. Having officially cleared immigration and customs in Auckland, I was not supposed to stop anywhere - but what the heck, I had been known to be naughty before. Whangaroa Harbour is a glorious waterway where a small marina became home.

Taped diary:
Tuesday 30th May

I'm at a marina for just $15 per night and $2 for a shower. I can pop over to the pub for a beer, so life's not too bad, but gee, I'd like to be out of here and heading home.

Email from Clouds: *"First front is through now, several more to come, in fact more than you could possibly count. It makes things very hard for you, but not impossible. Waiting is best for you"*

Taped Diary:
Wednesday 31st May

Still in Whangaroa, frustrated at not being able to leave. I have things to do, places to go, gotta go find some money, need to see my wife and family.

Email from Clouds: *"I can't see you getting away for another 2 days yet. It's a windy cold place in mid-Tasman right now. Suggest you keep hanging out."*

I was frustrated BUT there is a time to push the envelope and a time not to and I wasn't ready to push, just yet. Additionally, the lessons of the '98 Hobart were causing me to make reserved choices.

Taped Diary:
Thursday 1st June

The weather is still average, last night it blew really hard here at the marina with heaps of rain and very cold. God fucking knows when I am going to get out of here. I have to go soon or else I will go off my fucking tree.

Email from Clouds: *"Hi Tony, more of the same, the Tasman is still a very nasty place today and tomorrow"*

Taped Diary:
Friday 2nd June
I am still here.

Email FROM Clouds: *"The outlook is grim with another low set to sweep the Tasman. Does not look too nice for you. I suggest you leave the boat there and catch the plane home, but I am a wimp."*

Email TO Clouds:

1) *"I am a wimp too.*
2) *I can't afford the fucking airfare so I am leaving at daybreak in the morning."*

I'd had enough.

It was time to go.

On Saturday morning I apprehensively headed off, knowing the forecast was still bad. I rationalised my decision based on the premise that when sailing around the world I would not be able to pick and choose the weather. I would have to deal with whatever conditions were thrown at me, so we may as well get started. I wasn't happy to leave but I knew I had to look it in the eye.

I had to take it on.

Email to Jordan and Holly:

Dear Jordan and Holly, thank you for your nice emails. I really like reading them. I finally left this morning. There is a SW front coming through this evening at about 30 knots so that will make it very cold so I'll have to put on an extra jumper. Hope you had a good time at Nan's. Was the Bar b Que good? See you soon. All my Love dad

Despite the bravado in my email to Clouds I was desperately torn between staying or leaving.

However, the overriding thought was that I HAD to maintain momentum, even if it meant more anguish for my family and I. It was as if I had painted myself into a very tight corner when committing to the world trip 3 years before and the ONLY way out was to leave Whangaroa and press on.

Taped diary:
Sunday 4th June

I'm at the top end of NZ and there is a goddam stinking fucking westerly blowing. I have had just the storm jib up since yesterday afternoon. This morning at 8 am a squall caught me off guard blowing 60 knots for about 10 mins. It is fucking blowing 50 knots at present.

I am going to have a cup of tea. I am pretty tired but this has been a good test so far. It's not the sort of thing you want but it has to happen.

It's definitely not hot, dry or dusty out here.

Taped Diary:
Monday 5th June

Getting shit belted out of me. Very slow progress. There is another low pressure nearby which is sending more fucking drama my way.

Taped Diary:
Tuesday 6th June

I am covered in sand fly bites. I have about 50 on each leg plus 10 or so on each arm so 120 infected bites all up. At Whangaroa, the little bastards were sucking blood out of me, getting big and fat and now the itch is unbelievable.

I was starting to feel a little more relaxed, although it troubled me that my overall schedule was falling behind. I had originally planned on arriving back in Newcastle on 6th June, but I had another week to go. The saving grace was that the boat was handling the conditions really well.

The enormity of what lay ahead of me from 15th October onwards was really starting to hit home. At least I was getting it out on the table up front. Once you commit, you have to keep going, cos you are committed.

Taped Diary:
Tuesday 6th June (late arvo)

I have had a shit of a day with North Westers pumping 30-40 knots and rain squalls this afternoon that you wouldn't fucking believe. One was so heavy that I was flat out seeing the front of the boat 10 metres away. It was like solid water falling out of the sky. I have been toughing it out.

Like many, when the opportunity presents itself, I am a voracious reader. On this trip, in between fighting lions and tigers, I read as often as I could. I devoured a Bob Geldof Autobiography, "Is That It?". Part way through I was compelled to copy the following excerpt:

"*But I still don't believe that contentment is part of the plot. I don't think that I can ever be content. There will always be a push and pull of an internal conflict, the tiresome civil war that screams on perpetually in my head, the constant tedious questioning and analysis of motive. I felt then, and still feel, that the purpose of life must be more than going to work and coming home and going to bed. I don't believe in the work ethic, I don't believe in the rich man poor man lie about the dignity of labour. There is no more dignity in labour than there is in not working. I never felt ashamed to be out of work. I just felt broke. The dignity and value of a man is not in his labour or abilities. It is in his worth as a human being. The value and dignity of a man is humanity. The purpose of your seventy years seems to be about discovering what your brain and body are capable of. Seventy years is nothing, so you may as well push yourself right to the extremes of your capabilities. I find it interesting to test myself so long as I don't hurt other people. I am capable of doing more than some people and less than others. So is everybody else but as you can only be capable of so much and as you will always wish to do more and will probably be dissatisfied with what you have already done, then you can never be content.*

The only real sin is wasting time."

Taped diary:
Tuesday 6th June (late evening)

I set the alarm for 2 hours, got up and luckily went on deck to tack. The fucking breeze came through at 50-60 knots for about 20 mins with blinding rain and lightning. It was just fucking blowing. I have just sailed through the back of it into a starlit night with about 15-20 knots of breeze and it's a glorious night now. It's unbelievable the number of, and the viciousness of, the fronts and squalls that are ripping through.

Taped Diary:
Wednesday 7th June
Progress is painfully slow.

Email from Clouds: *"Things should improve for you today and remain that way for the next 2 days until that final front comes up on Friday night."*

It had been a rugged 4 days, but on reflection, a valuable 4 days as I was becoming at one with the boat. I was getting to know her idiosyncrasies and how to set her up. The value of being there was not completely apparent to me at that point, but there is no doubt that in the overall scheme of things it was a great proving ground for both of us.

She performed magnificently, shaking herself off after each wave and plugging away toward home.

Taped Diary:
Thursday 8th June

The hard work of the last 5 days is now worth it as it has finally cracked and we are to have a couple of days of decent sailing and should chew up some miles.

I am hungry. Am gonna cook some 5 day old sausages for breakfast and see how they go. I am much happier this morning now that the weather has broken. I still have 800 nm to go and I reckon that will take 6 days or so to knock over so I won't get home until Wednesday or thereabouts but so long as I get home, that is the important thing.

Taped Diary:
Friday 9th June (morning)

Had a great sleep last night for quite a few hours. It's a beautiful blue sky morning. I am sitting here in a pair of shorts and a full mainsail up. This is the first time in ages, on both counts. We shouldn't get extreme weather from here to home, so won't that be just ducky?

(afternoon)

I am motoring on a glassy ocean so we must be in the centre of the high. There is not a breath of breeze. What an amazing place the ocean is. I've had shit belted out of me for 5 days and now it is so tranquil and beautiful.

Email to Snapey:

Hi mate, been out here now for 7.5 days with another 4 or so to go. Maybe a bit quicker if the low pressure off Qld coast pumps some good SE breeze my way. Got flogged the first 4.5 days only averaging 65 nm per day. Headwinds 35-40 knots with plenty of 50 knot squalls and some 60 knot "adventures".

Snapey, I found quite a few skeletons in the closet but with each wave I crash off they diminish little by little, but it will take a long time to eradicate them. This trip has been a great shakedown as it was intended to be.

All my Love, Tony.

Taped diary:
Sunday 11th June
393 nm to home. 2.5 days or so to go.

1) *I am not going to die wondering.*

2) On my death bed, I am NOT going to wish that I had spent more time at the office.

Was about to have a cup of tea and discovered that the last of my fresh milk, bought 8.5 days ago, has soured and gone chunky so that's the last of that. I've been eating vegemite sandwiches and they are pretty good after picking the mould off and slapping on plenty of butter. I have plenty of food left and been grazing a lot. I'm like a vacuum cleaner hoovering up any food in sight, which of course, is one of my favourite pastimes.

I have been sailing the boat quite conservatively. You don't need a lot of sail to push the boat and why stress her. I am keen to get back. I have found out what I wanted to find out and now it's time to get back.

I have been gone for 29 days, originally anticipating 24 days.

I have been on edge today. I dug out some old cassette tapes and found a Shania Twain one which I have fired up. Her music gives me a different, calming perspective. I've just realised how much music can positively impact my mood out here so it's a priority to have a variety of good music.

Being at sea for 6 months or more is going to be a long haul and I need to make sure I have plenty of things to keep my mind occupied, amused and interested. In the last month, I have read 7 or 8 substantial books. I need to take plenty of books. About 100 I reckon which equates to a book every 2 days which may seem like overkill.

I suppose I could just take 50 and read the fuckers twice.

For 11 days, I have been insulated from the outside world. I don't know anything about what is going on except what is happening on this boat.

I am living in an area that is equivalent to a box trailer with a canopy. It is where l sleep and eat and includes the bunk I crawl into to sleep. I have one seat to sit on and one spot to stand at the galley to make a cup of tea.

That's it. That's my living space.

I need to make that area as comfortable as I can.

Taped Diary:
Monday 12th June
245 nm to home

Last night was a wild and woolly night but I made some good miles.

I haven't stopped pissing lately. Talk about piss. I don't know if I have something wrong with me or if it's the constant movement of the boat making the body shed its excesses or what. Christ, today I would have had 8 or 9 pisses, maybe more.

I will be glad to sleep in a proper bed and right through without the need to get up.

Fish and chips and a beer will be pretty good too.

Taped Diary:
Tuesday 13th
84.5 nm to home

Time to get back and sort out a lot of financial matters, see my family, sleep in a bed, have a shave and shower, sit at a table, eat with cutlery and maybe even eat off a plate. Out here I eat from the saucepan.

When I go around the world all I will need is a saucepan, a frying pan, 2 × bowls, 2 × plates, a knife, fork and spoon.

In the pre-dawn hours of Wednesday, whilst the city slept, Solo Globe and I eased our way past Nobbys into Newcastle Harbour. If all went according to plan, in just 4 months we would slide past again as we took off in pursuit of a world circumnavigation. At 4 am I dropped anchor to wait for daylight and to meet with customs and immigration to process me and the boat officially back into the country. The rules stipulated that one must stay on their vessel and no one is allowed on board until officially processed.

Lorraine, Holly, Jordan and Baz appeared on the shore and it was so good to see them, even if they were 40 metres away.

I was relaxed. I was feeling pretty chilled. I was feeling pretty good.

Getting to this point was a huge achievement in so many ways.

I had done it!

Thus far.

The customs and immigration officer arrived and he most definitely had been a member of the polished shoes and tucked in, ironed shirt brigade when he went to school. I'm going to call him "Billy" after "Billy Bunter" (Google it). Billy had an ironed uniform with a name badge, was very efficient with paperwork, had a distinct lack of empathy and was not interested in small talk. He let me know who was in charge of the show, and it wasn't me. I wasn't too impressed with him after what I'd been through, and took it very personally when he told me that I needed to pay $187 to allow me entry back into my own country. I took exception but didn't let it show. It's difficult to explain why I was so pissed off but it was all to do with what we'd been through in '98.

We processed the paperwork (in quadruplicate) and "Billy" asked for payment. I told him I had no cash, nor a cheque book or credit card, so I would have to drop it in to the office.

I never did pay the $187 and never received any follow-up.

Baz and I sailed the boat back to the lake that afternoon.

CHAPTER 18

How much did it cost?
How do you pay for it?

After safe return to Lake Macquarie, I took stock:

Where was my head space and had I erased any Hobart demons?
I had definitely flushed some skeletons out of the closet. There was no doubt that I was still tentative, but I didn't necessarily see that as a bad thing. On a few occasions, I had been downright scared, but I had managed to work my way through it. I knew that I was sailing more carefully and conservatively than previously, but felt that this was not necessarily a bad thing, particularly as the world attempt would be an endurance event, not a mad sprint.

The first 4-5 days of the trip back had been particularly tough and my willpower and mental state had been stretched super taut. My brain had whispered,

"You can turn around and go back."
"You can change your mind and decide not to go around the world."
"You can make up an excuse."
"Pretend you broke something."
"You don't have to prove anything to anyone"
"Come on mate, you don't need this"

Then, rational thought kicked in and I got into a steady rhythm.

Where was the boat at?
I had given the boat a hell of a work out, falling off a heap of very big waves. The mast was still standing and looked flash. Apart from a slight sail tear and a partially chafed rope, there was no damage. The

work that we had done had passed the test with flying colours but it was business as usual. I still had a job list bigger than Ben Hur but somehow or another I figured they would be whittled away.

Would I be ready to attempt the world trip?

I now realised that 6 months or more at sea was going to be a bigger challenge than what I had originally thought. Every journey has a start, a middle and an end. The start phase of the world trip would be, ever so dauntingly, 2 months. The middle bit would be another 2 months and the end bit would be another 2 months or longer. Fuck, that is a long time.

Coming back from NZ, I'd had 60 knots for a relatively short period. How would I go with 3 or 4 days of 60-70 knots with the accompanying massive seas?

My overall conclusion:
Let's go get 'em!

5 days later I quit my job with Flano. There's nothing like jumping in at the deep end to find out if you're going to sink or swim! Despite my very ordinary personal financial situation, I now had no form of regular income. Quite a lot of people questioned my sanity about the decision, however for me it was an easy one.

I still needed to find approximately $70,000 in cash and kind to get us through to the projected end date of April 2001. I only had 4 months to find it. If I continued to work for Flano, I would have earned about $25,000 over that period, but the problem was that I needed to go there 5 days a week in order to get it. Resigning meant I had 7 days a week available to focus solely on preparation, including hunting down the badly needed $70,000.

Resigning was a liberating decision, as it was another step in following my passion and unshackling convention.

Working for Flano would turn out to be my last grown up's job.

Don't get me wrong. Since then, I've done it bloody tough financially a lot of the time and really scraped the bottom of the barrel, BUT that was the last time I reported to a 9 to 5 employer.

One small matter was that I now wouldn't have a car as I had been driving one of Flano's. I considered this a relatively minor matter that would work itself out somehow.

Where to now?

With the job out of the way, I was now able to look ahead with sharper focus. The marketing vehicle that was the project was primed and full of unique opportunities for sponsors that could share the vision. It was time to find them.

When I was beating the bushes looking for $100 bills to fall out, I was in my mid 40s, articulate, well presented, personable, media savvy, had a track record in sponsorship relationships and a strong selling background. I also had a reasonable media and public profile and I'd had success as a public speaker. I thought it fair to assume that a significant sponsor would be relatively easy to find.

It was not to be. The reality is that it's a war out there.

In my opinion, sponsorship should be viewed by both parties as a serious commercial partnership. My goal has always been to provide a return on my sponsor's investment, ideally exceeding, but at a minimum, commensurate with their input.

In other words, I always want to leave the bar not owing anyone a beer.

Another problem I encountered was prospects thinking, "Solo sailor, he'll probably sail off over the horizon and we'll never see him again". One can't blame some for thinking that way, cos they may have been right.

We created a variety of sponsorship packages that I thought had a great chance of success.

Gold Level Major Sponsor:

A gold sponsor (and there could only be one), would receive naming rights of the project and boat, virtually owning me for 1.5 years. This was pitched to national or multinational organisations.

Investment: $75,000

Silver Sponsor:

Two Silver sponsors would receive smaller versions of the gold package, customised to suit their needs.

Pitched to large local organisations with multiple retail outlets like building societies, credit unions, fast food.

Investment: $25,000 each

Sponsor me for 1 or more days:

180 days in 1, 2, 3 or 7 day bundles

A single day sponsor would receive a bound copy of my logbook, their name on www.sailsolo.com and cross links to their web site etc.

A multi day sponsor would receive the single day offering but with other items added including a signed limited edition print, speaking engagement/s etc.

Investment: $500 per day.

The "Sponsor me for a day" option became a valuable tool. If a Gold, Silver or other significant prospect declined the opportunity but liked the way I "parted my hair", (if I had any), it was a shame to leave the table empty handed, so I would try to sell them a single or multi-day package.

Small fish are sweet.

Goods and Services Sponsor:

The outcome of these arrangements varied. At one end of the spectrum, a supplier might give me something free of charge, expecting nothing in return because they were inspired by what we were doing.

Conversely, someone else might sell me something at their cost price or a little less than retail, still turning a profit, but then think they "owned" me, expecting thousands of dollars of exposure and a huge return on their imaginary "investment". An "investment" that cost them absolutely nothing or that they actually turned a profit on. The more desperate I became, I unwittingly became a slave to many.

My energised team and I spent weeks putting together and mailing out 200 Gold and Silver proposals. Where possible we addressed each one personally to the heads of marketing. It was mammoth effort and I was sure that the hard work would be worth it. I was TOTALLY convinced that it would produce results. I sat back and waited for the phone to ring.

The phone didn't ring.

What did happen, was that I received a barrage of form letters, which in many cases did not even have a human signature. A favourite theme of the cookie cutter, formatted replies, was, "We are sorry but our budget is exhausted." Another stereotypical reply, that really pissed me off, was "Sorry, we already have a charity, or charities that we donate to."

Fuck me! I am not a fucking charity.

I was, and am, very aware that high profile organisations receive many sponsorship requests. Responding in the way that most did showed me that no one had taken the time to even briefly peruse our document, which I found insulting. For them, I felt it was embarrassing and foolhardy.

How do you know when the goose, (me), with the golden egg might waddle past?

You never know when a great opportunity comes knockin'.

Having said that, it is my strong view you will get a lot further in life by focusing on the positives as against the negatives. Not all replies to our mail campaign were negative. Some pure cream floated to the surface.

Kennards Hire is a very successful family owned, Australian hire company specialising in hiring equipment to Do It "Yourselfers" and small to medium builders. The patriarch of the company is a wonderful man, Andy Kennard. Their national marketing director was based in Newcastle.

The day after their proposal went out, I got a phone call.

Rose: *"My name is Rose Lines from Kennard's Hire. I've received your sponsorship proposal and I want this. How do I own it?"*

Me: *"That's easy Rose, all you have to do is write out the cheque."*

I thought I'd hit the fucking jackpot!

Laughter erupted from both of us as she told me that it wasn't quite that simple, as she had to have the approval of Managing Director Peter Lancken, from Sydney head office. For $75,000 I could see her point.

She had already rung to tell him how excited she was and had express couriered the proposal to him for his urgent attention.

This was indeed, very encouraging.

She wanted to meet and the next day we did so for a relaxed and enjoyable chat. Rose was enthusiastic and energised, recognising great possibilities in what I was offering. I left her feeling extremely positive.

The next day she rang to tell me that Peter had considered the proposal and that unfortunately the bulk of their marketing budget needed to be directed elsewhere and sadly the answer was no. Rose and I were both very disappointed, as we could both honestly see great value for both parties, and we lamented Peter's decision.

She and I went around in circles on the phone and in the end, I asked, *"Rose, can you get me a meeting with Peter Lancken?"*

She was hesitant but went back to him again, affirming her strong belief in the project, and managed to coerce him into meeting with me in Newcastle a week or so later. I was allocated 20 minutes.

The appointed day arrived, I donned my best, and only, suit and tie. I waited nervously and when we met, it was obvious that Peter was a man on a mission and would not suffer fools easily. He arrived 10 minutes late, shook my hand apologising for his lateness and said that I now had just 10 minutes.

I was a tad pissed off but with a smile, said "No problems, sit back, relax and enjoy the next 10 minutes while I give you both barrels". Peter laughed and I knew we were off to a good start. After 10 minutes, the meeting concluded.

The next day Rose rang again, apologising profusely telling me that major sponsorship was still a no BUT said Peter really liked my style and had instructed her to give me a no strings attached, $5,000, for which I never had to do a thing in return.

Whilst I was very disappointed to lose out on $75,000, I was fucking ecstatic to have five grand coming my way. Rose asked me when I would like to get the cheque, and I laughingly told her I had jumped in my car and was on my way as we spoke.

The contact with Peter and Rose (and later with Andy Kennard), kicked off a friendship that quickly transcended money and sponsorship, and endures today 25 years hence.

Ken Stokes is a retired Pommie school principal, so he's got a couple of things going on that make me a tad wary of him. Despite his ex-vocation and his heritage, he is a bloody champion bloke. Ken emigrated to Aussie in the 90's and I had the good fortune to become close friends with he and his family. Ken is a shining example of the numerous people that put their shoulder to the grindstone to help in many different ways.

Admirably supported by Cookie and Snapey, Ken organised a fundraiser at LMYC to raise money to help us personally. It was a fantastic night raising enough money to give us some breathing space.

I am often asked "What did the around the world trip cost?"

One possible answer could be, "A full head of hair and the small amount of mental stability that I possessed to kick off with".

There are so many different ways to look at it.

We had 2 residential investment rental properties that we sold to fund "the beast". Each had about $25,000 equity, and I ploughed that $50,000 into the project. A few years hence, they had appreciated by at least $300,000 each, so if you were to cost in lost asset appreciation of $600,000, the total "cost" escalates but in my mind, that is not a true indication.

I went on an asset reduction program, and it worked magnificently. But it's no good complaining about that. One cannot commit to a task as daunting as it was and worry about the balance sheet or profit and loss. One needs to come to terms with that at the outset.

I never kept a tally of expenditure, however the figure that I normally quote is $350,000 which was a fair chunk of change in the late '90s.

In a worst case scenario, if I perished, Lorraine would have the family home, my life insurance proceeds, a cash kitty and be debt free.

After resigning and having no regular income, I identified the $500 per day sponsorship option as a viable tool to keep us afloat. The first thing I did every Monday morning was contact potential day sponsors seeking a commitment. I would do nothing else until I had 2 × $500 sponsorships in the bag.

If I had succeeded by lunchtime, I would then redirect my attention to the job list or attempt to secure bigger sponsors. If, however, it took me until Tuesday lunchtime, then I would stick at it until then. I knew that once I locked $1000 worth of sponsorship in, that equated to a week's salary and somehow or another the flow-on effect would keep my family and I ticking over financially.

It was like a sausage factory. I had to keep shoving the ingredients in the front end before I could expect them to pop out the back end. I viewed it as mini-employment, chasing down that $1000 at the start of each week to create a weekly pay packet.

As the 15th October rushed at me, I quantified the time left in days, not months. It was easy to be lulled into a false sense of security thinking that I had 3 months to go. If I said that I had 97 days left, then this created a lot more urgency. As the number of remaining days dipped to 100, it became patently aware to me that If I were to spend 1 day of that 100 on a task, then I had just used 1% of my available time.

With 50 days to go, 1 day represented 2%, so my time management had to be efficient and get better as each day slipped by.

Update #15
28th June
Only 109 days before we sail.

I previously mentioned having on board a recent innovation, Satcom C to allow me to email via Satellite.

The capital cost was $4,000, which was not an insignificant amount but the major problem was the service charges which were 1 cent per character to send or receive.

A dot or a space was counted as a character.

Economical it was not.

I negotiated a part sponsorship of 50% of the $4,000 purchase price.

I also managed to secure a part sponsorship package for the service charges.

It was not cheap but the Satcom C was worth every dollar and saved my arse more than once.

15th July
91 days before we sail.

Companion Credit Union were my financial institution of choice at this time however since then the name has disappeared as they morphed into a Bank.

They had a number of branches throughout our region and I felt they were admirable prospects for a Silver sponsorship of $25,000.

I had some meetings with their Marketing Head who was enthusiastic but told me that they had recently, for the first time, engaged an external advertising agency to assist with their marketing and that he/we/they needed to engage with the agency as they would be an integral part of any decision.

Our discussions and their deliberations dragged on getting virtually nowhere, and it seemed to me to be a classic example of not being able to grab the bull by the horns and make a decision.

There were far too many cooks stirring the broth and it frustrated the hell out of me.

If the answer is no, tell me no and we can all go our separate, more productive ways. If the answer is yes, let's get on with it and maximise your return on your investment.

But no, let's have another fucking meeting.

As October drew nearer, Companion asked what they would receive should they decide to throw $10,000 into the ring instead of $25,000. It became obvious that they wanted the $25,000 package for $10,000. In the end, out of desperation, I agreed, BUT they still couldn't make a decision and on and on it went.

Finally, the day arrived when I had an absolute gut full. I rang, very bluntly asking, "Are you in or out?" When pushed into a corner they said that they had decided to offer me a $3,000 no strings attached donation, as they wheeled out the good old chestnut, "Our budget is exhausted". Well, so was fucking I! A bloody donation! I didn't have to do a thing in return?

What sort of a bright fucking marketing decision was that? If they didn't want to invest $10,000 then why would you give me $3,000 and not ask for a thing in return? I wasn't going to look a gift horse in the mouth but their decision didn't make any sense to me.

To say I was disappointed would be an understatement, after the huge amount of time invested in discussions. But of course, I wasn't about to walk away from $3000, as lousy as it was for all the time I'd invested and the heartache. I told the guy that I was not a charity, that I was not looking for donations, and that I would ensure that upon return I would do something to repay them such as a couple of speaking engagements or similar.

Unbelievably, he went from "We are giving you $3000 no strings attached" to "Can I get that in writing about the speaking engagements?"

Fuck me!

CHAPTER 19
How much toilet paper do I need?

Taped Diary:
28th July
Only 79 days to blast off.

Yesterday was the worst day I have had trying to cope with the pressure however today is a watershed day.

This morning was freezing but I needed to get out on the boat, on my own and do some serious thinking. At 7 am Solo Globe and I headed out onto Belmont Bay and we spent 3 hours motoring around almost aimlessly but testing the engine repairs. It was so cold that I had to continually jump up and down and stamp my feet to get the blood circulating.

Those 3 hours re-energised and invigorated me.

It was cathartic. I have turned a corner.

I am not happy that I have put myself in this situation. I have such a tremendous amount of self-belief, determination and positive attitude. I have such a good marketable product and am so determined and committed.

On the 15th October at 1 pm my boat and I are going to "take it on" regardless.

A necessity was food.

In early August I received a welcome phone call from Bi-Lo supermarkets. Bi-Lo was wholly owned by Coles Supermarkets back then but does not exist today. As the name implies, it was focused on the low-cost, no frills segment of the market. When we sent out the sponsorship proposals, I jotted a handwritten note on the cover of the Bi-Lo copy suggesting that if they weren't interested in a cash partnership, then possibly an "in kind" food sponsorship might appeal. The phone conversation with a senior member of their marketing team (don't get me started again on marketing) was encouraging.

It had a nice feeling and I was quietly hopeful.

Update #20
5th September
Only 40 days to blast off.

What do you eat on a trip like this?

I'm very happy to say that because of Bi-Lo's sponsorship I will be sustained in grand style. Their support and concern also extends to Lorraine, Holly and Jordan as they will be able to keep the pantry stocked whilst I'm away.

How my family were to eat has been a real concern.

It is only when you are **fully 100%** committed that people around you recognise and relate to that full on commitment and respond to help you realise your goal. The manner in which it will happen is not always clear. What is clear is that it **will** happen.

Bi-Lo have recognised, related and acted.

Their package provided me with $8,000 retail value of food, plus $150 per week of groceries for Lorraine from a local Bi-Lo store. Later on, the local manager surreptitiously removed the $150 limit giving Lorraine carte blanche access to whatever she wanted. The Bi-Lo partnership was a huge relief.

In return, I agreed to a number of things which included putting the Bi-Lo logo on the hull. It was a simple, bold, "jump out at you" design, and they hit the jackpot as their prominent clean logo made it appear as if they were the major sponsor. Gerry Masters was the CEO of Bi-Lo and a finer gentleman one could not wish to meet. The relationship between Gerry and I quickly transcended that of sponsor/sponsee.

Gerry Masters, I salute you.

I decided I wanted to film for a possible documentary. Sony's Australian head office in Sydney was daunting. The main reception area had not one, not two but three receptionists smiling away as little old Tony lobbed there one day in early August without an appointment.

You DON'T have an appointment? Shock horror!

I may have appeared unprepared BUT I had done my research and knew that Ashley Roan was the Marketing (be nice, Tony) Manager of their "Professional and Broadcast Quality Equipment" suite of products.

I asked to see Ashley and amazingly within 2 minutes he was standing in front of me at reception. My tried and tested, (not always successful) approach again went:

"*Good morning Ashley, I am going to sail solo, non-stop and unassisted around the world. I am going to make a documentary. You have the equipment that I need. Is there a chance we could do something about that? Also, I need it sooner rather than later and I have no money to pay for it.*"

He laughed out loud, which told me that there was a chance of success. From that first meeting with Ashley, there was nothing but positive vibes from he and Sony. A giant leap forward came when they provided me with equipment to allow me to film comprehensively. I was ecstatic.

All I had to do was remember to make sure the batteries were charged, take the lens cap off, load the film, allow for the light, get the sound levels correct and yell "action" or "cut". That shouldn't be too hard for the guy who could only just make coffee in the microwave and didn't have a hope in hell of tuning in the TV or video at home. Somehow or another, surely, I'd be able to find the "record" button.

Sony's gracious offering had a retail value of $25,000. In return, they did not try to suck me dry. They were the opposite, being super relaxed and confident that I would repay their faith in me along the way, and they were right.

After the trip, I spoke at their national conference, became an ambassador for the Sony Foundation, featured their logo prominently on the hull, plus did a lot of other "stuff" for them. Although Ashley and I don't see each other regularly, he and I are still firm friends even though he has moved on from Sony. He is a great guy and was an absolute breath of fresh air when I so badly needed one.

One evening, in a rare moment, I was on the lounge trying to veg out in front of the TV and I came very close to losing the plot. In a nearby bedroom, Holly wasn't well with a stomach bug and was crying as Lorraine comforted her.

My mind started to race, thinking about the fallout that the kids and Lorraine were experiencing, the enormity of the project, and how much more I still had to do over the next 54 days. Then I thought of Cape Horn, out there on my own and getting belted and bashed. I just about lost it. I had to concentrate really hard, fingers gripping the lounge, to keep myself from tipping over the edge of a full-blown panic attack.

It was bloody scary and not at all like me.

That night I slept in Holly's bed as she slept with Lorraine in our bed. My mind raced again, and it hit me for a second time. It took ALL, and I mean ALL of my resolve to keep the panic at bay.

Update #19
29th August
Only 47 days before departure

In late August, the Olympic torch relay passed through Lake Macquarie and I was the MC in front of a crowd of approx. 15,000 and it was a hoot.

The sense of anticipation and the tingle down the spine as the flame was carried to the stage to light our cauldron was just sensational. It was indeed a wonderful community event.

Reality check.

Back to the job at hand.

Taped Diary:
30th August

Yesterday I was in a pretty bad state and my brain was not coping very well.

I am certainly not being a good father nor a very good husband. I am not handling the project and my discussions with potential sponsors very well. I feel that I am not getting ahead.

I am uncomfortable with a heap of things.

There will have to be some light at the end of the tunnel come the 15th October.

The problem is that, when Tony Mowbray stops, it stops.

When I flew to Melbourne to meet with Bi-Lo, I was, as always, broke scraping together enough for the airfare, taxi and a night's cheap accommodation. The following is an almost verbatim description of my "experience" at the motel.

Taped Diary:

"Stayed at a motel in Footscray and what an exciting fucking adventure that was. A cheap doss house for $75. In room #3 and, the television doesn't work.

Shifted to room #4 and got that TV going. Got some take away Chinese, stuffed myself with dim sims and fried rice.

Didn't worry about a shower. Not very often I do that but I was tired and on my own and so I said stuff it.

Woke at 5 am thinking about a whole lot of stuff and got very nervous worrying that I leave in 42 days and am I under prepared? I have so much to do.

I decided to get out of bed, make a cup of tea and get positive.

I shouldn't have got out of bed, or at the very least, got out of the other side.

I ran the hot water for a shower and there was no hot water. I rang reception to be told I have to run the hot water for a while. Well, I have been running it for 7 fucking minutes but I give it another couple of minutes and still no hot water. Call the girl again. She goes to the laundry and says she found the problem and fixed it.

You will have hot water soon but I never did get fucking hot water.

I wanted to iron my shirt and long pants so I ask for an iron and an ironing board. She brings it down. I am wary of irons in motels because they can spit shit onto your shirt.

I put water in the iron and sure enough it spits out crap. I clean that up.

I checked the bottom of the iron for other shit that may mark my shirt and there is none so I put the shirt on the ironing board and start ironing and then discover big lumps of grease on the back of my shirt and lo and behold there is grease on the underneath side of the ironing board. Then I dropped the iron on the carpet and it burns a hole in it plus I ended up with burnt carpet stuck to the face of the iron.

My breakfast cereal and toast arrived.

I put the tray on the ledge and fuck me if it doesn't fall off and the glass shatters on the floor. The milk spills everywhere and so then I've got soggy toast and broken glass on the floor. A shit fight to clean up. I get on my hands and knees to pick up the broken glass and clean the milk up. Still no hot water so it's time to have a cold water shave. There is no plug for the sink. I stuffed my dirty sock, from yesterday, into the plug hole and have a shave. I think I have given the hot water long enough. Fuck em. I boil up a bit in the jug and have an armpits and crotch wash from the basin with sock for a plug.

It reminded me of Fawlty Towers with Basil and Sybil. I was Basil.

Taped diary:
14th September

How am I travelling? I wake up in the morning with a sick feeling in my stomach and my brain starts thinking about what I may have forgotten or the things still to do. The sick churning feeling in the stomach is there constantly from when I wake. No matter what time it is I have to get out of bed and get active to try and get my mind off it. Usually I get out of bed between 4-5 am. The sick feeling stays with me all day until I go to bed. If I don't go to bed exhausted then I toss and turn, thinking, thinking and more thinking.

It is 31 days to go which is getting pretty scary. It wasn't long ago that it was 108 days to go.

Bring it on. This is the reason that I have been flapping my gums and putting my family through so much pain and agony.

Financially I am still rooted but the boat is in pretty good nick now.

I still have some major things to get like a life raft plus test the new sails.

Have to take the boat sailing.

I woke up this morning breathing.

I have had breakfast and 2 cups of tea.

What more can a guy want?

When I committed to the trip I thought I had an idea as to how tough it was going to be to get to the start line, but after 3 years and 3 months I knew that I had been very wrong. It proved to be far more difficult than I ever imagined.

I hoped that the sailing component would be the relatively easy bit. The logistical challenge was very complex. How do you correctly identify and get on board all of the nuts, bolts, food, tools, equipment, and 1001 other items to sustain you for up to 9 months?

Try this as a challenge:

Take as long as you like, visit the supermarket as often as you want over as long a period as you wish. Maybe take a couple of years? Compile a list of all of the food and consumable items that you will need to exist on for nine months. Ensure the finished list is absolutely correct because if you forget the jelly babies or chocolate you can't go back for a second go. The list has to be finite and correct.

Once you are happy with the list, you then need to go back to the start and work your way through it again, quantifying each item.

How many milk crates of tinned food? 17
How many kg of LPG gas for the stove? 40kg
How many matches to light the stove with? I can't remember.
How many teabags? A fucking lot!
How many litres of long life milk? 130 litres.
How many Bi-Lo light fruit cakes? 45! …and I ate 'em all in the first two months!
But the big question is:
How many toilet rolls?

Those that do the household shopping will know that it seems like a whole aisle is dedicated to just toilet paper. There is thick, thin, soft, hard, some resembling 80 grit sandpaper, printed or plain. Ribbed is my current favourite.

Then there is 2 ply, 4 ply, 6 pack, 12 pack, 24 pack, 36 pack. Throw in the weekly specials and you need a fucking university degree to buy toilet paper.

On the day I did the major provision, standing in the aisle, I pondered the great toilet paper question. I thought, I normally "go" once a day. So, I multiplied that by 9 months and couldn't believe the answer. I walked out of Bi-Lo with a mountainous box of toilet paper that I couldn't jump over.

But the logistical challenge doesn't end there! What's to say that you take that big box of toilet paper back to the boat, stow it in a locker, head off around the world and that locker leaks the first night?

We broke the box down in to smaller bundles and the team wrapped each bundle in heavy duty plastic to waterproof them. Next, we secured the package with duct tape and then wrote on two sides the contents e.g. "8 × toilet rolls". We employed this moisture proofing system with a variety of items such as batteries, torches, matches etc.

We then stored the toilet roll packages in various lockers around the boat to minimise risk.

One of the key elements of any reasonably important decision we take on a day by day, hour by hour or even minute by minute basis is the risk factor. If this (whatever it is) goes pear shaped, what will be my situation?

I work as hard as I can to minimise risk however once I have minimised it, it is time to do it.

The toilet paper example is a micro example of the macro picture illustrating the length that sometimes you have to go to increase your opportunity for success.

Update #22
27th September
18 days to go.
Now it's getting very, very scary.

The sick feeling in my stomach is still there. Never mind, it will go one day.

We pulled Solo Globe out of the water on Saturday morning for a final paint job and had a near catastrophe when a support arm on the slip cradle partially failed and the boat fell forward as she was hauled up the concrete ramp. She was headed for a big nose dive onto the concrete (all 8.5 ton of her) which would have resulted in unthinkable damage at this stage. I was very fortunate to have good mates there who pitched in and within an hour we had her sitting back upright.

There are still a lot of "hard yards" to cover over the next 18 days but somehow, we will be there.

I badly wanted positive things out of this for Lorraine, Holly and Jordan and it wasn't money. Money was important, but down the list.

I remember my line of thought being as follows:

If I can achieve this, might I come back to my family better equipped in some way? Might my intellectual asset base be enhanced so that I can do things for my family that I may not have been able to do before.

Might I, by broadening my horizons, be better equipped to help my family broaden their horizons.

Might I be able to build a bigger, more stable, stronger platform from which my children can springboard into their future lives.

Might my children inherit by osmosis or association some of the values that we as a community hold high? Loyalty, trust, integrity, honesty, a strong work ethic, friendship or just plain old "having a go"?

Holly tells Jordan, "You know Jordan, if ever it all goes to crap and everyone else has deserted us, we'll turn around and Dad will be the last person standing behind us".

I cry as I type.

I tell Jordan that when he is 73 years old and I'm 110 years of age, I'm still going to kiss him on the cheek in front of his mates. He wants me to.

When Holly was in primary school, she was elected school captain and I helped her write her election speech and still have it on my computer. I was never a chance to be a school captain. They used to make me stand outside Principal's office a lot and I say it was because they recognised me as a future leader and I was there to observe the running of the school. Apparently, that wasn't the case.

When Jordan was 7 years old, I dropped him off at school one morning but this morning was a little different. At that hour of the day, 7 year olds are only concerned about getting to the playground to join their mates. This morning he had the door open, a foot planted on the ground dragging his backpack behind him when spontaneously he stopped, turned, looked me squarely in the eye and said, "You know Dad, the other day Jordan Sibthorpe said to me, Jordan your dad is really cool". He paused, thoughtfully. "You know what Dad? I think you are too." With that, he charged off to the playground leaving me slumped in the driver's seat, heart beating out of my chest and tears of love flowing.

I can do things for Holly and Jordan that I could never have done before.

10 days before departure things were chaotic. I had been to Sydney for more meetings attempting to lock in financial support. It had been a tough and demoralising day. Back in Belmont, attired in my one and only suit (again), I called in to the yacht club for a couple of beers before heading home.

The McCloy family are long time residents and part of the fabric of Belmont. Don McCloy, the patriarch, had been a very successful builder and had a number of children around my age who all went to Belmont High School. A son, Graham, was at the bar and casually asked how things were going. He caught me at a weak moment and I poured my heart out, sharing some of my financial woes. He said that he would like to help, but currently had commitments that precluded him from doing so. I was aghast that he thought I was sharing my problems with him looking for money.

"Macca, you are a mate. I'm not looking for anything from you!"

I headed for home, not thinking much of it.

A couple of days later, the yacht club office rang to tell me that there was an envelope there for me. When I picked it up, I was stunned to find 2 × $1000 cheques. One from Graham, one from Don.

I rang "Macca", telling him that there was no way in the world I expected this from him or Don and that I was overwhelmed. He said he wished it could be more. I asked if there was anything I could do to show my gratitude.

Don had been a game fisherman all of his life, however advancing years and a leg amputation now prevented him from getting on the water. Additionally, his wife had recently passed away and he was struggling. Graham suggested a visit to see if it might perk him up a bit and I jumped at the opportunity.

On Thursday morning, three days before departure, my life was absolutely frenetic but I was determined to visit Don and Graham. Graham's older brothers, Jeff and Steve were there as well.

Jeff now ran the very successful McCloy building company. I chatted mostly with Don and Graham and as I did so, I came up with the idea that as I reached major milestones, like rounding Cape Horn, I would ring Don on my Satellite Phone for a chat, so that he could, in part, vicariously live the adventure. He was enthused and we could see his demeanour lift as the conversation flowed. As we spoke, Jeff asked about my financial situation.

I welled up as I told him that I did not have all of my bases covered but regardless, come Sunday, I was going to leave and give it my very best shot.

As Jeff saw me out, he asked where I was off to next and I summarised the million and one things on my "to do" list.

He suggested I call to his office as there was an envelope there for me cos he wanted to help too. There was no way in the world that I expected anything more from he or his family and I told him so. He looked me straight in the eye and told me that if he thought I expected it, then he wouldn't be helping. At his office, there was a cheque for $5,000.

That $5,000 was the equal highest amount of cash that any individual or organisation contributed. I was totally gobsmacked.

You will recall that I had borrowed $3,800 from mum's funeral fund.

I had not been able to repay her and nor did I have any idea when I would be able to do so. On that day, a huge burden was lifted when I was able to give mum her money back using the bulk of Jeff's generous donation.

On 1st October, I had turned 45 years of age, but there had been no time for celebration.

On 5th October, we did our main shop at Bi-Lo, and were there from 7 am to 4.30 pm. We ended up with 11 extra-large trollies, stacked to the hilt with non-perishable supplies. Media outlets jumped on the bandwagon and Bi-Lo got HUGE media exposure.

In the last week or so I largely gave up worrying about money, as I knew the trip was going to happen regardless. I chose to focus primarily on logistics, making sure that the boat and I were as best prepared as could be. Almost coinciding with the switch in focus some money started to flow. They weren't huge amounts, but when added together it meant that I could sail away knowing that my family were going to be okay. Whew.

So, what was our financial situation at that point?

When I was 15 years old, my parents prompted me to take out an AMP life insurance policy for which I had paid $1 per week for 30 years. It matured 15 days prior to departure, and I received $6,500. I also received some free shares worth about $4,500 when AMP demutualised. I purposely kept this $11,000 aside for Lorraine and the kids. They also had the weekly shop at Bi-Lo, plus Henny Penny Chicken were to regularly supply free take home meals.

A large raffle had been organised by friends who spent countless hours selling tickets. All of the proceeds went to Lorraine to keep the household finances ticking over.

When I review my taped diary, sift through my memories and notes from this time, in so many ways I am affronted by my actions and look upon them as if, at times, they were of another person.

I don't know what to say about that.

Taped Diary:
Thursday 12th October

John Denton did a mast and rigging check whilst I was with the McCloys

Many people helped over a long period but the week preceding blast off saw people like Anthony "Pato" Patterson, Steve "Chappo" Chapman, Steve "Blower" Boyd and Mark "Schrodes" Schroder put in huge hours. It was not uncommon for them to be still on the boat at midnight working. It was rip, tear and bust.

**Taped Diary:
Friday 13th October**
Out of bed at 4.30 am.

In the KOFM Radio studio at 6.20 am for interview with David and Tanya. Then down to the boat for an outdoor broadcast TV interview with Steve Liebman on Channel Nine's, Today Show.

After Steve's interview, the producer commented, "2 million people just watched you on TV"

Scott Donaldson is a real character and shares my sailing addiction.

A year prior he had pledged to assist me but said he would only decide how he would do so, just 2 days before I left.

Through the course of the year, I tried to glean from him what level of financial support he was thinking, but his stock standard answer was, teasingly, "Wait until there are two days left".

On the Friday, I finally only had two days left, so I rang Scott and told him that "now" was the hour.

He asked what was particularly worrying me.

I shared that I needed to pay $550 each month to service the bank loan that I had taken out to buy the boat and that I had no idea how I was going to find at least $3300.

In an incredible gesture, Scott deposited $550 each month into the loan account for the next 6 months. Scott Donaldson can present a "gruff" exterior but he has a heart of gold. I will never forget his generosity.

He is a bloody champion regardless of what he tells you.

On the morning of the 14th October, 2000, we loaded the last items aboard Solo Globe and she ended up well down on her the designed lines, floating 150mm lower than normal. The amount of extra weight on board was crazy. You couldn't jump over the stuff and I thought it may have been too much.

Did I have too much food?

There was 1 ton of liquid, made up of 640 litres of water and 350 litres of diesel. Every nook and cranny was crammed with food, spares, sails, clothing, tools, nuts, bolts and a vast array of bits and pieces. She sat so low in the water I was genuinely concerned that at sea she might go through two waves before getting over one.

That afternoon "Baz", "Blower", Cole Butterworth and Vicki Engert from the Australian Master Games and I sailed her to

Newcastle, retracing the route of my 1st ocean sailing experience when I was 14 years old. We berthed her and handed responsibility to Biggles who had volunteered to sleep on her as security.

In less than 24 hours. it would finally be time to get going.

I was mentally and physically exhausted. Back home that night, I packed the last of my clothes and as I made my way to bed, stopped in at each of the kid's rooms and gave them a long gentle kiss on the cheek. I collapsed into bed at 1 am, completely stuffed.

4 hours later, at 5 am, I was up again.

The big day had arrived: Sunday 15th October. Ken Stokes and I were at Bi-Lo at 6.30 am to pick up fresh food. We were at the boat by 8 am and from then on, the morning ended up a bit of a blur.

Despite the blur, I do remember very clearly that my dear friends Craig and Jenny Butters along with their three sons, Alex, Nicholas (Nic) and Coen had sailed their boat from the lake to the harbour to see me off. In 1995, prior to his 5th birthday, Nic had been diagnosed with an aggressive Medulloblastoma brain tumour. Craig and Jenny were fighting with every ounce of their being to give Nic the best possible chance of recovery, however his long term prognosis was not good.

My heart has a special place for Nic.

He presented me with a small toy koala bear, the approximate size of a tennis ball. I immediately christened him "Billy the Bear" and told Nic I would take our furry friend on the ride of his life. I cable (zip) tied "Billy" to the mast below decks in the cabin, where he could keep a keen eye on proceedings.

At 11.50 am speeches kicked off, taking half an hour or so plus the raffle was drawn and then it was time to go. Tears were aplenty as emotions overflowed.

I walked along the wharf with Holly, Jordan and Lorraine.

Holly got extremely upset, as did I.

One of the hardest things I have ever had to do was kiss and hug those kids that last time before stepping on the boat.

There was no avoiding it.

It was now time to do it!

Solo Globe Challenger hull. A mini battleship.

Torch, batteries and boxes of matches, plastic wrapped to keep them dry.

Tin of Milo stripped of label.

Same tin of Milo 25 years later.

Stripping labels off tins and varnishing to prevent rust. In carport at home.

Heading to Newcastle the day before departure.

Solo Globe in Newcastle, primed and ready to leave the next day. Note, Monitor self-steering at stern.

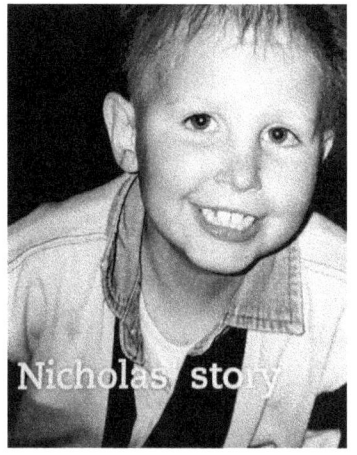 

Nicholas "Nic" Butters. Billy the Bear.

Biggles crawled into my bunk and wrote this.

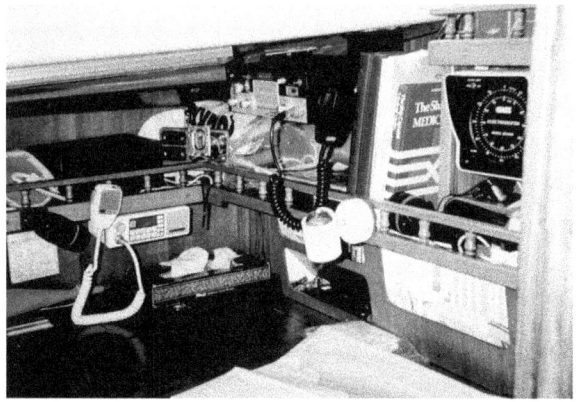

Navigation area where I spent much of my time.

The Nav seat upon which I sat endlessly. Keir wrote the message for search aircraft in Bass Strait.

The galley. Sink, gas stove, fridge (only used for storage) and step up to cockpit.

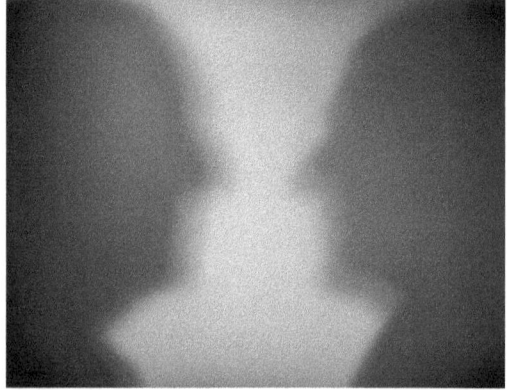

My imaginary friends, Kevvie and Frankie Babe. They were great listeners!

CHAPTER 20

Time to introduce my imaginary friends, Kevin and Frank.

On the 27th and 28th December 1998, in Bass Strait, my 7 mates and I had a go.

Just 1 year and 10 months later, with the help of many, we had rebuilt the boat and on 15th October 2000, I headed back out to sea to have another go.

Only this time I was on my own.

I motored away from the wharf, and hoisted the mainsail with 1 reef to reduce its size, as the breeze was reasonably fresh. I unfurled part of the big headsail and with a truckload of emotions in play, in front of roughly 500 people, I crossed the start line at 1 pm on the knocker as Holly fired the start gun.

Making my way down the harbour, I stood up on the aft stainless safety rail to get a little higher, craning my head to prolong the view of my family as they got smaller and smaller, eventually fading from sight.

Down the harbour I went for a couple of miles before turning right at the end of the rock breakwall off Nobbys headland, and set course for the southern tip of New Zealand, about 10 days away.

With luck, I would be back there in 6 months or so.

Was I good enough to get the job done?

I was accompanied for a time by Craig and Jenny as well as mates, Steve Lamb, Peter Cummings and John "Seagull" and Lyn Edwards on their yachts. The time came to wave my last goodbyes and I spent the afternoon disquieted. Eventually, I forced myself to settle down, by cranking out a couple of mugs of tea and taking a breather.

At 5 pm I did my first log entry.

Logbook:
Day #1

I have now realised the enormity of this task and just how long I am going to be away from family and friends. I was very pensive this afternoon as I sailed along the coast but now that land has just about disappeared I am getting better. I rang home and spoke with Holly to make sure she was okay.

I had borrowed a satellite phone but I needed to pay call costs. Billing was in US$ and at that time the Aussie currency conversion wasn't real flash so it would cost an incredible AU$11 per minute.

I obviously would need to use it sparingly.

The breeze was coming from ahead and was fairly fresh. I knew the angle would improve in the next 36 hrs so I decided to stooge along, sail conservatively and settle the boat, and me, down.

I thoroughly enjoyed my first meal of steak and eggs with garlic salt as I started my first book, "Lionheart", about Jesse Martin's solo circumnavigation of the globe. Maybe this solo sailing around the world thing might not be too bad.

Even though I was worn out, having existed on 4 - 5 hours sleep a night for the preceding month, I was not able to sleep for long periods. I regularly needed to check for other vessels, as we were still relatively close to land, crossing busy shipping lanes.

On the first occasion that I decided to have a rest, I wormed my way into my bunk, laying there with the underside of the deck just 200mm from the tip of my nose. As my eyes adjusted in the gloom I realised that someone had scrawled a short message directly in my line of sight.

Tony "Biggles" Purkiss had had the forethought to climb into my bunk when he had been on security duty the night before and with an indelible marker pen wrote, "**YOU CAN DO IT! from purkiss**"

Those scribbled words from my mate, would be a wonderful comfort on many occasions in the future.

Stepping down from the cockpit into the main cabin, immediately to my port (left) side was a much smaller cabin with a small seat at the navigation table surrounded by electrical switchboard, radios, clocks and navigation equipment. This was where Snapey spent most of his time navigating and operating the radio in the 98 Hobart. Immediately aft (behind) the Nav area was my bunk, as all other bunks were crammed full of food, spares, sails etc. This was the bunk that I had been in when the skylight imploded.

This small area and the bunk would be the centre of my universe for much of the next six months or so. The Nav seat would be my chosen location to sit and ponder many a thing, including the meaning of life and my belly button.

I had a variety of music genres on cassette tape and found a handy shelf to keep them. Younger readers may wonder what a cassette tape and player is. Google it.

Email to Holly:

Dear Holly, Thank you for your lovely message. I am missing you very much as well, and Jordan and Mum too. I have your photographs on the door in the Navigation area and I look at them a lot. Yes, I do worry a little bit but I just have to sail around the world and I hope you will be proud of your old dad for at least having a go at it. I hope you do well at the sports carnival. Do you remember how well you did in the sack race that time? Thank you for thinking of me so much

I love you and will see you soon, Dad.

I had a variety of photographs, particularly of Holly and Jordan. One featured Jordan sitting cross legged on the boat a few months prior, grinning like a Cheshire cat. There was another of him at school with a chicken perched on his head as part of a show and tell. Another was of Holly standing beside her favourite teacher with the chicken in her hand smiling. Holly was smiling, not the chicken. Another photo was one of Holly resting her head lovingly on my shoulder. I'd stuck the photos to the door of the tiny cabin so that when in the nav seat I could kick back, feet up, and contemplate them at length.

I laughed out loud as I looked through my diary to make sure I hadn't missed anything in the mad rush.

Monday	9th	Chaotic
Tuesday	10th	Chaotic
Wednesday	11th	Chaotic
Thursday	12th	Chaotic
Friday	13th	Chaotic

Saturday	**14**th	Chaotic
Sunday	**15**th	**LET'S GO!** (Circled in pen)
Monday	**16**th	BLANK

One extreme to another. How does one cope with that extreme change?
I was about to find out.

Update #23
16th Oct

What a day yesterday. After 3.5 years of planning and work it is now happening. That was such a fantastic send off by so many well wishers. Everything is working well so far (touch wood). I managed to grab some sleep last night but only in 30 minute naps since I had to get up to check for ships.

The last few weeks have seen so much work and effort by so many helpers. Thank you all.

Update #24
16th Oct

I win the prize for goose of the day. When we overhauled the steering system, we fitted new cables and chain and made a spare set.

I have left the spare set at home in the garage.
Idiot!

Two flexible stainless steel cables were integral to the steering system. One end of each cable connected to the steering wheel and the other to the head of the rudder so that when the wheel turned the rudder would move in concert and steer the boat.

The cables passed through a series of pulleys and one of those could not be perfectly aligned so the guaranteed result was that over an indeterminate period of time, the cable would wear at a greater rate than normal. I did not know how much more quickly.

I had built a spare set of cables, being fairly confident I would need to swap them because of normal wear and tear, let alone any extra damage caused by the misaligned pulley.

When corralling last minute sundry items, I had hurriedly gone to the garage, hoisted the roller door, quickly scanned the interior and decided that there was nothing in there I needed.

On the second day, it hit me like a ton of bricks.

The spare cables were neatly coiled in a white plastic shopping bag, laying on the garage floor. Fuck me! You are an idiot. Spare cables could be essential to the success of the trip. My knee-jerk reaction was to go back, grab them, and without any fanfare, restart.

I thought about it and decided that if I had realised my error at Cape Horn or in the Atlantic Ocean, then going back would simply not have been an option. I came up with a couple of ideas as to how I MIGHT be able to jury rig the steering should a cable break. I wasn't confident that the backup plans would work, and I wouldn't know until I really needed to know.

I also pondered that I may have forgotten other important things.

I could not repeatedly go back and restart.

I decided to continue.

In keeping with my philosophy of breaking the big goal down into a series of smaller goals, my immediate goal was to round Snares Island, off the southern tip of NZ, in good shape.

Taped Diary: 19th Oct
Day #4

592 nm to Snares Island. I have been having a pretty good run with a triple reefed main and small headsail averaging 7 knots in a 20-30 knot NE breeze and minimal swell. The boat is performing bloody brilliantly as is the Monitor steering the boat beautifully. It's very overcast and I haven't seen the sun for a couple of days. It's a very lonely ordinary place out here. I am roughly equidistant between NZ and Australia, smack in the middle of the Tasman Sea. It has been an incredible journey over the last 22 months from when we went arse up in Bass Strait. The effort and help from so many, whether it be with money, emotionally or working on the boat is staggering.

I don't know how I can ever repay them.

Most don't want repaying of course.

Many people have the impression that a solo sailor is continually on deck, braving the elements, steering hour after hour, day after day. I had spent countless hours/days/weeks designing and installing various systems, and the overall result was looking pretty encouraging, as I was finding the boat relatively easy to sail.

The Monitor vane was steering the boat exceptionally well and I found that I was not needed on deck apart from adjusting the course or the sails occasionally or keep an eagle eye out for shipping. The weather was settled, and I found myself padding around the cabin in socks and thermal long underwear, reading, listening to music, stowing items more efficiently and generally recovering from the gigantic effort that it had taken to get us there. I actually felt a tad guilty that I wasn't spending more time in the cockpit but the guilt soon passed as I settled into another cup of tea and turned the pages of my current book.

Five days after leaving I was interviewed by Luke Grant on Newcastle's radio 2HD's breakfast show. It was the first of many pleasant interviews with him. Before departure, I had been a guest of Luke's in the studio on several occasions and really liked his style. He was insightful, humourous, perceptive, knowledgeable and personable. When he asked a question he actually allowed you to answer it rather than answer for you, which some broadcasters fall for the trap of doing.

Paul "Chief" Harragon is a Belmont boy first and foremost. He was a legendary rugby league player at the highest level representing Australia, NSW and the Newcastle Knights and to top it off is a bloody good bloke. Chief worked with Luke as support co-host.

Throughout the project, I was interviewed by some excellent media broadcasters including Luke and Chief who I rated a "10/10".

As the trip unfolded, Luke's personal interest grew to match his professional involvement. Apart from on-air official interviews we regularly chatted pre/post interview off air and I grew to like him.

For the first week I enjoyed very pleasant sailing but an air of expectation hung in the air. The further south I got, the closer my first serious belting got.

For a long time, a common question was: "How do you think you will cope with the loneliness?" I used to waffle on when in fact, I didn't have an answer.

Cookie came up with a brilliant solution. He suggested that I should tell people that I would be fine because I would have my imaginary friends with me. I thought I would test it out.

One day, I was working on the boat and there was a guy on the wharf checking us out. The inevitable question was asked. Keeping my head down but watching him peripherally, I nonchalantly answered that I wouldn't be lonely because I would have my imaginary friends with me. I swear he physically took half a step backwards.

I loved it.

We were on a winner.

From then on, I referred to my imaginary friends regularly and for those in on the joke it was a good laugh. For those that weren't in on it or didn't get it, they usually didn't ask too many more questions.

It didn't take long for me to christen them Kevin and Frank, which added another dimension. Later on, Kevin morphed into "Kevvy" and "Frank" transitioned to "Frankie Babe". Some people used to ask why I didn't have a female imaginary friend so I used to ask, "How do you know Frankie Babe isn't a female?"

Update #26
21ˢᵗ Oct
Wind North 15 knots
Air temp 13 °C

*Time to introduce my imaginary friends, Kevin and Frank. They are both new to the sport of solo world sailing. Generally, they're pretty good blokes but they do sleep a lot, eat heaps of my beaut **Bi-Lo** food, don›t do too much around the boat and don›t tidy up after themselves. I had a chat with them about lifting their game and they both were a bit taken aback as they said they were modelling their behaviour on my example.*

Taped Diary:
Sunday morning, 3.30 am.

The moon has just risen in the east and is about quarter size. It is a brilliant starlit night, with stars everywhere whilst the boat is floating along with a beautiful motion on a gentle breeze.

The absolute sheer beauty of the moment is breathtaking

At the horizon, there is a clear definition between the light sky and the jet black dark ocean. There is not a cloud in the sky and it is overflowing with brilliant stars. I can see the "saucepan" along with the Southern Cross and its two pointer stars.

The moon has an aura around it and is glowing.

Taped Diary:
23rd October
Day #8

I am only 35 nm from my turning point at Snares Island and there is a SW front coming through. In readiness, I have a triple reefed main and a bit of the small headsail out waiting for it. It's forecast to be 30-35 knots. There is always that air of nervous anticipation before they hit. I am sitting in the hatch watching it approach. It's overcast, raining and grey and I can see the front bearing down on us. It's a big line of white cloud coupled with the dark grey, almost black of the front.

Another bastard on its way to get me.

I was nervous as I waited for my first, and way overdue, cold front of the trip. I needed an emotional pick me up, so I rang home. Holly was very excited to tell me that her and I were the two most popular people in her class.

Email to Jordan:

Dear Jordan, how is my favourite boy? Have you been swimming a lot in the pool? I have your green nippers bag with me doing a good job with some of my clothes in it. How are you going at nippers? I bet you have a suntan now with all the hot days. Have you had any of your friends over to stay lately? Write to me and tell me what you have been doing. I have some of your photos here that I look at a lot. I like the one of you with the chicken on your head at school. I love you, Daddy

Email from Jordan:

Hi dad how have you been? Is it very cold? Seen any icebergs? I haven't been swimming much. I've had a cold. I went to hospital one night in an ambulance. I had croup. I didn't stay in hospital long. They gave me medicine to help me breathe. I have been very good at nippers but I haven't done the swim yet. No suntan yet. Dean has slept over twice. Love Jordan

What can I say?
On the way back from NZ in June, I had knocked over the first 200 pages of Nelson Mandela's totally inspirational book, "Long Walk to Freedom". I was now devouring the remaining 600+ pages and noted in my log that he regretted not spending more time with his children.

I too, regretted that but was determined to rectify that in the future. Looking at their photos in the Nav area didn't make it any easier.

Early that evening, the ominous grey black line of cloud passed by leaving me all dressed up with nowhere to go. It was a fizzer. I didn't complain.

One of a number of criteria that I had to satisfy in order to achieve the requirements of the circumnavigation, was that I had to pass to the south of the 5 great Southern Capes. The first was South West Cape at the southern tip of New Zealand, but I opted to go further south, rounding Snares Island.

Number 2 was the legendary Cape Horn at the southern extremity of South America.

Number 3 was The Cape of Good Hope at the bottom of South Africa.

Number 4 was Cape Leuwin at the SW tip of Western Australia.

The 5th and final cape would be South East Cape at the southern extremity of Tasmania.

To give you some relativity, the bottom of Tasmania is close enough to 44 deg south of the Equator and for those lucky enough to have visited Tasmania, you will know that it can be very cold at times.

The southern tip of NZ is 240 nm (445 km) closer to Antarctica.

The granddaddy of them all, Cape Horn is 720 nm (1340 km) further south than the bottom of Tasmania.

As I hunted down Snares Island, it got incrementally colder and more uninviting. An entrée of what was to come in the Great Southern Ocean.

Update #27
23rd Oct
Wind NW 20-25 knots
Air temp 10 °C

Some people are meant to have a library card, a box trailer with lights that work and a tidy tool shed.

I'm not one of them.

I've got 2 reefs in the main and a partially furled big headsail doing 7-8 knots. It's very bleak. Only shades of grey out here. There was fog last night and visibility was down to 50-100 metres which was very eerie.

I had to have Kevin and Frank on deck all night keeping a look out. I've dug out my ski pants, gloves, beanies and thermal gear. It's not a very attractive look. Boat doing a great job, performing so well.

Update #28
25th Oct
Wind SW 25 knots
Air temp 8 °C

Reporting from the South Pole? Not really. It's so cold that it seems like it.

We've had the staggers in the last 36 hours with progress slowed by light breeze. We had to work into a 20-25 knot easterly headwind yesterday morning and then it died out through the afternoon and night and we drifted in circles. At 2 am this morning, a light SW breeze arrived and has built nicely. In another few miles we will be on the longitude of SW Cape. I have 4600 nm to reach Cape Horn. We're getting down towards 50 deg S.

There was a close encounter with a ship two nights ago. I woke up, looked out the window and uh oh, lights. I rushed on deck and after some time I worked out that it was ahead, having already passed about 1.5 nm away whilst I was asleep. Yesterday afternoon we came across two very big Russian fishing vessels in the distance. I spoke with one on VHF radio. I think my close encounter a couple of nights ago was with one of these two boats. Kevin and Frank have been a bit quiet since the ship incident, but they will come good.

From Snares Island the course to Cape Horn presented two broad options, either of which I was free to take.

Option #1 was to head north into the more benign warmer conditions of the Pacific Ocean, encountering less destructive winds and waves, be more comfortable and generally safer. That option would have got me to the mid section of South America relatively easily and then I could have dived south at the back end of the leg to slip around Cape Horn.

Option #2 was to head further south into a very hostile part of the world.

The furthest south I had ever been was the bottom of Tasmania.

The "Roaring 40's" is a 1200 km wide band between 40 and 50 degrees south of the Equator.

The "Furious 50's", is further south and is the next 1200 km wide band straddling 50 to 60 degrees south of the Equator.

The "Screaming 60's" is even further south encompassing 60 to 70 degrees south of the Equator. It is an "interesting" place to say the least. They say there is no law in the "Screaming 60's".

At the conclusion of the trip, I didn't want to come back wondering.

I was not prepared to take a soft option.

I wanted the answers to some questions.

I wanted to learn.

I wanted to learn more about me and I wanted to learn more "stuff".

I'd read and thought about the Great Southern Ocean, lapping up the exploits of great sailors like Chichester, Knox-Johnston, Tabarly and Motissier since I was a teenager.

I wanted to know what it was really like.

After rounding Snares Island, I launched myself into the Great Southern Ocean which was akin to sailing through a trapdoor into a whole different world. I set course for the "Furious 50's". I went looking for some answers to some questions.

I did not want to die wondering.

Three days after rounding Snares Island, I sailed into more new territory when I crossed the 180th meridian of longitude which meant that I was exactly on the opposite side of the world to Greenwich and crossed from east to west of Greenwich in the blink of an eye.

We racked up another milestone on Sunday, 29th October when we nosed across the 50th parallel of latitude to officially enter the "Furious 50's".

The Great Southern Ocean is an amazing place, like no other on our planet. It is a world of large relentless tumbling, rolling waves marching to their own beat. They girdle the southern reaches of our planet unimpeded. The water and air temperatures are very cold, largely because of the proximity to Antarctica. Because of the almost continual grey overcast conditions, the waves are colloquially called "greybeards".

Now that I was in the 50's, I headed East, tracking roughly the 51st degree in search of, what is for me and many others, the Holy Grail of sailing, Cape Horn.

Update #31
2nd Nov
Position 50 deg 28' S, 167 deg 52' W
Wind NW 20 knots
Air temp 9 °C
Water temp 8.8 °C
3618 nm to Cape Horn

'tis another day above 50 deg south. What a place this is. Yesterday we saw the sun for the first time in ages. Down here it is just shades of grey and bleakness. It's either cold or bloody cold. It gets dark at 8.30 pm and light again at 3.30 am, so just 7 hours of darkness. We are in fog a lot and visibility is down to 100 metres at times, but generally around 200 metres.

We have only seen one pack of dolphins but plenty of glorious albatross. The weather has been good to us. Monday saw a 20+ knot NE. The wheels fell off a bit on Tuesday and Wednesday, with lighter winds and we drifted in circles. Clouds' forecast for next few days is stronger following winds up to 35 knots, so we should eat up some miles. We have averaged 5.5 knots since leaving.

I have been catching up on some reading, but I find myself wanting to sleep a lot. Is that because of the cold? The only **Bi-Lo** fresh produce left are some eggs, carrots and onions along with 2 oranges, 1 apple and 2 tubs of margarine. Kevvy and Frankie Babe have been okay. I had a really good talk to them the other night. As the trip progresses, I find that I am understanding them better. All in all, we have a pretty happy ship here.

One of my favourite media commitments was with Newcastle radio station, KO FM, participating in many enjoyable interviews with breakfast announcers David Collins and Tanya Wilks. We always enjoyed good banter.

In an interview, I asked if they knew of anyone with the following habits?

1) Would not shower for 2.5 weeks
2) Would not shave for 2.5 weeks
3) No personal hygiene
4) Eats exactly when and what he wants to
5) Eats from the pot
6) Doesn't wash up

7) Inconsiderate of others, particularly his imaginary friends.
8) No dress sense whatsoever

Tanya and David laughed loudly as Tanya blurted out, "It sounds just like David". Said I, "Well, it's obvious, David has the credentials to be a long distance, solo sailor".

Since leaving nearly 3 weeks prior, the maximum wind strength had been 25 knots on a couple of occasions and up to 30 knots once. Generally, it had been a pedestrian 5 to 20 knots. I considered myself extremely fortunate not to have copped a serious front but knew it would inevitably happen.

Logbook: 3rd Nov
Day #20
20 mins after midnight
Wind SW 10 knots, Air temp 7 °C

Just Gybed to starboard. There is a front on the way. On deck with no gloves, the burn of the cold is incredible. Particularly my thumbs, more so the left thumb.

1.15 am
Wind SSW 30 knots, Air temp 7 °C

Front came through about 25 minutes ago straight from the South but settled at SSW. Down to triple reefed mainsail and nothing else. Averaging 8 knots. Daylight soon.

3 am
Wind S 40+ knots, Air temp 6 °C

It freshened. Now down to bare poles. i.e. no sail up. Helm lashed. So very cold. Hands on fire when on deck.

Update #33
5th Nov
Air temp 5 °C
3197 nm to The Horn

The party is officially over. I've had a good run to get to this point unscathed, but 65 hours ago payback time arrived. We are now coming off the back of two successive cold fronts that have had us firmly in their grip since 1 am Friday morning. 45 knots from the South started the fun and it is only in the last hour or two that the breeze has faded to around 20-25 knots. When the breeze is on down here, it is full of grunt. It is absolutely relentless when it's "on"

The seas have been up around 30 ft with us being "taken out" plenty of times. Solo Globe does not falter. She shakes herself off and pushes on. The beautiful thing she is.

Kevvy and Frankie Babe were a bit quiet while the two fronts were on. At one stage I heard Kevvy tell Franky Babe that he needed a good cup of tea and a sit down. He also asked if he could borrow a handkerchief?

A cabin temperature of 8 °C necessitated keeping the hatch closed at all times but my much higher body temperature caused condensation below decks, which became a real problem.

The bigger the disparity in temperature, the quicker the condensation formed, and the more prolific it became. Droplets formed on the underneath side of the deck, the ceiling of the main cabin and also, very inconveniently, directly above my bunk.

I had to regularly sponge down the two surfaces and the amount of water wrung out each time was incredible. If left to their own devices the droplets increased in size eventually joining, becoming rivulets flowing to the nearest low point as the boat rocked and rolled. At a low point, the rivulets would pool and any items of food, clothing, or tools in that area would suck the water up like blotting paper. It would be a very long time before I would be able to dry things out, or worse, the water might damage a vital piece of equipment.

I found it particularly annoying when I was in the bunk and as my body temperature increased and the disparity of temperatures grew, the condensation became rampant. It would almost "rain" down on me so I needed to burrow my head and face under the bedclothes to avoid the relentless drip, drip, drip.

As I rearranged some shelves trying to control some of the condensation, I found two pairs of shorts. Laughing aloud, I stowed them away for possible future use.

The fronts had given me a nice old pasting, providing a stark reminder of what this playground could throw up to anyone game enough to get on one of the rides.

On Day #21 the log recorded that I had had a rough day mentally.

"When depressed, eat" was my motto, so I cooked two fried eggs and hot chips for lunch. I cranked up Dire Straits and read some of Billy Thorpe's book, "Most people that I know, Think that I'm crazy"

It was a nicely triangulated collection of rebellion.

Then bugger me, the barometer started to drop like a stone again heralding more bad weather. By 6 am the next morning another front had swept over me and I had wind from the west at 40+ knots. My comment in the log was that it was "Full of grunt".

Email to Holly:

Dear Holly, my favourite girlfriend. How are you sweetheart? Have you been looking at the map to see where I am? I am at 51 00s 140 48W and I have 2638 miles to Cape Horn. Have you stayed at Nannie's or Grandma's lately? How are your stomach pains? Do you want me to send an email to your class? If you do then you better tell me the address. Have you been swimming much? I have your photos stuck up on the wall in the navigation area and look at them all the time Write and tell me all your news.

I love you, Daddy

Email from Holly:

Dear Dad, how are you? I have been looking at the map. I would love it if you send an email to school. The class don't have their own address. My tummy hasn't been too bad. I don't sleep with my light on anymore. On Wednesday I got a very special Certificate at assembly for participating in discussion in class. I love you Daddy and I miss you a lot.

Love, Holly

Logbook: 5th Nov

Had some wild rides and been dumped on plenty. Edge of your seat stuff. Cannot reduce sail any further and do not want to go to bare poles because of sea state. Don't want to get beam on like in '98. Wave and swell height about 30 ft Relentless stuff. When it decides to blow, it fucking blows. This is not fair dinkum stuff yet. What about when we get 50, 60, or 70+ knots?

It blew hard for another couple of days until a small window of reprieve popped up. I hoisted a triple reefed mainsail and noted that

I had not had any part of the Mainsail up for 4.5 days. The reprieve provided an extra bonus in that I was able to open the hatch and ventilate the boat.

When I set out, I was not intent on breaking any records or beating a particular time. I simply wanted to get the job done and time did not matter. My strategy was that when I needed to pull my head in, similar to a tortoise, I would do so. I needed to look after the boat at all times as it would be a real test of endurance for her. However, when I was comfortable to pull the trigger a little and let her have her head, then I would do that and let her go for a gallop. Thus far, my approach was working and my confidence in her and my ability to cope, was increasing.

The longer the trip went on, the more at one I became with the boat and the environment to the point that we blended almost seamlessly, so that I ended up an extension of both. I developed a very highly tuned sixth sense enabling me to detect small changes in wind direction or strength sub-consciously when below or even asleep.

Eventually, I also knew the origin of every creak, groan and squeak that Solo Globe emitted as she burrowed through and over each wave. If an unusual noise popped up, my ears would prick up and I would, metaphorically speaking, look like a deer caught in the headlights.

We all have comfort zones and are happy to be in them, however from time to time, either through necessity or by choice, we venture outside them. Sometimes we discover it's not too bad out there. Other times we beat a hasty retreat. The longer we remain outside our comfort zone the more comfortable the new zone becomes. It becomes our new normal and if we venture further afield then another new normal is created and so on.

If on day #1, if I had 30 knots of wind and 25 ft high waves there is no way I would have been below deck, feet up, reading and drinking cups of tea. In the Great Southern Ocean, a new normal had evolved. A new comfort zone had been created.

On the first day after clearing the harbour, I changed out of my "street clothes" into my sailing attire. I put my shoes, socks, long pants, belt and shirt in a white plastic shopping bag and knotted the top. I placed that inside another plastic bag knotting it as well. I then stowed the package in a locker that I thought had a good chance of staying dry.

The one item that I kept wearing was my underpants.

At day #7 they were still in pretty good condition so I decided to continue wearing them. On day #14 I came up with a plan. You've got to have a plan.

I decided that I would continue to wear my undies until I got to my previous personal best time of 27 days that I set sailing around Australia with Morrie. If all was going well on day #27, then I would venture into previously unexplored territory to maybe 30 days, setting a new PB. This of course, would provide no end of amusement for my mates. I hoped that no one would tell Mum because she had told me that if I needed to be rescued, I had to make sure that I had clean underpants on because I was brought up properly.

On day #27, the 10th November, the old underpants record toppled. Should someone have advised the Guinness people?

I needed to keep my mind engaged and reading was one way of doing that, but recording and updating various statistics stimulated me. I recorded all manner of things.

On 11th November:

I had 2344 nm to go to Cape Horn.

I had covered 3700 nm at an average speed of 5.7 knots. The trip was 17% complete.

If we were to maintain a 5.7 knot average Cape Horn was another 17 days away which meant a projected elapsed time of 44 days for that leg. Whilst time was not important, I was pretty happy with a predicted 44 days as I had originally thought 50 days likely.

Rounding Cape Horn would be an absolute highlight of my life. As each day ticked over, I became more focused on getting there and it was increasingly in my thoughts.

I'm not a very creative person but I penned a poem:

Ah, 'tis the dawn of a new day
In fact, a Thursday I t'ink
In the bunk longer I could lay
But there are miles to be sailed, quick as a wink

For I hear the call of my mistress strong, loud and clear
Through the ocean, the sky, the albatross, Cape Horn beckons, she is near
Only when the Horn is rounded will I consider the task able to be done
There are 2,700 miles left until I meet her, at the end of this run.

There is no doubt that I underestimated the freezing temperatures of the Southern Ocean and the effect that it would have on me.

The cold permeated every bone of my body, worming its way into my very being and was a constant enemy. The outside air temperature was around 6-8 °C. On 12th November, a new air temp record of 4 °C was reached and the next day that record toppled when it bottomed out at 3 °C. The air temperature was one thing, but the real killer was the wind chill. Throw 30 knots of wind onto an icy 4 °C and I can assure you that the cold/pain experience goes to a whole new level.

Taped Diary:

The cold burns. It's impractical to wear gloves when changing sails or working on deck because they are awkward, not allowing fine work. After a short while ungloved whilst handling wet ropes, the pain is unbelievable.

I am wearing 2 pairs of very thick socks that I have had on since I left and have not taken off at any time.

It's bleak, it's always a shade of grey, its cold, its damp, its relentless, it's hard, its devoid of land. Occasionally I am surrounded by birds but most of the time I am not. I haven't spent a lot of time on deck because it has been so cold.

I always wear my super thick thermal pants that Gary "Gus" Telford lent me. They are akin to wearing a full sheepskin on each leg. I am so pleased I have them. When need be, I put my black ski pants on over them. Down below, during the day, I usually get around in Gus' pants then put the ski pants on over them in the late afternoon and then wear them all night. On my torso, I wear 2 thermal tops plus a long sleeve top, short sleeve shirt and a heavy jacket. Often, I will put another top and jacket on as well. When I go to bed I simply take my shoes off and hop in. I lay on top of a Doona to keep my back warm then pull a blanket and sleeping bag over the top. I quite often wear a balaclava rolled up acting as a beanie during the day and also when in bed. I use 3 pillows to bury my head, attempting to stop my world record sized "melon" from rolling around as I sleep.

If you're thinking, why the hell didn't he turn the heater on?

It's because there wasn't one.

Update #35
9th Nov

Wind NW 30-35 knots
Air temp 8 °C
Water temp 6.8 °C
2650 nm to The Horn

Currently we are reaching before a fresh 30-35 knot NNW with another cold front hunting us down. I expect this new dispenser of wind, cold and discomfort to be here early this evening with around 40+ knots from the NW. Currently have the small headsail only up and are making 7.5 knots due E. There has been no shortage of wind for the last week.

Melbourne Cup day came and went. I tried to get a sweep going but there was a distinct lack of participants. Kevvy reckons he couldn't find his wallet and Frankie Babe says he didn't even bring his. I sure don't accept cheques out here.

I broke out the rolled oats for brekky two days ago. The great unsolved mystery of where the sultanas and the main stash of lollies are is yet to be cracked. I wouldn't miss this for the world. I reckon it's heaps better than mowing the lawn or going to work.

We went through a couple of days of near calm, at times losing steerage, drifting in circles on a listless ocean with the wheel locked off.

I launched a "message in a bottle". I used an empty glass stubby beer bottle which I christened, "Sailing Vessel Stubby" and at position 50 deg 55 mins S 128 deg 33 mins W I sent Stubby on her maiden voyage with a note inside inviting the finder to contact me, plus I included a business card and 2 × 5 cent pieces. "Stubby" has not been heard of since.

In the preceding 29 hours, we had covered just 48 nm whereas normally we would expect to roll out 160 nm, however it was a welcome break from the continual fierce action of the boat that had dominated my life for the previous couple of weeks. My current read was "Schindler's List". I noted how well written it was but despaired over the subject matter.

I had a recurring dream where I had left the boat at sea on its own and had gone back home to buy something that I needed to work on her with. As I walked around people were asking me what I was doing back there? Then I would get upset and worried because by being there I had negated the unassisted component of the challenge and would be disqualified.

On other occasions, I also dreamt that there was someone else, not Kevvy or Frankie Babe, on deck looking out for me sailing the boat.

That particular dream intrigued me.

Taped Diary:

Generally, I sit at the Nav station and read. I have crossword and puzzle books that Marina gave me. The puzzle book is a bit hard. I do a few crosswords to distract me. I play heaps of music as I decide my preferences. (Kenny G was a favourite at that time)

When it blows hard I am cocooned below. I sit, look at the stove and think, yes, I will have a cup of tea. I make a cup of tea, sit down and drink the cup of tea. Then I have a piss in the plastic hospital bottle and tip it over the side. Then I have something to eat, navigate a bit, look at the barometer, write up the log and do some calculations.

I estimate that if I maintain my current average I will take 160 - 165 days.

CHAPTER 21
Houston, we have a problem!

Near disaster was looming and I had no inkling.

Logbook 16th Nov
Day #33

Very gentle breeze. You would not know we were in the Southern Ocean. Sun out all day. No swell. Perfect. Had my first shave.

Spoke with David and Tanya. Tanya can't get over the fact that I haven't had a wash yet. Put fishing line out. Not many miles being covered but that will come again. Today has been magic. It's the reason, one of them, why I keep coming back.

It's too easy at the minute but rest assured it will change.

Little did I realise just how much it was about to change.

Logbook 18th Nov
Day #35
7 am

Averaged 8.2 knots for last 10 hours. Just furled the big headsail and now just the small one out and still doing 8+ knots

Might put the 3rd reef in the Mainsail. Don't want to load boat up too much.

8.45 am
DISASTER!

Update #39 18th Nov
Position 51 deg 02' S, 113 deg 18' W
We have a huge problem!

This is another challenge!
How do I get around this one?

A chainplate is a substantial piece of stainless steel bolted to the boat below deck, extending up through the deck, to which mast rigging wires are attached. All components are subject to massive loads.

Late morning on day #35, I made my way forward to the toilet steadying myself with my left hand, as I normally would, on the upper shelf near the mast. I realised the shelf had water sloshing around on it, which was completely abnormal.

My eyes were then drawn to a spot under the deck near the port, (left side) chainplate. I initially thought that the sealant around it had popped, allowing water in. As my eyes adjusted, and my brain computed what I was looking at, I realised I could actually see water running in, not dripping, as each wave splashed onto the deck above AND I could see daylight through a large gap between the deck and chainplate.

Fuck!

Hang on a minute!

That's not right!

I was horrified. A section of the chainplate had sheared through, allowing it to lift up similar to a partially prised up jam tin lid. The deck was drum tight, bulging upwards under enormous and unsustainable load. Should the chainplate fail further, the surrounding deck would have been ripped off leaving a gaping hole and the mast would come crashing down.

In a blind panic, I rushed on deck, dropped all sail and changed course so that the waves would hit the starboard (right) side, reducing some of the load on the disabled port side. I drifted on the wind and waves. Vital rig tension had been lost, allowing the 16 metre mast to gyrate in a wild arc, about to snap and topple over the side at any moment.

In a desperate frenzied attempt to stabilise it, I attached all of the spare halyards to the aluminium toe rail on the outer edge of the deck and winched them tight, mindful of not over cranking them and ripping the rail off. This helped a little, but the mast continued to sway back and forth alarmingly. It was a hair's breadth from crashing down.

Point Nemo is the point on Earth that is the furthest distance from land in any direction, and would you believe that I was almost smack on top of Point Nemo. Outer fucking space was closer to me than land was.

A lovely situation, in the middle of fucking nowhere.

Back below deck, I maniacally lashed the chainplate with rope, managing to stabilise the situation a micro amount more. Or was it wishful thinking?

I racked my brain trying to think of what else I could do as an emergency quick fix but couldn't come up with anything straight away. We had a fairly big sea running and I needed it to abate before undertaking the next step. Whatever the next fucking step was?

I hurriedly emailed Clouds for an updated weather forecast, hoping like hell for good news.

With no sail up, we were drifting toward Antarctica.

Seriously?

Antarctica?

I had figured that I'd like to see Antarctica one day, but not that day or any day in the near future.

As I collected my thoughts, the overriding emotion was of profound disappointment, but I needed to accept the situation. One of my mantras was that you are only as good as your weakest link, and I had just found one.

It was no good crying over spilt milk. We had to make the best of the situation.

Clouds' email was good news. A SW change was due the next day followed by a progressive settling of the conditions.

We would have "roughish" conditions for a while, but it would calm down in 24 hours or so.

Why had the failure occurred? The chainplate had been welded together at manufacture and the welds ground flush and polished to make it look pretty. Grinding the welds in pursuit of aesthetics had weakened it, leading to a structural weld tearing apart.

My mind raced, and I sprang into action. I drilled some holes through the deck beside the chainplate. Through them I threaded some really strong rope and tied the ends off below deck, creating a loop above deck. I attached a pulley to the loop.

I then climbed the mast to the bottom set of spreaders, (cross arms) about 4 metres above deck, and lashed another pulley to the end of the spreader. Between the two pulleys, I threaded rope, creating a block and tackle purchase system and tensioned it trying to take some load off the damaged chainplate and provide a backup should it completely fail. The mast was not moving as much but was still flexing and pumping a terrible lot and was still very close to snapping like a twig.

The sheared weld had left a jagged sharp gap, which was alarmingly opening and closing a disconcerting 20 mm as she rode each swell.

Taped Diary:

Even if I can save the mast I reckon I will still have to stop at The Falkland Islands for repairs, about 450 nm past Cape Horn and 2000 nm from here. I can't see how I can go on without doing that.

I might be able to get her trussed up so that I can sail her in normal weather BUT I still need to allow for extreme conditions like 80-90 knots. The fucking loads in 80-90 knots are bullshit. I don't think I can truss her up to cope with that.

The chances of success are pretty slim.

By stopping at The Falklands, I would disqualify myself from the non-stop and unassisted components, which for me, is the essence of the trip. If I eventually got home after stopping there I could still say I'd sailed around the world solo but big fucking deal. However, if that's the way it has to be, then that's the way it has to be.

I wouldn't have another crack.

It's been a hard road and the price it has extracted financially, physically and emotionally has been huge.

I might think of a solution.

I try never to say never.

Tomorrow is another day.

I am mentally rooted.

If nothing else, I've had a go.

I emailed Craig Butters, asking him to investigate ports of entry in Chile, 1400 nm away, should I need to divert there instead of The Falklands.

In another email to a closed group of supporters, I mentioned that things were pretty grim and whilst trying to be positive, but looking at it objectively, the fat lady was in the wings gargling, meaning that the show was nearly over with the final act nigh.

I started to cannibalise the boat, raiding it for bits and pieces that I could put to better use.

I did not have a battery-operated drill as these were the days prior to efficient battery-operated tools. The only drill I had on board had been fortuitously given to me by Mark Schroder. It was old fashioned eggbeater type, only suitable for soft materials like timber and thin fibreglass. That morning, using Schrode's trusty drill, I drilled a heap of holes and using cannibalised fittings, bolts, screws, rope and pulleys to further stabilise the rig.

Around lunchtime, the new 25 knot SW change swept in, freshening a tad as the afternoon wore on, before backing off to leave reasonable conditions for a few days hence, I hoped.

As work continued, the mast became incrementally more stable and the fear of it falling out of the boat reduced little by little however it was still almost a certainty that we would have to go to land.

To soften the sudden jerky action of the boat, I decided to tempt fate by unfurling a bit of the small headsail to try and smooth the ride and it helped.

Taped Diary:

At this stage, I have turned a micro corner. I don't want to go to Chile if I don't have to however I've still got 17-18,000 nm to go and I have to be very careful that I don't be a dickhead as this place will bite you on the arse.

On the 3rd day of repairs, I emptied the cupboards around the problem area and removed the doors. Inside the cupboards and on/through the structural bulkhead, I drilled, chiseled, smashed, bashed, gouged and generally bludgeoned a number of holes to which I attached a variety of fittings and yet more rope, in a further attempt to reduce the load on the crippled fitting.

I rang John Denton to discuss options. One I put forward required trussing the mast up in such a way that I would not be able to use the mainsail for the rest of the trip but he knocked that on the head. I was comfortable to sail without a main, prepared to do whatever I had to do to stay out there, but John felt that it might create other problems later on. A foolish man would ignore the sage advice of John.

Taped Diary:
Monday 20th Nov 11 pm

I have had a big day. The work is not easy. Just when I get the tools set up a big bastard of a wave cleans us up throwing them everywhere. I have been in perpetual motion for five fucking weeks. The body does not stop moving. Ever!

We now have bugger all breeze. We are doing 2.6 knots heading at Cape Horn but I am not worried about speed. My sole aim is to get the mast set up so that I can sail the boat in 60-70-80 knots or more and complete the course without stopping.

I don't care if I have to limp it home. I will do anything I have to, to finish the job. If it takes 10 or 11 months then so be it. I would then have plenty of time to read the 100 books I have.

It's 11 pm, I have knocked off for the day and am rewarding myself with some smoked Oysters, barbecue chicken rice crackers, pickled onions and salami as I down a second beer.

I'm leading the life of Riley. Whoever the fuck Riley was or is?

I had a lot of encouraging emails today including some from Biggles, Keir, Schrodes and Hugh saying that if anyone can do it, I can.

I hope they are right. We will have to see what happens.

I felt I had achieved the short-term goal of saving the rig.

The medium-term goal was to reach Chile or the Falklands without it disappearing over the side.

Could I achieve the long-term goal of going all the way around without stopping or getting assistance? That was the burning question.

To win the day in the long term, I decided that I needed to carefully work through my options by slowing the process down a tad. From then on, each morning I would not jump out of the bunk to start work but force myself to lay there and think, searching for a fresh perspective, pondering what we had done and what we might still be able to do. I sketched diagrams, perused containers of spares and cast my beady eyes around the boat looking for more fittings that could be unbolted and used for a greater purpose.

With finite resources, I needed to be a lateral thinker. One day I was very close to drilling a hole through the centre of a frying pan to use as backing plate for a bolt.

Once I had completed the review/planning/thinking process, only then would I start on the physical work for the day. The old adage of "proper planning helps prevent piss poor performance" was alive and well.

All the while, in the back of my mind I kept thinking, there has to be another/better/different ultimate solution.

I had her trussed up unbelievably and the bloody thing was still moving an unacceptable amount. The jagged opening in the sheared chain plate still had 10mm of movement and at its extremity was still a disconcerting 20mm wide. I had to reduce that somehow. I hacked out more timber cupboards and internal linings around the troubled area, exposing more raw hull and deck.

When raiding the boat, I unbolted 2 stainless steel base plates from the bow. Each had an upside down U welded to it and was attached with 4 × bolts nuts and washers. They are commonly called "pad eyes". I decided to bolt these to the outside of hull, about 100 mm below deck level, and use them as part of yet another support system.

Taped Diary:

I drilled through the hull from the inside and the drill was like a battering ram rather than a drill. The bloody drill bit kept coming out of the chuck.

I was stuffed by the end of each hole but eventually, I bludgeoned 8 holes through. Bludgeon is the only word I can use.

It is freaky to be deep in The Great Southern Ocean drilling holes in the hull of my beloved boat. When I punched the first hole through I looked through from inside and could see daylight and ocean and thought, what the fuck am I doing?

After lots of grunting, groaning and general whingeing to myself, using the drill as a mini battering ram, I managed to get the pad eyes bolted on.

I then threw yet more rope up and over the bottom spreader and assembled 2 more cascade rope purchase systems which I attached to the pad eyes. I had that many purchases it was easy to tension them by hand, with no need for a winch.

I now had a multitude of systems and bindings holding the shooting match together and was starting to feel better about our prospects. I revisited everything I had done, refining and strengthening the weak points. By Thursday afternoon, I thought we were back in the game but something didn't feel right. I forced myself to take time out and review our position again.

I had now taken the chainplate and some of the mast rigging out of play with the mast now, primarily supported by my jury rigging. The chainplate was secondary.

John Denton, forever in my corner, urged me to get the chainplate back to work. He wanted me to try and get the boat rigged as it should be, with the tensioning systems I had created, secondary, rather than primary support.

John was 1000% correct. If I were to be out there for another 4.5 months and 17,000 nm, this was the time to make sure the remedial work was as good as could be. It was not the time to fall short.

His advice meant backtracking, disassembling and rearranging a fair bit of the work I had done. Psychologically, that was a bit tough to cope with, but I had to accept it. Just like in life, it can be difficult to do an about face after running down a particular track, as I had been for the last 6 days, but that is what I had to do.

I spent all of Friday, well into the evening, preparing for a big day the next day. I worked out my method of attack, prepared the job list and got the materials together.

On Saturday I started at 5:30 am, disengaging some of the systems I had installed.

I then hacked, hammered, bludgeoned, bashed, hit, tensioned, gouged, lashed, belted, roped, winched, climbed in and out of the hatch at least 1000 times and swore the whole fucking day.

Finally, I got the metal tear that had once been a weld, to within 10 mm of its original position and only opening an additional 2 mm as she rocked on each wave. After a mammoth 11 hour day I had achieved the goal. In total, I had put in 7 days of full on effort.

I was totally fucked, BUT enthused.

It was now or never.

For the first time since the drama occurred, I hoisted a double reefed main and coupled with the small headsail, set course for Cape Horn.

Chile, Argentina or the Falkland Islands as a stopover were no longer on the radar. I decided that we were going to sail to and around Cape Horn and carry on with the job at hand.

Update:
Wind West 15 knots
Air temp 7 °C.
YES, YES, YES, YES

Solo Globe Challenger and the boys are back in business. The fat lady can pack her bag and fuck right off. No stopping, no mucking about.

We are now as ready as we're ever going to be to try and finish the job we started. After 7 days, the work is complete and I feel bloody good that we have survived to fight another day. We are as good as we are going to be.

I feel so relieved. Only 5 Australians have completed this goal and I thought my chances of being #6 were gone.

However, we are not in the clear yet. We still have 17,000 nm to cover together and there will be all sorts of problems to overcome. I hope they are not as monumental as this one, but if they are, then so be it.

__P.S.__ If you are wondering if it's still cold down here. Two days ago, whilst in the bow cannibalising the boat, I sliced open my index finger with a Stanley knife.

It started to bleed today.

Taped Diary:

I am so emotional. Before taping I was a blubbering idiot for half an hour and couldn't talk. I'm still having trouble as I mop tears away. We are not stopping anywhere. I have done the best I can do. I am happy with the result and we are onwards and upwards. Amazing what a bit of willpower and determination will do. 7 days ago, I didn't see how it was possible for me to fix it, however, it was possible AND we have done it.

I was so emotional that morning as I thought about a lot of things including Dad, hoping that he would be proud of me, if watching from somewhere.

I also thought a lot about my surrogate father, Snapey. It really got on top of me and I stood in the cabin crying my eyes out and I am not ashamed to admit it.

Email to Snapey:

Been lots of tests for us since I sat in the dining room at your home when I was kid and asked you about the Spinnaker pole in the corner. We nailed this one too mate.

Thinking of you and maybe you can have a beer for me tonight?
All my love
Tony

How determined had I been to repair the problem and what lengths would I have gone to? Throughout the saga, I filmed at various times, and on one occasion, when using Schrodes' battering ram of a drill, I turned to the camera and said that I would wreck the whole inside of the boat to stay out there, and I meant it with all of my being. I would have torn apart and gutted the complete boat internally, back to a bare hull and a deck leaving a shell only, if that was necessary to be able to stay out there and get the job done.

What did I take away from the experience?

The week long process was evolutionary.

First thought: I'm done. The rig is going to go over the side. I'm buggered.

Next thought: I think I can save it, but it looks like I need to go to Chile.

Next thought: I don't need to go into Chile cos I think I can get around Cape Horn but I'll still have to go to the Falklands.

Next thought: Hang on a minute. If I think I can sail around Cape Horn then maybe, just maybe, I can keep working on it and not have to go in anywhere.

And so on.

I guess the lesson in there for me is that so often in this life the outcome is quite different to that imagined at the outset.

The public were able to sign up to allow them to email me direct via the Satcom C, but they needed to pay for the air time. For me, it was enticing from a financial point of view because for every $1 an email cost the sender, I received a credit of $.50 to help offset my costs. I would never do it again though. At times, it was wonderful and a real-life saver but on occasions it was terribly onerous.

When working on the mast problem, as you might expect, I received more emails than normal from my inner sanctum which was fine. The number of emails from the general public increased as well, but was a real burden as I felt obligated to reply to each which I did so eventually, but taking a lot of time to clear the backlog.

A lot of emails fell into one of two distinct categories.

One category typically went along the following lines:

"You haven't really failed. You can come in now. It will be okay. Life goes on. Don't worry about it. Give up. No one will think less of you"

Really?

Earlier I wrote:

In another email to a closed group of supporters, I mentioned that things were pretty grim and whilst trying to be positive, but looking at it objectively, **the fat lady was in the wings gargling**, *meaning that the show was nearly over with the final act nigh.*

The second category of email was typified brilliantly and succinctly by this one.

"Piss off Mowbray, the fat bitch isn't even the building let alone got the cap off the water bottle to gargle with"

Cape Horn here we come!

Update #45
26th Nov

Since rounding New Zealand, I've sat on approx. 51 deg S. Cape Horn is at 56 deg, 300 nm further south than my position and I have altered course for the run in. It is 938 nm away and should take about a week.

Useless fact: I am averaging 5.8 cups of tea each 24 hrs. You were dying to know that, weren't you?

Taped Diary:
27th Nov Day #44
8.25 pm

I am in an exceptionally good mood, standing at the hatch. It is overcast as usual and we have a pleasant 15 knot SW breeze.

Am cooking pasta in the liquid from a tin of tuna mixed with a little water. Going to add a chicken and sweetcorn soup sachet along with a seafood bisque sachet plus the tuna. I have just had half a glass of Verdelho which was left over from a little tipple last night plus I tipped a bit into the pasta as well. I am now drinking a Bourbon with Golden Circle Apple Lemon and Lime juice from a tetra long life carton and it is just beautiful!

The Eagles are belting out "Hotel California"

Read some of Kay Cottee's book to compare her experience in this area to mine.

I go to bed around 11 pm each night and don't get up until 5-6 am which means I am racking out for 6-7 hours straight each night. I certainly didn't think I would do that. I figured I would sleep for an hour or two at a time. I've become very familiar with my surroundings plus not seeing any other boats day after day after day leads me to ponder. What's the fucking point in getting up and looking?

Since leaving, from time to time, I've had up to 50 knots but have not had a serious pasting yet which is fortunate. Clouds reckons it is going to be good for the next 3 or 4 days so there is a chance I may get to the Horn without a serious flogging.

Lorraine emailed this afternoon. I would like to call her and the kids but the bloody sat phone isn't working so will email.

This Bourbon with Apple, Lemon and Lime juice is bloody beautiful.

I'm going to hide the Bourbon and juice from Kevvy and Frankie Babe.

I haven't read a newspaper, listened to a radio and don't know what's going on in the world and I don't care. I wonder what it is going to be like when I get back? I'm sure I am going to be a cot case. I am a cot case now as well as a goose.

I was taken aback by the number of people that emailed about the mast problem and were resigned to the fact that the ONLY option was to retire. It's similar to before I left, when I was experiencing problems and my schedule got tighter and tighter. Some people would automatically default to, "Oh it's okay, you can delay departure"

They don't understand the commitment, passion, drive and determination I have to get the job done.

Fuck me, this Bourbon with Apple, Lemon and Lime juice is good!

Alcohol is not something that I look for at sea for a number of reasons including that it is not the place to be partly or wholly inebriated. On a 10 day run across the Tasman to NZ it would not enter my mind to have alcohol on board nor have a drink at any stage, although I would happily tip multiple beers down my throat at conclusion.

I love a beer and used to jokingly say that the only reason we all went sailing was to drink beer afterwards, which I guess is true of so many team sports. Similar to the 19th hole at the bar in golf.

When provisioning, I seriously considered not taking any alcohol but then I thought that there would probably be times when the occasional drink in moderation would be nice. I would only ever have a drink when the weather forecast for the next few days was favourable and I generally limited it to two or maybe three and only around sunset. The effect of alcohol seemed roughly doubled, which I guess was caused by being in a state of perpetual tiredness. Two drinks kicked like four. My original alcohol inventory consisted of 2 × cartons of beer, (48 stubbies), 2 × 40 ounce bottles of Bourbon, 6 bottles of wine, which was so fresh off the press that I almost had to clench my teeth together to sieve out the grape seeds and skins as I drank.

Cookie also gave me 6 cans of premixed Bourbon and Cola.

My favourite drink by far was Bourbon and "boat temperature" Tetra Pak long life Apple juice. I loved 'em. The funny thing is, that after the trip I can't remember ever having another bourbon and apple juice.

CHAPTER 22
Now I can wear an earring!

As I refocused on getting to the Horn, the mostly inhospitable Great Southern Ocean continued to live up to its reputation. The periods of grey were relentless. Regularly I could not remember if it had been one day, three days, a week or perhaps a month since I'd seen the sun. No matter how hard I racked my brain, I could not remember. I graded the days as light, medium or dark grey.

My regular companion, fog, continued to cloak me in a world of damp with its curtain of white sitting 100 metres or less ahead. I moved, it moved, I moved, it moved. I never, ever got to the curtain. What if a ship burst through the curtain and ran me down? It was common for fog to enshroud me for three days and nights straight. A common misconception is that fog happens mostly when there is no wind but that is not the case, at least in that part of the world. Down there, mostly, fog operates in tandem with wind.

I had finished repairs late on Saturday and 72 hours later, the wind was blowing hard from the North at 30+ knots. The barometer was dropping, heralding more crap weather. I had 3 reefs in the main and a small amount of the headsail out. It was raining and my constant companion, fog, was there as well. The strong breeze and good sized swell was whacking us on the prone port side. It was the first good test for the remedial work and I was nursing the boat. The repair held up well, however the deck was still leaking a bit. I had now moved onto the paper navigation chart that would get me to, and around the Horn, which I would be VERY pleased to do.

Grey, Grey, Cold, Cold. It doesn't take much to turn this place ugly. How could you live here?

The next day I had 539 nm to go. I spoke with Mum on the Sat phone. She worried but I knew she was proud of me for having a go.

What is it with Cape Horn?

Apart from anything else, Cape Horn is the Holy Grail of sailing. It is a headland on Hornos Island, one of a cluster of islands that form the Tiera del Fuego archipelago, at the very southern extremity of Chile. Chile occupies the western, Pacific Ocean side of South America and Argentina is on the eastern, Atlantic Ocean side. The towering and imposing Andes mountain range, running north to south, is the spine that separates the two countries. The Andes has a dramatic impact on approaching weather systems.

As they sweep across the Great Southern Ocean from Australia and New Zealand on their relentless march around the planet, the systems are blocked by the Andes, unable to heave themselves up and over the massive mountain range. As they stall at the impenetrable barrier, each system compresses, generating and spewing out increased energy, with wind strength off the Richter scale, at times.

In the very south, the contour of The Andes geographically tails and feathers away to the SE, finishing near the Horn. Each weather system is forced to parallel the mountain range looking for a non-existent way through, and is pushed inexorably South. The way through, coincidentally, happens to have Cape Horn smack in the middle so the surrounding waters are blasted like you would not believe.

After passing the Horn, each system settles down and backs off the power. It dissipates a little as it enters the South Atlantic, and gets ready for its next lap of the globe and its next head butt with the Andes.

Add to the equation that The Atlantic, Pacific and Southern Oceans collide at Cape Horn, creating some very strong, confused currents in relatively shallow waters. This collision of oceans can generate waves known to reach as high as a 10 story building, not unlike the conditions that led to the horrors that the Bass Strait Eight faced.

The waters around the Horn have claimed more than their fair share of sailors, and it is estimated that between the 16th and 20th centuries a minimum of 800 ships were shipwrecked with over 10,000 lives lost.

It can be bloody freezing to boot, with the Admiralty pilot book noting that it can snow on any day of the year. Top it off with a water temp of 6 °C in summer and you see it is an extreme part of the world.

I was busting to get there and see what it was all about.

I had read, dreamt, thought, written and spoken about Cape Horn in one way or another since I was a teenager. I was now within striking distance and she wanted to play games with me, or so it seemed.

On the run in to the horn it ended up a series of "stop/starts" with a bit of the "slows" and the occasional "fuck me" thrown in as I inched my way towards that granite hard, black foreboding piece of rock known as "Fin del Mundo", Spanish for, "The End of the World".

Logbook:
Day #47
8 am *Headwinds slowing the show up*
9 pm *Becalmed 448 nm to Horn. Making me wait.*
11.15 pm *Only 6 nm covered in last 10.25 hrs.*

Been so slow but a little breeze now and we're slowly heading toward my "Mistress" again. I feel like the Horn is playing a game of cat and mouse with me.

Logbook:
Day #48
1 am

BANG. Breeze and plenty of it. A 45 knot SW front came blasting through about five hours ago. I have a tiny amount of the small headsail out and the main lashed to the boom. It's so cold. The cold on my hands is incredible, particularly my thumbs. It makes me cry out in agony moaning and groaning uncontrollably. I light the stove, put the kettle on, wrap my hands around it as it heats up. I then wrap them in a pair of tracksuit pants. Bloody painful. Barometer just starting to rise so hopefully this will piss off.

That one did piss off, fading to about 20 knots and providing some reprieve. The Horn was extracting a toll from me physically and mentally.

Logbook:
Day #49
8 am
Air temp 5 °C
Cape Horn 317 nm away

How do I feel about the Horn? I feel as if it is a wily seductress. At times, she gives me hope when I have a pleasant breeze and a good sea, allowing me to head straight for her at speed. Then, in the blink of an eye she's left the bedroom and with her goes the breeze and I am becalmed. Upon her return, she decides that any reward for being patient cannot be handed over too quickly, so she belts me with a 45 knot SW to remind me of who's in charge.

Am I losing it?

The repairs have had a good test and are holding up well, but I find it hard to relax completely.

I can't believe it's the first day of the Southern Hemisphere Summer.

While it was quiet, a day or two ago, I tensioned and greased the steering cables and can report they look okay. In the process, I ripped a massive chunk of skin and flesh off the top of 3 fingers when a cockpit locker lid fell on my hand and I instinctively pulled my hand away.

If I can maintain an average of 5.5 knots I will be at the Horn on Monday afternoon. I would love to round in daylight so my wily seductress and I can come face to face. Maybe she will be benevolent just once and allow me to get close enough to take some photos?

At this time, my meals generally consisted of:

Breakfast: Porridge with reconstituted sultanas, dried apple and apricots, my favourite breakfast in the Southern Ocean. Then, after throwing down a couple of mugs of steaming tea I was ready to take on the world.

Lunch: A packet of Chicken Chow Mein mixed with a can of prawns.

Dinner: A sachet of pasta mixed with a tin of tuna and a sachet of chicken and sweet corn soup.

I reckoned I was going okay on the food front.

I developed a very sore right nostril, which extended to behind my right eye, then across to my left eye and down to my left nostril to keep everything symmetrical. My nose bled intermittently for 10 days or so. You would think it had to have been caused by the cold.

On each ear, I had lumps just under the skin, starting at the top working their way down the back edge to the bottom of each lobe. Apparently, they were chilblains. I wore a beanie continuously for a few days covering my ears to warm them up, in an attempt to improve circulation. The burning, stinging and itching eventually retreated.

I still had not changed any of my clothes since leaving, including my underpants. The old 27 day non-stop underpants record was now well and truly smashed. A new, magnificent (in my eyes and the eyes of some others), "Personal Best" had been established. I planned to change them at Cape Horn. They were just about rooted, with holes worn through the arse. I emailed Dave Marshall appraising him of the new benchmark and detected a note of jealousy and awe in his reply.

Imagine wearing the same pair of underpants for 49 days.

That's terrible.

Is it?

I really wanted to round the Horn in daylight to get a good look at it. I needed to keep on the pace to get there by Monday afternoon. Otherwise, I decided, I would back off to round on the Tuesday morning in daylight but the weather took that decision out of my hands.

Around 150 nm out, as I closed the Chilean coast, the breeze started to funnel in. It was coming from over my left hip out of the WNW at 20+ knots, then 30 knots, then 35 knots and increasing as the Andes flexed its muscle.

Update #48
3rd Dec
Position 55 deg 46' S, 70 deg 27' W
Air temp 5 °C
107 nm to Cape Horn

This is a place of extremes and anything can happen but our ETA is somewhere around midday tomorrow. I currently have 35 knots from the WNW. It's raining with visibility down to 1 nm. I've just crossed from the deep ocean into the shallow band of water around the land mass. The depth instantly went from 2000 metres (2 km) to 46 metres. What a ride! I've picked up a couple of knots of current and with only the back end of the small headsail out and the main down, we are doing 8.5 knots straight at the mark. Nearest land is "Islas Ildefonso", 36 nm away and just about on my track so I will have to be wary.

Logbook:
3rd Dec
1 am
Wind WNW 30-40 knots

Just saw the lights of a vessel off the starboard quarter and called him on VHF. They responded but not in English. I think he is heading away from me. Rang Keir to try and speak with Lorraine and kids who were there for a barbecue but they had just left.

Big sea running, about 25-30 ft cork screwing us and whacking us on the side. Still just the back end of the small headsail out

Horn 71 nm away.

6 am
Wind WNW 40 knots

Still blowing. Barometer dropping further so does that mean more wind?
A very inhospitable place.

8.30 am
Blowing 50 knots

9.15 am
Wind WNW 50 knots
Land sighted to port. Still blowing its arse off

Update #49
4th Dec
Position 56 deg 00' S, 67 deg 16' W

Let the record show that this magnificent boat, Solo Globe Challenger passed Cape Horn at 3.25 am AEDST (12.25 pm local time) on Monday 4th December, 2000. Time taken since departure was 49 days 14 hours 25 minutes. We copped a belting yesterday, last night and early this morning with 40-50 knots coupled with some ordinary seas, rain and very poor visibility. I thought our chances of seeing the Horn were remote. However, as we neared land and got some protection, the breeze started to drop off, the rain cleared and the seas abated. The result was that we passed within 1 nm of this absolutely majestic piece of our planet in a comfortable 15 knots of wind.

What a sight, with the majestic snow and ice capped jagged peaks of Argentina and Chile in the background.

Thank you SO MUCH to all those who've helped get me here.

Having rounded at approximately 3:30 am Aussie time, I had to work super hard to contain myself before ringing anyone at home. I managed to get to 6 am and then couldn't stop myself. Snapey was very proud. Don McCloy wanted to chat about the weather back home and how they were experiencing a cold snap of 21°C at that time and it was forecast to blow a "cool" 10 knot sea breeze at Belmont.

Tears flowed all round when I spoke with Lorraine, Holly and Jordan. I was scheduled to do a heap of media interviews as well, however, the sat phone disappointingly went on strike. I emailed support company, Electrotech, and in essence the reply was, "*You won't be able to fix it out there*" so that stymied my voice communications for the time being. A tad inconvenient but that's boats for you.

The calmer weather held, and I had an opportunity to reflect on what we had just achieved.

It was an amazing day in the life of little Tony Mowbray from Belmont.

Don't be fooled though. It was not a solo effort. It was a long way from being a solo effort. When I rounded Cape Horn, I was not on my own. On board with me in spirit were all of the people that helped me over many years in so many different ways, like the enthusiastic helpers that had plastic wrapped a multitude of items to keep moisture at bay.

Tireless helpers like Lorraine's Mum Noelene, sister Nyvonne and Ken Stokes were always ready to lend a hand, including stripping the labels from each tin of 17 milk crates of tinned food. They then lined them up on wooden planks in our carport and on the top and bottom of each can they wrote the contents using a black felt tip. They said they were going to write beetroot on each one!

Then they hand lacquered (varnished) each individual can to impede the onset of rust over the 6 - 9 months I'd be out there. They were with me at the horn.

All those that had put up with my bullshit for years, supported me financially, given me "stuff", gave willingly and freely of their time over a long period, in at times, trying circumstances, were all on board as well.

Why do people do that? Why do people jump into the breech like so many had?

It is simple.

I was 100% committed.

Logbook:
4*th* Dec

The loss of 6 lives in the 1998 Sydney to Hobart race affected my crew and I deeply. What took place in Bass Strait left an indelible imprint. Being there and experiencing the conditions in which these men fought to survive, and being fortunate enough to have lived to enable me to be here now pursuing this challenge is something I will be forever grateful for.

I have therefore decided that, on behalf of Bob Snape, Glen Picasso, Keir Enderby, Keith Molloy, Tony Purkiss, Dave Marshall and Dave Cook, to dedicate Solo Globe Challenger's rounding of Cape Horn to the memory of the six men who gave up their lives and their family and friends who have been affected in so many ways.

Bruce Guy
Phil Skeggs
Glyn Charles
Mike Bannister
Jim Lawler
John Dean
Gentlemen, rest easy.

At that point, the journey was only 27% complete, and we still had a lot of water to pass under the keel and past the rudder to get to 100%. However, if the trip now went off the rails, at least we had achieved this. I was so relieved and proud to have rounded Cape Horn. It had been such a focus in my life for so long, and it was surreal that I had finally got there. For me, it was as if I had added a tangible, bricks and mortar asset to my life that could never be taken from me. I felt pretty bloody good about it.

It was phenomenal to think that just a little under two years prior, my seven blood brothers and I had been fighting to keep the same boat afloat in Bass Strait and struggling to within a hairs breath for survival.

Now, I was at Cape Horn, on the same boat, on my own.

Traditionally, a sailor who had rounded the Horn was entitled to wear a gold hoop earring in their left ear, the one which had faced the Horn in a typical eastbound passage, and was allowed to dine with one foot on the table. If the same sailor had also rounded the Cape of Good Hope they could place both feet on the dining table. I might forego the earring, but I had one foot on the table and was on my way to both.

I hope I don't sound conceited, but, "How many people do you know that have sailed around Cape Horn solo?" The answer is, fuck all.

Maybe I don't know too many insane people?

The boat had done a fantastic job thus far and the chainplate repairs seemed to be holding up well, but I was still nervous. The conditions I experienced through the night and early morning prior to rounding had been a huge test for her. The poor old girl had copped some really bad ones whilst I had cringed below in the Nav area chewing my finger nails.

The now, benign conditions, gave me an opportunity to rejoice and have some fun. I was able to film and photograph merrily. Pete Collins had donated hundreds of packets of his Old Pete's Beef Jerky and all he wanted was a photograph of me holding a packet with the Horn in the background, so I obliged.

I wanted to give Bi-Lo a good run for their money and so I filmed extensively for them. I shot a very humorous piece holding up a Bi-Lo light fruitcake perfectly, after trialing a lot of positions, with me and the horn in shot, whilst I extolled the virtues of their products in general but more specifically their fruitcake.

The narrative went something like, *"Bi-Lo light fruitcake is my favourite. I break it off by the chunk full and have it for breakfast, dinner and tea. It's Yummo!"*

All the while, I was hamming it up I was chewing a big chunk whilst filming. That piece made it into the documentary that we eventually made and everyone, and I mean everyone, that sees that bit of footage gets a huge laugh. The return on Bi-Lo's investment in me was re-paid in spades with that one clip.

I first sighted land at 9.15 am and had it in sight until sunset. I was completely taken in by the rugged landscape of Chile and Argentina and the island cluster close to me. The view was mesmerising, partly because I had not seen land for 50 days, but particularly because of nature's staggeringly beautiful creation.

I promised myself that one day, when I had time, and I could afford to stop, that I was going to come back to explore the area. That is a story for another day. Maybe?

Where to now?

Any journey has a beginning, a middle and an end, regardless of whether it be the journey of life, a trip to the supermarket or to the toilet. I had previously decided that getting to the horn would be the start of this journey. I figured that it would probably be pretty tough psychologically and I had been right.

I hadn't looked too far beyond the end of the "start" section, but now that it had been achieved it was time to lock in the next goal of knocking over the "middle" bit, which would encompass the South Atlantic and Equatorial region.

The next rounding point would be Tristan da Cunha Island group, a British flagged territory of a remote group of islands in the mid South Atlantic, about 2450 nm away.

I thought we would rip this shortish leg off pretty quickly but once again, I was wrong.

CHAPTER 23
Underpants off after 70 days

Rounding the Horn had taken me to the southern extremity of the trip, and I now set an ENE course to Tristan, about 20 days away. On this leg, I would slowly get North, which I was super keen to do (read: fucking get me there now), to be in warmer, more benign conditions. At Tristan, I would take a sharp left turn and head due north toward the Equator, escaping the clutches of the Southern Ocean more quickly, eventually swapping out rough, tough freezing sailing for sunglasses, shorts and heat.

Around five years prior, I had suffered my first serious back problem when I was on a yacht and felt something "go" in my lower back. Fortunately, I was with three others, including Keir, because within an hour I was completely incapacitated. Laying on a lounge below decks, the ONLY thing I could do was raise my head about 25 mm. I could not roll over, sit up, stand, put weight on my elbows. Nothing. If the boat had been burning to the waterline or sinking, there was no way I could have saved myself.

I was nearly 100% incapacitated and it was a pretty scary experience.

The crew at that time had considered calling for a chopper to airlift me. This option waxed and waned until eventually we discounted it as arrival to port got closer, plus, I began to slightly improve. 6 hours after the initial onslaught I was able to get myself on deck, albeit very painfully. On land, an ambulance whisked me off to hospital for an overnight stay.

It took a couple of weeks to recover aided by anti-inflammatories, massage, yoga, a chiropractor, exercise and whatever else came along.

In the years following I suffered more attacks with the diagnosis being a sciatic nerve problem. The pain in my lower back and left leg could be shocking. At the height of an attack I would collapse to the floor, unable to stand, at best walk, stooped over with a crabbing sideways gait.

Some attacks were worse than others. A full blown one typically saw an initial 4–5 days of increasing discomfort until it reached a peak, plateauing for another 4-5 days at which time the pain was a force to be reckoned with and I was generally immobile. It would then taper off to normal over another 4-5 days.

As I closed on the Horn my back had been "niggling" me, and I was worried that it might develop into a full-blown episode. This was definitely not the place to be incapacitated. After rounding the Horn the "niggle" built to the "here we go again" level, and it was obvious that I was in for a tough time.

I had read that the colour of the Atlantic Ocean is very different to the Pacific Ocean and it was. It was almost as if I had sailed across a dashed line as the morbid grey was replaced with a deep rich blue. 36 hours after rounding the horn I was almost becalmed, however as a result of two intense low pressure systems colliding not too far away I was subjected to massive loping swells. These caused the boat to be tossed around, disconcertingly, like a cork bobbing on the ocean.

However, on this day, the sun was framed by a beautiful cloudless blue sky and life was pretty good, even though the air temperature was only 5 °C. As I slowly gyrated my way toward Tristan da Cunha, I found myself just 130 nm south of The Falklands and able to tune in to BBC radio. It was wonderful to listen to sport, world news, music and political comment. It had been great to be insulated from the outside world for a couple of months, but I now realised how much I needed this in my life as well.

As we dawdled along, I was surrounded by about 50 magnificent albatross and many other bird species. On this day, the albatross would fly ahead and land approximately 150 metres away, and form a structured circle with them all facing inwards, as if they were having a mother's club meeting.

Solo Globe and I would eventually waddle up to and past. Once we were about 100 metres ahead, they would all take off simultaneously, landing 150 metres ahead again, form another circle and wait for me to catch up. The process went on all day and I was thoroughly intrigued having previously never witnessed this behaviour from these magnificent creatures. I was enthralled. What a day!

I had entered the Atlantic thinking that a switch would flick and the weather would improve almost instantaneously. I thought my "Albatross, sun and blue sky day" was clear evidence that the weather from now on was going to be much more favourable but as usual, I was wrong. The Southern Ocean would not let me out of her grasp easily, as I would find out.

With a break in the weather, I tidied the boat up a little, but not myself.

I had intended on having a tub up including fresh clothes and a change of underpants however, after checking them, they seemed to be doing pretty well so I decided to extend my "Personal Best" further. How long could I make one pair last?

I replied to a backlog of emails, mainly congratulating us on rounding the Horn.

I was upset that the sat phone had given up the ghost, as voice contact with the outside world was cherished. Not to be thwarted easily, I decided to see if I could prove Electrotech wrong and repair the troublesome unit. If you haven't gathered by now, I don't like throwing the towel in and love a challenge.

They had said that I required a special screwdriver and that I *"wouldn't have one on board"*. It just so happens that I bloody well did.

The fault code flashed "antenna down".

I managed to prise apart the moulded handset and found the antenna cable termination was pretty well stuffed, but made intermittent contact when I wiggled it.

Being inventive I used:

1) The stump of a pencil
2) A stainless washer
3) A screw
4) A pair of nail scissors
5) Sandpaper
6) Duct tape
7) 2 × toothpicks

The above is an unlikely combination I will admit, however, voila, problem solved. It wasn't a 100% perfect remedy but was better than nothing.

Update #50

RE SATELLITE PHONE *I've managed to find a wire that has an intermittent fault. If I "jiggle" it a certain way, the wire that is, and hold my tongue correctly, I can get it to fire up. I'm still talking about the phone! We are operating in a harsh environment for electronics, and every other bloody thing, so problems like this are bound to occur. We have to roll with the punches. I will do my best to maintain communications and keep you all informed.*

It is worthy of note, that it is a strong possibility that at some stage I may lose all communications and that should not be cause for immediate alarm. I have safety equipment like EPIRB's to fire up if I'm in trouble. If all communications fail I will continue to sail the boat toward our objective and try to let the outside world know that I'm okay through some means, like contact with a ship etc.

I will not stop just because I can't communicate.

A bloke called Captain James Cook didn't have satellite email/phone.

Update #51
7th Dec
Air temp 6 °C
Water temp 5.7 °C
95 nm SE of the Falklands
Some fun facts and useless information:

1) *My overall average speed has dropped from 5.4 knots to 5 knots*
2) *I have TWO pair of very thick socks on that have been on for over 40 days straight.*
3) *I have only run the motor for a total of 11 hours as my solar panels and wind generator are doing a great job charging batteries.*
4) *I have read 22 books totaling 7019 pages averaging 130 pages per day*
5) *I left with 640 litres of fresh water.*
6) *I left with 4 × 9 kg bottles of LP Gas and 1 × 4.5 kg bottle. I am still on my 1st bottle so I should have plenty to get the job done.*

My bad back was getting worse. How far would this attack spiral? I also had a very sore left inner elbow. My left knee was having a go as well, as a result of my marathon days. My Chilblains were giving me plenty but slightly improving. My nose still bled from time to time but was improving a little. Both hands were very sore with various cuts, swelling and stiffness. Where I had ripped the skin off my fingers was healing slowly but I constantly knocked it and it hurt a bloody lot, every time.

A picture of health I was not.

My book of choice at this time, was *"The Falcon and the Snowman"*, a true story about Andrew Daulton Lee and Christopher John Boyce from the US. Set in the mid 70's, it involves espionage and the Russian KGB.

I love true crime and the associated intrigue. I was enthralled. What drives some people to do bad things?

In 1977 Lee got life imprisonment and Boyce received 40 years. They were eligible for parole in the 90's. I was super curious to know if they were still in gaol.

Logbook:
7th Dec
No Sun.
How could you live here?
Iceberg!
This one on my course. How big is it! 20 nm × 20 nm!

From Argentina Marine Safety:
NAVAREA VI 0201
PROVINCIA TIERRA DEL FUEGO, ANTARTIDA E ISLAS DEL ATLANTICO SUR
DEC 2000 ICEBERG ADRIFT:
A-22 B AT 51-24 S 039-18 W SIZE 20 × 20 NM

I ventured into more new territory. My previous longest continuous time at sea was 54 days and I now eclipsed that. A new air temperature low was set when it dropped to 2 °C plus it bloody well snowed again. Yep, I was spot on with my prediction regarding the weather improving.

My back had worsened and mobility was shot to pieces. Regularly, the pain would drop me like a sack of potatoes as I cried out involuntarily.

I had shortened sail to minimise visits on deck and tried to stay in the bunk, resting it as much as possible. I mostly had to crawl around the boat.

Logbook:
11th Dec
10.20 am

Some blue sky, snow gone. Yesterday was very cold. Spent the day below reading with heaps of clothes on including gloves. Had porridge, raisins, sultanas and dried apple for brekky. Bored with crook back.

Logbook:
11th December
5.15 pm
BECALMED

Turned out a great day. Blue sky, some warmth in the sun. For the first time that I can remember I wanted to sit in the cockpit and did so for 4 hrs reading Peter Cook Bio. Had smoked oysters, cheese, salami and Jatz for lunch followed by a little sleep in arvo to rest back.

I knew I was a genius at this weather forecasting stuff.

Then the wheels fell off the bus.

To prove me an idiot, yet again, and to remind me who was actually in charge, the wind gods sorted me out with a 35-40 knot NE gale. My course to Tristan was almost directly from where the wind was coming from so progress was minimal. It was a very uncomfortable night and morning with a vicious, short, sharp, boat breaking sea. I shortened sail to just a triple reefed mainsail to ride it out, almost stopped, not overly worried about making forward progress.

This was the start of a very trying period.

On the 13th it blew 35 knots all day from the West, which was behind me but only temporarily. That day I was bashing my way into the residual sea generated by the previous strong winds from the opposite direction which created its own set of challenges. I only had a tiny portion of the small headsail out and was forced to sail as if picking our way through a minefield, which I was, sort of.

My back had started to improve. Hallelujah.

Bring on the tropics. I'm ready.

That evening the barometer dropped yet again heralding a new assault.

The breeze dropped off for a few hours before hammering me again from the NNW at 45 + knots.

Logbook:
14th Dec

These strong breezes from the Northern sector will not give in. 45 knots all last night plus on the nose. Backed a bit to the left and dropped off a touch. It seems like this one thing forever. Blow like buggery from the NE, NNE, N, NNW. I want something different. Give me some gentle stuff.

I just took a wave on the side that takes the prize for force exerted. How the windows didn't cave in, I'll never know.

Later that day, the breeze finally abated and I increased sail and made some forward progress, but was now shrouded in thick fog.

If things weren't bad enough, on 15th December, to my absolute horror, I discovered that salt water had contaminated a large portion of my fresh supply. This had the potential to bring us completely undone and bring the challenge to a premature end.

Water is the staff of life.

I HAD to find a solution.

I left with 640 L of fresh water, 260 L in a tank under a bunk, 300 L in a tank under the main cabin floor and 4 × 20 L plastic drums. For a number of reasons, including cost and electricity requirements, I did not have a desalinator. I knew from previous experience that if I were reasonably frugal with fresh water I could exist on 3-3.5L per day. I estimated that I had used about 3L per day to that point.

To get by on such a meagre amount you need to wash dishes in salt water ALL the time and NEVER have a freshwater shower. You must wash clothes in salt water and use a tiny amount of fresh as a "rinse cycle" in a bucket. You should guard your freshwater reserves as if your life depends on it, because one day it might.

For the early part of the trip, I decided to initially draw from the tank under the bunk, being reasonably miserly but not overly so. My plan was to check consumption after a while to assess if I needed to be more frugal. With 640 L, a hoped for 180 days at 3.5 L (maximum) per day, I expected to use no more than 630 L. A safety margin of 10L over six months? No problems.

I hoped to catch rainwater in the tropics.

On this day, I switched tanks to start drawing from under the floor and was horrified to discover its contents not only salt laden but had a lot of black algae/mould/gunk in it as well.

Houston, we have another problem.

The leak around the chainplate repair, had allowed salt sea water in, which worked its way down to the floor of the main cabin from where I sponged it up from time to time. When I pieced it together later on, I realised that some of the salt water on the floor had seeped into the underfloor tank because of some degraded silicon sealant around an inspection port. The water from the tank was now undrinkable.

You're bloody kidding me, aren't you? Here we go again.

I had to solve the problem.

I transferred the remaining "good" water out of the under bunk tank into containers, and then relocated the bulk of the "bad" water into the under bunk tank so that it would not be further degraded. I decanted the remaining "bad" water into more containers. The under floor tank was eventually empty and remained so for the rest of the trip.

The tropics were still a fair distance away but in any event, I could not rely on catching rainwater. I had to make do with what I had to get me to the finish line. If I caught rainwater, it would be a bonus.

I experimented, blending "bad" and "good" water, deciding that 65% "bad" plus 35% "good" was drinkable even though it had a salty overtone and left a lingering, almost permanent salty aftertaste.

By following that ratio I would still have some "bad" water left over at the end that could not be factored into my calculations, but I kept it just in case I could mix it later with any rainwater that I might catch.

I then calculated the total amount of blended water I would have and divided that by the estimated days left to calculate the maximum amount I could drink in any 24 hour period.

The answer was 1.5 L every 24 hours, which was bugger all.

I ratted an empty 2L plastic milk bottle from the rubbish. Everything on Solo Globe had a 2nd, 3rd, 4th or more, possible use apart from its original application. That milk bottle, in the 2nd phase of its life cycle, stood me in good stead for the next four months - but not to hold milk. It had a moulded ridge near the top which conveniently was at the 1.5 L mark.

From then on, every day at midday precisely, with almost religious fervour and huge anticipation, I would blend 35% "good" with 65% "bad" water filling the bottle exactly to the ridge and no further. That was all the water that I would/could allow myself for the next 24 hours. At 6 am the next morning, if my 1.5 L ration was gone, I would not mix up a new brew until midday. I had to be focused and strong.

What about the black algae/mould/gunk I hear you ask? This presented another challenge. I strained my "bad" water through a piece of paper towel shaped as a small cone, to trap the black rubbish. It was similar to using a filter paper in science lessons at school but not quite the same. Each day I very carefully set aside the paper towel to dry, as you wouldn't want to waste it. Prior to reusing it the next day, I flicked away the now dehydrated mould.

I then compiled a detailed inventory of every other bit of drinkable liquid on board and calculated an average daily allowance that could supplement my rationed water.

70 L Long Life Milk (undiluted)	600ml per day
15.5 L fruit juice (dilute with bad water)	200ml per day
47 × 375 mm cans carbonated soft drink	125ml per day
36 × 600mm PowerAde (dilute with bad water)	250ml per day
Total	1175ml per day

The maximum amount of life sustaining liquid that I could consume in a 24 hour period was 2.675 litres, a portion of which was salt affected.

These calculations surmised a 180 days at sea. If longer, the numbers would be worse, so I had to be strong and keep as much in reserve as I could to allow for a longer stint out there.

I HAD to be miserly.

There was also liquid in tins of vegetables such as corn, beans, peas, beetroot etc., all of which I would consume but didn't include in the numbers. I would cook noodles in beetroot juice and eat/drink the pot empty.

This new regime had significant consequences, apart from the worry. Upon waking, I would moisten my lips to be greeted with a salt taste which wore thin when it was day after day. From that point onwards, I wasn't getting enough water and my level of dehydration rose exponentially as I got closer to the Equator. My urine became darker each day as I entered a state of partial dehydration, but I was prepared to pay the price.

Would I be able to catch a meaningful amount of rainwater in the future?

Over the years I have been asked many times if I ever thought about quitting. I can, with my hand on my heart, say that the thought never ever, ever crossed my mind.

Never!

My mindset was always that I would do whatever I had to do, within some reason, to stay out there. My reasoning might not be considered mainstream, but, so be it.

I was 100% committed. Boots 'n all.

This part of the trip was becoming a real pain in the arse. I was hard on the wind yet again, still bashing toward Tristan. The barometer plummeted as I sailed on with a pocket handkerchief amount of headsail.

Logbook:
16th Dec
8.50 am

Had a testing week. You can't relax. Just when you think you've got a break the Barometer drops and off you go again. Just poking along to ride yet another one out. The whole week I've been on edge.

   10.30 pm Blowing a bastard again. Sick of 'em.
   10.50 pm Make it 50 knots.

Logbook:
17th Dec
4.30 pm

Breeze has dropped to 15 knots and swung. I'm now left with a huge confused sea and am being rolled everywhere. One wave put us on our beam ends. I'm glad I'm in a strong boat like this and not some modern "eggshell". I'll wait for the sea to abate and hoist some Main. Just had a cup of tea and some Bi-Lo fruitcake.

Eventually, a new SW front filtered in but before its arrival we were subjected to an incredibly confused and massive residual swell, which saw us madly rolling gunwale to gunwale for about 5 hours. I needed to get my head together.

When in danger or in doubt, eat. So, I did.

Dinner was rice, a small tin of prawns, some smoked chicken and a packet of seafood bisque soup mixed together. Further evidence that I was living the dream. It was bloody glorious.

Update #55
17th December
Air temp 8 °C
826 nm to Tristan

Today I am on the opposite side of the world to home and nearly level with the bottom of Tasmania. Progress has been slow of late. The log for the last week or more records a continuous stream of wind around 30-35-40 knots and yesterday for about 10 hours I had 50 knots from the NNE (my course is ENE). A very nasty sea built and we were punched by a few absolute rippers. There is a long way to go and I don't want to "trip". When conditions are "on". Preserving the boat is more important than making miles.

It looks like I will arrive at Tristan on Christmas Day. I hope the big guy in the red suit brings you what you want.

We were way less than 50% complete but the fact that I had reached and crossed the Meridian of longitude on the opposite side of the planet from home allowed me to now think of home being ahead, and not behind. It's a mind game apart from anything else.

We finally got a break in the weather and I had an easy day catching up on some reading, dried some socks and shoes in the oven, as you do. I cooked a sultana cake at the same time as the socks and shoes were in the oven. The cake was surprisingly moist.

That morning there was clear blue sky, bugger all breeze and I was belting out Neil Diamond. What a brilliant entertainer.

2NURFM is a Newcastle community based radio station. I liked the volunteer hosts, Judith and Bob, who surprised me that day when they had Lorraine, Holly, Jordan and Trevor in the studio. It was a great interview which lifted my spirits immeasurably however the downside was that it left me with an aching heart. Poor Jordan could not utter a word because he was so emotional.

Prior to departure, Holly fretted badly, thinking that I might never come back. Jordan, on the other hand, hadn't been so concerned because he thought that Dad was just going for another long sail and would be back soon enough. As the trip progressed, their view and emotions flipped.

Holly eventually realised that there would be an end to it. For poor Jordan, the longer the trip went on, the more convinced he became I was never coming home. It was so tough emotionally for all concerned. I have an emotional debt to my children that will be with me until the day I die. The kids, of course, say I owe 'em nothing.

We were in a period of no Moon and coupled with thick cloud cover that night, it was so dark that I could not see the front of the boat. A black abyss into which I sailed.

705 nm to Tristan da Cunha.

Do you remember being a child in the back seat of the family car on a long and boring journey? When the boredom got too much you would ask, more than once and to the chagrin of your parents, "How much longer Dad?"

Well, "How much longer Dad?"

On the 19th we had a stunning blue cloudless sky but bugger all breeze and we either drifted in circles doing doughnuts or had just enough wind to achieve a knot or two in the general direction of Tristan, so I took the opportunity to carry out some maintenance. It was an incredibly harsh environment on both me and the boat and I had to look after both. Part of the "Looking after Tony" program that day included having my 3rd shave in a tad over 2 months. I was overdoing the personal hygiene bit I know.

The weather had been unstable for ages and that evening the instability continued. Two low pressure systems to my south head butted each other and consequently sucked the wind from where I was to them. It rushed away like a steam train to fill the atmospheric void and as a result I was yet again down to minimal sail area, using a triple reefed main and small part of the small headsail.

Let this bit be over. Let me get to Tristan.

I promise I'll toddle around the corner and be on my way.

Update #57
20th December
Press Release
From Heidi Pollard
Public Relations Manager
John Hunter Hospital
Solo sailor lives it up for Christmas

Well known Lake Macquarie yachtsman, Tony Mowbray, who has been at sea since October 15, 2000, will be celebrating Christmas in a very different way this year.

"Looks like Christmas is going to be spent very close to the Tristan da Cunha Island Group in the South Atlantic," Tony said today. "I'll probably be asleep when Santa comes but I'll leave a bourbon out for him."

Tony explained that his Christmas Day will consist of:

- *Bi-Lo Christmas pudding and custard,*
- *Opening presents he took with him from his children, family and friends,*
- *Calling home*
- *Putting up Christmas decorations if the weather is calm enough although some of them had got wet so he's not sure what state they are in.*
- *Considering he is already talking to himself, Tony figures he may as well sing some Christmas carols too even though he professes to not being able to "sing for nuts",*
- *If the weather is okay he may have "a celebratory drink of either wine, bourbon and apple juice, rum or beer. If it is a really good day, I might have the lot"*

Tony said. "I really miss my children"

His message to everyone back home was simple: "Those that have children please make sure that they really appreciate and love them. Give them lots of hugs and kisses all the time, not just at Christmas"

NEVER, EVER GIVE IN!

It was another glorious day with a powder puff cloudless blue sky, married to a gentle ocean, coupled with a gentle breeze. That night the stars were switched to peak brightness and clarity.

An absolute cracker of a day.

Update #58
21ˢᵗ Dec
Air temp 16 °C
Water temp 13.9 °C
480 nm to Tristan
1900 nm WSW of Capetown, South Africa

I reckon that childbirth and long distance ocean sailing have a lot in common. Both parties push the bad memories to the inner recesses of the mind, never to be completely forgotten, while fondly remembering the good times, which is why you go back for more.

Today was one of the good times. Blue sky, amazing deep blue ocean, gentle 10 knot NW breeze, no swell, loping along at about 4 knots, sunglasses on for the first time, 16 deg heatwave, listening to one of Biggle's cassette tapes called "Mariner" which on the cover is described as "Haunting Pan Flute and warm orchestral strings, gently awash with ocean waves. Stirring and soulful. This beautiful recording takes you on a relaxing journey over the ocean"

(I loved that tape Biggles.

See, I do have an appreciative artistic side after all.)

Yes Sir, it doesn't get much better than this.

It looks like I'll round Tristan late Christmas Eve or early Christmas Day Maybe I will be able to raise someone on the radio. I might even see a human being.

Logbook:
22nd Dec
3.40 pm
350 nm to Tristan.

Blue sky, fresh breeze, getting warmer. Been getting some absolute corkers of encouraging emails. It makes me feel very proud to be out here having a go. Just rolling along square, poled out with the wind behind me.

Logbook:
23rd Dec
3 pm
Still running square. Double reefed Main and poled small headsail
    Breakfast was cereal and long life milk that was turning sour.
    Lunch was Suimin noodles using liquid that I saved from a tin of corn and a tin of tiny taters from last night. Making every effort to conserve liquids.
    Had 2 Bourbons last night using the remnants of 2 × cans of orange carbonated soft drink that had corroded through and partially leaked their contents. The soft drink was flat but the Bourbon helped.
    Now that we have stepped through a doorway into the 30's of latitude I hope the weather is more like this, benevolent, for the next couple of months.

Logbook:
24th Dec (morning)
131 nm to Tristan

A gentle breeze from ENE. Hard on wind, blue sky, slight sea. Going to get Xmas presents and decos out. Just crossed another time zone.
    Had my 4th shave AND my first all over wash, shampooed hair and everything.
    Took my underpants off after 70 days. New record!
    Smashed the old record of 27 days. Hit it right out of the ballpark.
    I might have some "Gala Spumante" from the Xmas presents stash to celebrate.

I fully accept that wearing my underpants for 70 consecutive days might polarise opinion. Many, I believe, will be in awe and then there may be those who possibly don't see my 70 day effort as being admirable or something to aspire to. Not only had I worn them for 70 days but they had not left my body, having been no further than my ankles. If the trip went to the pack from that point, I would still have a world class achievement to hang my hat on and dine out on at dinner parties for the rest of my days.
    The undies were green and had small koalas printed on them. Because I had spent so much time sitting, I had abraded the 2 sections that covered each arse cheek and they were razor thin. These two sections were joined at the centre by what resembled a macramé weave with more holes than fabric.

I felt this was a cornerstone day. I made up a sign recording the date they went on, the date they came off, and prompting that it may have been a new world, or anywhere else in the universe. I sat on the engine box lid, put the sign around my neck with said underpants perched on top of my head, all the while taking selfies and videoing myself.

When I got home, Lorraine washed them and to this day they are sealed in an airtight plastic bag never to be worn again. They are a treasured and valuable family heirloom, to be passed down from generation to generation and spoken of in hushed revered tones.

Logbook:
24th Dec (early afternoon)

In shorts and short sleeved shirt, and fresh *Undies. Been beating to windward all night, getting carted way off course. At one stage steering 115 deg when the Island was bearing 75 deg. Island now 63 nm away Greased the steering cables and pulleys to get rid of a squeak. The Starboard cable is wearing. Have to watch the wear and keep it well greased. Took compass out of binnacle and greased steering chain where it goes over sprocket.*

I knocked over some "Summer Wine" last night which was a Xmas present. It did the job

There was a big chance that the cable would not make it to the end. It had me worried so from them on I increased the frequency of greasing and checking to every couple of days.

I still had my back-up plans but in my heart, I knew they weren't brilliant.

However, I was 100% sure that if it broke, it would not stop us.

Logbook:
24th Dec (still!)

Bloody North Easter. Tristan is 44.7 nm away and this NE breeze is coming straight from there. It looks like I won't see the Island. I've been planning on getting in close to see if I can see human beings but that might have to wait until I'm back here in a couple of months.

The course I followed in the South Atlantic created a massive circle, traversed in an anticlockwise direction. There is an almost permanent high-pressure system that sits over the South Atlantic, and in it the wind rotates anticlockwise. By sailing an anticlockwise circle, I hoped to get a slight overall advantage by going with the wind rather than against it.

The starting point for the circle was Tristan followed by St Helena and Ascension Islands, then on to St Peter and St Paul rocks, a group of 15 small islets and rocks 55 nm north of the Equator, about 510 nm east of the nearest point of mainland Brazil. By crossing the Equator, I would enter the Northern Hemisphere, albeit reasonably briefly but satisfying another cornerstone criteria. If you start in the southern hemisphere, at some stage you must pass into the northern hemisphere or vice versa.

After rounding the rocks, I would head south again to round Tristan a second time, thus completing the loop and then head underneath South Africa and across to Tasmania. It looked like I was going to see bugger all of Tristan on this first pass, if indeed any at all.

Logbook:
25th Dec
CHRISTMAS DAY
SIGHTED LAND ON STBD BEAM

Bugger it. I'm going to go in and have a look at the Island. Going in will cost me time but what the heck?

On Christmas Day I was battling headwinds, requiring me to tack. The favoured Port tack was taking me away from Tristan. Occasionally I would flop to Starboard tack and finally I sighted one of the islands just south of Tristan. I decided to stick with the less favoured tack in the hope of seeing land clearly.

However, the bloody barometer had dropped yet again and a new front arrived. The new wind hitting the old waves kicked up a vicious sea, and I found myself in boat breaking conditions fucking well yet again.

My main Christmas day meal was some instant mashed potato reconstituted with juice from a tin of carrots and some curdling long life milk to which I added a tin of sweet corn. It was seriously bloody good.

It was now dark on Christmas Day evening and the main island was just too dangerous to try and get closer to so I decided to forget

Tristan, hoping for a look at it when I passed by again later in the trip. That was a bit tough psychologically because I'd had a tough 3 weeks and was hoping to be rewarded with a good look at land. I did manage to see a vague outline through the haze, as the last rays of daylight faded and that was it.

Just like in life, it doesn't always work out how you want it to. So be it.

I rang home but the Sat Phone quite irritatingly kept dropping out, but, in the end, I had a beautiful chat with the kids hearing about their presents. I also rang Mum in what turned out to be an extremely brief conversation, courtesy of the fucked sat phone but at least I got through to her.

With Tristan fading to the background it was time to refocus and set a new goal. The next mark of the course was Saint Helena Island, 1335 nm to my north. It was our job now to knock that leg over and add it to the tally.

Red rope (and others) up and over mast spreaders to stabilise mast.

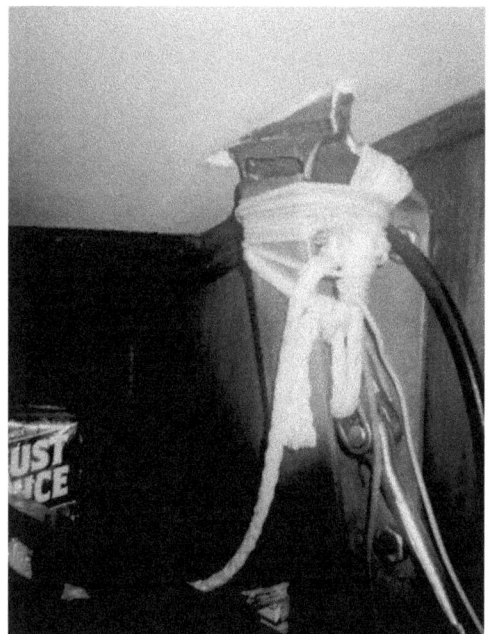

Chainplate at early stage of remedial work. Note, tear/opening in the weld at the top.

The block and tackle support systems to hold the mast in place on the Port side.

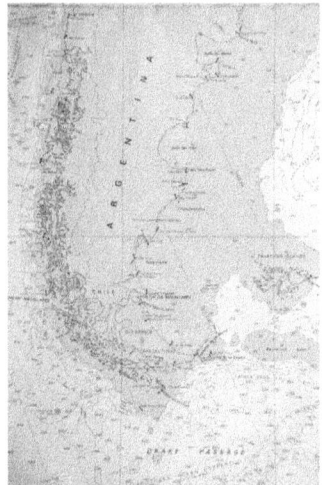

The contoured tip of South
America with Cape Horn in
the firing line at the bottom.

Cape Horn! Note, tiny amount of sail and
support system for chainplate.

Cape Horn! I had waited so long!

Cape Horn and Bi-Lo light fruitcake! Bloody beautiful.

Fresh water problem. A tally of drinkable liquid composed on 19th Dec 2000.

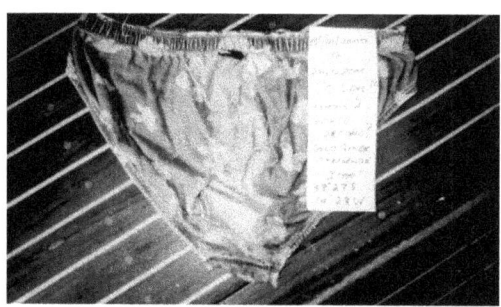

Underpants off after 70 days! A new world record?

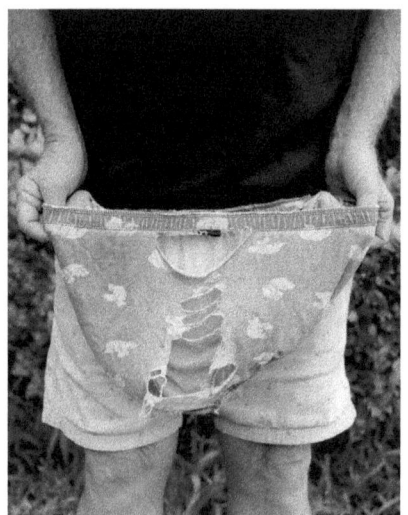

Underpants in 2025. A treasured family heirloom.

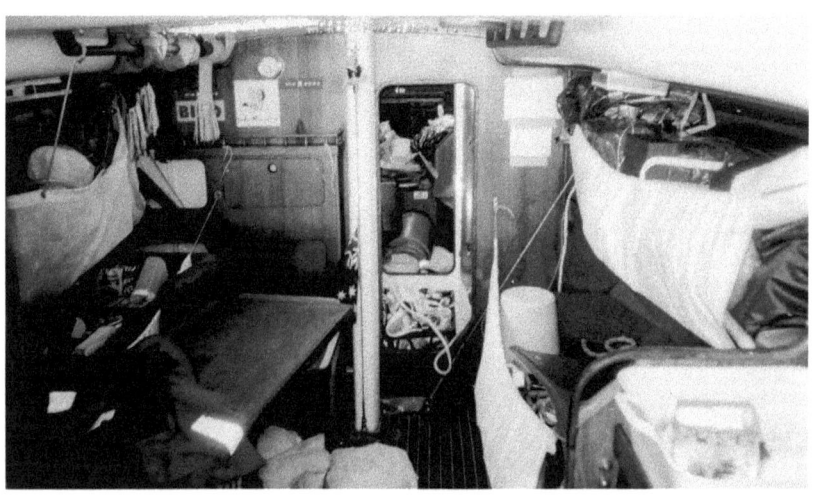

Main cabin. Repaired port Chainplate to left of Bi-Lo logo.
Billy the Bear at top of mast just under deck.

CHAPTER 24

It was like a canary perched on my shoulder

Saint Helena is a remote tropical volcanic island and a British overseas territory in the South Atlantic, 16 deg or 960 nm South of the Equator, so well and truly in the tropics. It is about 1000 nm West of Africa and 2100 nm East of Rio de Janeiro, Brazil, so a bit in the middle of nowhere.

Measuring 16 × 8 miles, it sustains a population of around 5000, and for about four centuries was an important stopover for ships heading to/from Europe and Asia until the Suez Canal was built.

St Helena is known for being the location of Napoleon Bonaparte's second exile following his final defeat in 1815. He died on the island in 1821.

The dawning of the first day of this new leg was Boxing Day and I pensively contemplated that back in Aussie, the Sydney to Hobart yacht race had started six hours prior. It was 2 years since the fight for life had begun in Bass Strait for us, and it was never far from my thoughts. It was like a canary perched on my shoulder, chirping away. On the 1st anniversary, at home, I had not coped and was very difficult to be around. On that 2nd anniversary, I only had myself to annoy.

On this first day of this new leg of the course, the temperature rocketed up to a scorching 20 °C. It was the first time, for a long time that the air temp had a "2" as the first number. As I tracked NNE in a moderate following SE breeze, I began to believe that by turning the corner at Tristan I had hit the "on" switch for some great sailing as suddenly shorts and T-shirt were the go. Yahoo! Would it last?

The next day we ticked over effortless miles, running with the wind behind us with a poled out small headsail and a reef in the Main. It was very cruisy for a change. Now that I wasn't under so much stress, I was keen to make some phone calls and found it extremely annoying that the sat phone didn't want to play ball, blinking unwaveringly, "Antenna link down".

My book of choice at that point was one that Mum had secreted on board as a Xmas pressie. "South Pole 2000" was about 5 women who trekked 600 miles to the geographic South Pole in early 2000. It was an excellent read, authored by the expedition leader, Caroline Hamilton.

She touched on their unsuccessful hunt for sponsorship, lamenting that their expedition was such a marketable package. Her words ran deep with me and fired me up on the spot. Memories flooded back about the negativity, procrastination, inept supposedly "professional" behaviour and laziness I had encountered. Many marketers would not know it if a golden opportunity bit them on the arse.

DON'T get me started again! Ha ha.

Then and there, I vowed that should I end up writing a book such as this I would give a huge fucking serve to some members of the marketing fraternity that deserve it. There are some bloody good operators, but many deserve a blast. More rantings and ravings about marketers and my hunt for sponsorship elsewhere in this subtle, unbiased, inoffensive, objective, non-opinionated and conservative book.

Update #59
27th Dec

Air temp 26 °C (ya fucking hoo)
Water temp 22.6 °C
1000 nm to Saint Helena
1400 nm due west of Capetown, South Africa

Today is day #74. We have sailed approx. 8,900 nm with approx. 13,000 to go, so about 40% complete.

Getting north quickly with some great sailing in moderate SE breezes, and a rise in temperature (26 beautiful degrees today). 9 hours ago, we were on exactly the same latitude as home (33 deg S) but the massive difference is that I'm on the other side of the world. Just 500 nm more north and we will cross the Tropic of Capricorn and officially be in the tropics. Scary.

My HF Radio continues to give me great enjoyment as I tune into Voice of America regularly.

It has not rained but I am confident it will.

Hope you all have a great New Years Eve.

In the previous day or two I had noticed a couple of pieces of rubbish in the water and this was the first that I had come across since leaving Australia. The waters from Australia to NZ, across to the Horn and of the far South Atlantic, were free of rubbish.

What I didn't realise on that day was that these first bits of debris were the precursor to what I came to view as a floating rubbish dump in the mid-Atlantic.

We now had a consistent trade wind pattern with a forecast of moderate SE breezes of 10 to 15+ knots for the near future. Through all of the boisterous sailing in the weeks/months prior I had got into the habit of using the small headsail, or a portion of it, plus small amounts of the mainsail to balance the changing wind dynamics.

The boat had performed well, but now that the breeze had consistently dropped off I unfurled the bigger headsail for playtime, as more sail area was needed to maintain speed.

That afternoon was glorious. One of those that we dream of. No swell, electric blue water, distinct horizon, a few puffy clouds in an otherwise beautiful blue sky.

Broadening one's horizons can be a wonderful and interesting thing. When I was 18, competing in my 1st 630 nm Hobart race was a MASSIVE achievement for me. 8 months prior to leaving for this trip, in one 4 week period I had racked up the equivalent to 4 × Hobart races and now I was in the Atlantic.

Keep the horizon moving I say.

Logbook:
29th Dec
6.30 am

Just woke to the dawn of a glorious new day. An absolute bottler of a day by the looks. Had a cup of tea and put the fishing line out.

(later on)

Keeps on getting more perfect. Blue, blue and bluer.

Pulled Sat phone apart again trying to find fault. Found a bit of green oxidisation on Antenna cable going into the black box but nothing startling.

Shorts and shirt off for a bit of sun. Reading about the first BOC single handed yacht race around the world in 1982. Now crossing into the 20's of latitude. Tropics just 380 nm away.

782 nm to Saint Helena

Had a couple of Bourbons last night then a fitful sleep because of the alcohol in my system. Woke to a light shower of rain so rigged the rain catcher over the cockpit and of course that frightened the rain away. Hopefully, it will come.

Breeze been progressively working its way around from SE to E to NE and now NNE so I can't directly head for Saint Helena and am being pushed out to the left (NW) a bit. Apart from that it looks like another great day. The Sat phone continues to give me the shits. I can't make calls and I suspect it's close to a terminal diagnosis.

That day turned out to be busy one.

My general rule is that so long as clothing is relatively dry then you can wear it, regardless of how much it smells. However, I could no longer cope with the stink of my Southern Ocean attire. I did my first load of washing, giving them a tub up in a bucket of salt water with some soap powder and a sparse amount of fresh water for a final rinse. I confess to mixing the colours and the whites.

My solar panels and wind generator were doing a fantastic job charging batteries but I was, as with every resource, frugal with my use of battery power. I had set out not relying on my 43HP Nanni Diesel engine for charging but I used to kick it over once a week to make sure she fired up. Whenever I did run her, it had to be out of gear otherwise I would have broken the rules of the attempt.

I kept a log of when I ran it and it is interesting to note that the longest period I went without running it to charge batteries was 3 weeks, which was bloody brilliant. The "enemy" of my solar and wind charging was windless, very cloudy days or night time.

The world is slowly but surely embracing wind and solar as a renewable energy source but we collectively still have a long way to go in moving forward with 100% commitment. There still is too much talk.

I ran the engine to check it was operational and then suddenly I was in a maintenance frenzy and by early evening, at the close of "business",

I had worked myself to a bloody frazzle. I lubricated the moving parts of the engine gear/throttle cables, and then launched myself into the Mainsail halyard winch, pulling it apart and servicing it.

What's next?

My sponge mattress and general bunk area were pretty gross, even by my standards, so the mattress came out for airing. I then went on a voyage of discovery into the inner recesses of my bunk, finding things that I thought were lost forever.

I had a micro storm sail, that Flano had made for me, clipped on at the ready on the foredeck. It hadn't dovetailed into my sail plan as I thought it might, so I stowed it below.

A rain squall dropped by, but by the time I rigged my rain catcher it had bolted, leaving me with a measly 1 litre. I then spent a couple of hours fine-tuning the set up so the next rain squall needed to be on notice. The catcher would be out and on with blinding speed, or so I hoped.

Whilst flopping around I had 3 or 4 fish, including a baby shark, milling around the back end of the boat looking for a free feed on some of the marine growth that was starting to attach to the hull. I nearly hooked one on an unbaited shiny hook. I then baited it with some smoked chicken but they wouldn't touch it. Bugger em, I thought, I'll eat the smoked chook myself if they're that fucking fussy.

I slept like a log that night which I guess was from the hard work and a hot sun.

The amount of rubbish/debris in the water continued to increase. There were fishing floats, bits of net, timber, plastic etc. There was rubbish everywhere, in stark contrast to my being lucky to see a piece of seaweed previously. One day I saw a hat float by and hoped that the owner was not underneath, still attached by the chinstrap.

The next day was New Year's Eve, so 2001 was just around the corner. When I went on deck to check out the new day, I was a little alarmed to discover that the Monitor, that I relied upon so much, had somehow or another disengaged itself and the boat was merrily heading off to South America. I re-engaged it on the correct course hoping like heck that it was not a sign of a developing problem.

Update #60
31ˢᵗ Dec 2000
Air temp 32 °C
Water temp 26.3 °C
More rigging problems.

(This latest problem was on the Starboard, opposite side of the boat that I had had the chainplate problem with, in the Southern Ocean.)

This morning I was horrified to find that the starboard Diagonal #1 wire has 2 broken strands at deck level and at least 1 is gone at the other end, where it connects to the mast. The kicker is that the Vertical #1 wire has done a strand in as well. For the uninitiated, this type of rigging wire is called 1x19 because it consists of 19 small diameter stainless wires wrapped around each other to form one wire. If 1 strand breaks you lose MUCH MORE than 1/19th of its strength. Both the partially failed wires are subjected to big loads increased substantially when falling off waves.

I have just spent the whole day in incredible heat carrying out remedial work.

I have a spare set of D #1's on board and I swapped them but I'm a tad worried that the new ones are a size down from those I took off. I can't change the V #1 out here, even if I had one, so I've rigged up a cascading block and tackle purchase system and installed it as back up in case the vertical wire fails. While at it I did the same for the D#1.

Poor old Solo Globe is trussed up like she's got five broken legs, a gammy arm and a crook back thrown in.

I climbed the mast to the top set of spreaders, which was painful, bruising and energy sapping but it had to be done. I was looking for failures elsewhere but couldn't spot any.

The D1's were increased in size before leaving at the insistence of John Denton. Maybe the extreme cold combined with the shock loads of the Southern Ocean are not a good combination.

I've had a huge day physically. I'm lucky that I'm an elite athlete (not). We survive to bat on a bit further.

We have the world's biggest, slowest moving high pressure system sitting right on top of us, which means NO WIND. Whilst carrying out repairs today, I had all sails down, and still do, as we have a "glass out" ocean.

I was totally buggered that evening. I filmed myself looking straight at the camera and in part, say something like, "I've had a hard life. I am

45 but I look about 105." When I look back at that vision, I look very haggard and way older than 45 years of age.

In fact, many people now say, 25 years later, say I look younger now than I did back then!

I had 3 hot beers, as I watched the sun go down and tucked into my favourite dinner at the time, tinned corned beef mixed with a tin of peas, a side serving of instant mashed potato and tomato sauce to taste. How good am I going? A recipe book to follow.

The previous couple of days had brought light headwinds so progress had been slowed. We were about 690 nm from Saint Helena but if I got a wriggle on I thought I might round near to Holly's 9th birthday. As I pondered this, the East Coast of Australia was getting set to stir from its collective slumber to ready themselves for the festivities to bring in the New Year of 2001.

Logbook:
1st Jan
3.40 pm

Welcome to 2001 Australia. I've been very tired today, spent a lot of time in bunk dozing fitfully. A bit quiet on it all day.

I made reasonable miles during the night spirited along by a fresh breeze using a small headsail AND a reef in the mainsail. Even though it wasn't so long ago that we were in the Southern Ocean and small sail area was stock standard, it seemed like a long distant memory and it felt a bit weird to have a reef in.

I had a consistent good breeze all day that allowed us to aim at the island with sprung sheets. A big rain squall passed in front of us and another out to our right, but not on top of us. Where is a good rain squall when you want one? They were starting to look very elusive.

Update #61
2nd January 2001
360 nm to St Helena Island
Media Note:

The Satellite Phone either won't play the game, so I have given up on it and 'tis time to enact Plan B. I have made contact with Capetown Radio and established that I can make phone calls through them 24/7 via my HF Radio. I need to be the one to initiate these calls and whilst I will do that as close as I can to your program schedule there will be factors out of my control that will require you to be flexible and "take me when you can" if you want an interview.

I have now officially entered the tropics having crossed the Tropic of Capricorn at 23 deg 30' S.

A VHF (Very High Frequency) radio is only effective up to approx. 20 nm

A HF (High Frequency) radio, given the right atmospheric conditions and time of day/night one can successfully transmit thousands of miles to a HF Radio elsewhere.

Via HF I contacted Capetown Radio in South Africa, which at that stage was approx. 1700 nm away, told them of my sat phone problem and asked if it were possible for them to act as an intermediary linking me via HF radio calls from time to time from me, into a phone call made by them, to Aussie.

Without hesitation, the answer was an emphatic yes.

Over the next two months, the team at Capetown Radio bent over backwards to help, going way above and beyond the call of duty. Without them, the black abyss in voice communications that had come to be, would have remained an abyss as all voice contact had been lost and would have remained so.

The always accommodating crew at Cape Town Radio kept a schedule of when I might call. They would listen out, sometimes straining to hear my signal/voice, then boost the signal by aiming a directional antenna at me 1,000's of miles away and then make and connect me into, a reverse charge phone call back in Aussie.

It doesn't sound too difficult, does it?

My time communicating with the team in South Africa left me feeling deep gratitude and a genuine fondness for them.

Logbook:
3rd Jan
5.40 am

The start of another day. Had a fitful sleep dreaming of home. Just out of bed. Sun not up. Sitting at Nav station and heard flap, flap on deck above

my head. It was a flying fish but he managed to flap himself back into water. Just had a beaut cup of tea.

11.45 pm
279 nm to St Helena
Making good miles

On the afternoon of 4th January, I had just 190 nm to go, having enjoyed another wonderful day of sailing.

As I got further north, I encountered an increasing number of flying fish and it became common for a school of up to 200 to take off suddenly, scarpering away at speed across the ocean top.

I was religiously sticking to my 1.5 L combo of "bad/good" water every 24 hours and was very keen to catch some rainwater, however getting all the pieces of the jigsaw to drop into place to allow me to do so was proving difficult. I mistakenly thought that when rain squalls dumped their load in the tropics that generally, it would be with no wind. I was yet again proven wrong when I realised that strong wind is, far more often than not, an integral part of a rain squall in that part of the world. The wind would cause my small tarp to flap wildly. The boat would lean, causing the waves slapping the hull to throw up copious of salt spray that lobbed fair and square in my tarp. That, of course, was whenever it might actually catch something.

That morning, a couple of rain squalls passed in front of and behind. I dropped all sail and set up the catcher, but once again there was too much wind and there was bugger all rain anyhow.

I realised I was going to have to modify my approach.

Bloody hell. I thought this was gonna be easy.

Logbook:
5th Jan
5 am
104 nm to Saint Helena

Another great night of sailing. Not far to Saint Helena now. I have been sleeping a heck of a lot. Maybe the heat is making me tired but having said that, it is not as hot as I thought it would be.

4 pm
35 nm to Saint Helena

Been belting along today close hauled. I managed to get through to St Helena radio via HF and a phone call compliments of Capetown. The guy at St Helena gave me some radio frequencies to call on but I am about to give up. I was going to try and drop some photographic film and video to a boat if possible and have it posted back to Keir but it's just too hard.

It appears as if I'll be off the eastern edge of the island about 9 pm tonight and by the time I get around the top it will be midnight or thereabouts so will then just head off towards Ascension Island

I knew land was close by and at 6.30 pm I spotted it.

At 9:30 pm I had officially rounded the island, inking in another milestone. Once again, it was a pity that it was in the dark but that's just the way things pan out sometimes.

It was now time to set a new goal within the overall goal.

It was now time to go and find Ascension Island, 702 nm distant.

CHAPTER 25
I could arrive back having gained weight.

I dedicated my rounding of Saint Helena Island to my beautiful daughter, Holly.

When I closed my eyes to replay in my mind's eye the time just after her birth, it seemed, and still does, that it had only been the day prior that I carried her out of Belmont Hospital as a tiny baby in her capsule, strapped her into the backseat and drove home no faster than 25 km/hr as nervous as I have ever been in my life, not paying any attention whatsoever to drivers behind, tooting their horn, trying to get me to speed up.

My heart ached to be with her, but it was not to be. I hoped like crazy that as she grew older she would understand that her old Dad just had to do this thing. I arranged for her godfather, and my close friend, "Gus" Telford to take her flowers and a card in which I asked him to write that she was my special princess.

Enlisting the support of Capetown radio, I put a call through to my beautiful girl for a lovely chat. After the call, I burst into tears and cried for some time. One day I would pay her back for putting up with this.

According to good old Wikipedia again, Ascension Island is also a remote tropical volcanic island and a British overseas territory that sits in the South Atlantic, is 480 nm South of the Equator, about 860 nm West of Africa and 1250 nm East of South America. Just like Saint Helena, it is a tad in the middle of nowhere.

Taking up approx. 88 km^2 it sustains a population of roughly 1000 and is home to a base operated by the Royal Air Force and was used extensively as a staging post during the Falklands war. I was intrigued to also to read that the island hosts one of four ground antennas that assist in the operation of the Global Positioning System (GPS). They drive on the left side of the road.

It was 629 nm away.

Update #62
6th January
Air temp 30 °C
Water temp 22.8 °C

1000 nm West of Angola, 1200 nm South of Ivory Coast and a bloody long way from home

I am now heading to Ascension Island 625 nm away (just a Sydney-Hobart race). As you would expect of Mowbray's (or was that Gilligan's) 180 day tour, I rounded Saint Helena Island in the dark, only seeing some lights and no humans.

I am well and truly in the tropics now with new territory coming up. Currently, I am on the same latitude as Cooktown, Australia. In another 300 nm, I will be level with Port Moresby, New Guinea which is the furthest north I have ever been so a new horizon will be reached.

The rig repairs look okay at this stage. The real test will come on the final 7,000 nm leg, in the Indian/Southern Ocean. It's been real trade wind stuff of late with SE to E to ENE breezes, 10-15 knots with generally blue sky and a brilliant blue ocean.

The trip is about 44% complete and I have to work hard to keep my mind occupied, stay focused and not look too far ahead.

It is indeed a test of the mind as much as a test of one's organisational and sailing skills, etc.

Boredom was something that I had to deal with a lot.

When the weather was as consistently benign and predictable as it had been lately, the reward for me having set the boat up well was some very long periods without any intervention required apart from a slight tweak here and there. This "nothing to do time" lead to boredom.

To counteract the boredom, I read a lot. I am a voracious reader when I have time and it was not uncommon to pick up a book and read it from cover to cover with the only interruption being sleeping, eating or taking a piss.

I played the card game, "Patience" regularly, listened to music and answering emails washed away time.

It was interesting to note that during the working week back home I received numerous emails, but come Friday lunch time when everyone was shutting up shop for the weekend, emails ground to a halt. On Monday morning, the yellow light on the Satcom C would flash and the thermal printer would burst into life as incoming emails fired up again.

In my (at times) approaching paranoid state, I would tell myself that they didn't give a fuck about me over the weekend. I knew wholeheartedly that it was not the case but my mind wanted to play tricks.

I thought about home a lot but I had to be careful that this didn't overshadow the reason I was there. I started to allow myself to think what it might be like to eventually turn the corner at Nobbys breakwater, line her up and sail to the finish line. If I was lucky enough to achieve that, then the feeling was going to be so very special and one that very few people would ever experience.

I couldn't allow myself to think about it too often though as there was still a lot of water to pass under the keel before Nobbys breakwater would pop up on the horizon.

Another antidote to boredom was eating. So, I ate.

When I was a kid, being fat was deemed healthy. If every other kid at school had one piece of cake in their lunchbox, I would have two and I ate both pieces every time, setting myself up with a lifelong cross to bear.

I have always been a 100% committed yo-yo eater, consistently eating until I have put that much weight on that I have to have a half time break, bending over trying to tie my shoelaces. When I reach peak weight, I get fed up and put myself on a strict diet, get back to a goal weight, then feel good about that but then stop the diet and start overeating again. This vicious cycle has repeated itself most of my life.

In the Southern Ocean I had consumed lots of calories in sweets and junk food through boredom but also trying to ward off the cold. It's easy to escape the fact that an extra kg or two (read: a fucking lot) has attached itself underneath numerous layers of thick clothing, however now that I was sailing shirtless a lot, it was not a pretty sight. As I continued eating through sheer boredom extra rolls of lily white, dimpled skin, were becoming apparent.

I had no doubt, that if I weren't careful, I would arrive back having gained weight which I know sounds completely bloody ridiculous but it was the case, 100%.

In the last 2 months, when back in the rough tough cold stuff, I would need to be vigilant so as not to arrive back fatter than when I left. A diet was not out of the question. Bloody hell!

As each day ticked by, the weather was a cookie cutout of the one prior, except, that as I got further north it generally got hotter, more humid and the breeze at times became slightly more unpredictable, but overall it was a wonderful time.

It was now "champagne sailing" day after day, night after night. It was superlative. In the early evening, when the heat of the day had waned I would lay in the cockpit with a pillow under my head, staring almost unblinkingly at the jet black velvet ceiling of the world, chock full of stars that looked like diamonds that might drip out of the sky all over me at any minute.

In Aussie and NZ, the Orion Star Constellation is colloquially referred to as the "Pot" (as in a cooking pot) or the "Saucepan", because of the way the configuration looks in the southern hemisphere.

I was reminded of the times that I took Holly and Jordan out into the backyard, pointed out the "Saucepan" and told them that the star at the top of the base was for Holly, the one at the bottom was for Jordo and the one in the middle was for Mummy. I had suggested that if they were missing their old dad whilst I was away, they possibly could go out to the backyard, stare at the "Saucepan" and maybe we could all connect somehow.

Those sorts of feelings and emotions cannot be bought, borrowed or inherited. You have to get them for yourself and when you do get them, they feel bloody good. I was, and am, a very lucky man!

7th Jan
800 nm to the Equator
It hasn't been very hot?

8th Jan
399 nm to Ascension

Just filmed dolphins at the bow. Only the 2nd lot I've seen since leaving. They were glorious. Still running square and poled out. Quite muggy this arvo.

8th Jan
324 nm to Ascension

More of the same. Square running. Email from NBN Television telling me the last of their sponsorship money is in the mail.

9th Jan
143 nm to Ascension

Still running square. Very predictable at present, beautiful day, cloud cover of last few days has cleared. Breakfast was "Just Right" with extra sultanas and Bi-Lo long life milk. Reading like a demon. 2,400 nm from Capetown Radio and amazingly I still get them on 4 MHz at night to make phone calls. This morning I did a 3D jigsaw puzzle given to me by the kids as a Xmas present.

As I closed in on Ascension, signs of human life began to pop up.

On VHF, I heard a supply vessel, "Saint Helena" call the yacht, "Annie M". I had a great chat with one of the crew on "Saint Helena", learning that she was 105 metres long, was based out of Capetown and her sole role was regularly servicing Tristan and Ascension.

I also learned that the "Annie M" was ahead of us making for Ascension, and it was suggested that I keep a lookout for her as she had not responded to any radio calls and would not be aware of us toodling along behind them.

10th Jan
7.15 am
33 nm to Ascension

At around 5.30 am it was still dark but with a full moon and I heard the VHF crackle to life indicating a vessel possibly close by. I did a quick visual and bugger me, on my Port quarter, close by, were the lights of a ship.

Another one!

I had a very long and enjoyable chat with Charlie, on the 300 metre long "Safmarine Nolizwe". She was on her way to New York, Baltimore and Charleston USA. It also hailed from Capetown and was crewed by South Africans. Charlie said he could see my radar footprint from about 12 nm away and said it was good.

It was quite eerie to sit on deck, watching her silhouette pass by without a sound, in stealth mode. It was a stark reminder that I had to be careful. She had appeared out of nowhere, without warning.

For once, it looked like I would round land in daylight and I did. With a lumpy SE swell behind me reducing the efficiency of the Monitor, the boat was all over the place so I did a lot of hand steering. I wanted to get close to land as I wanted to see a person, if possible.

I filmed and photographed a very pretty natural harbour with 20 boats in it, including 2 yachts, however, NOWHERE COULD I SEE A HUMAN BEING.

The topography was desert like, incredibly arid, rock strewn and brown everywhere with hardly any green vegetation. I called the island on VHF numerous times finally getting a laconic reply. Trying to be laid back and a tad humble, (it never works) I explained that I was not quite half way through a solo circumnavigation, that I had left Australia over two months prior and would be at sea for more than another three months. Blah blah blah.

His super laid back, "couldn't give a fuck" response was, "Okay then, have a nice day. Over and out" For fucks sake! Really? Jeeze Louise.

You have to keep laughing but sometimes it doesn't come easily.

Update #63
11th January 2001
Position 07 deg 53' S, 14 deg 30' W

Ascension Island was rounded at 1 am AEDST on 11th January 2001. We are now heading to the half way point, 700 nm away, and then to St Peter and St Paul Rocks. I will do a more comprehensive update later. Right now, I am hungry, hot, tired, thirsty, sunburnt and a whole lot of other things.

I dedicated my rounding of Ascension Island to my champion son, Jordan.

CHAPTER 26
Finally, I picked up the jagged outline of the rocks

Rounding Ascension was another brick in a bloody big wall. It had been surreal to be so close to land and not see a human being, which I was ever so keen to do, having not seen another soul since departure.

Forlornly, I watched the outline of Ascension shrink in the rear view mirror.

Update #64
11*th* January
Air temp 36 °C
Water temp 26 °C
Wind SE trades 15-20 knots

Yesterday afternoon I was physically and mentally off the pace however, a couple of hot beers followed by three watered down orange juices with a hit of rum in each consumed in a cool spot in the cockpit while watching the sunset helped a lot. Had a good sleep last night and I'm back to 100%.

Seeing land brings mixed emotions:

1) *It's good to see something instead of just water*
2) *The achievement of your current goal, followed by the need to refocus on your next goal (to reach half way, 573 nm away)*
3) *Land is the enemy and it hurts if you run into it*
4) *Land is a stark reminder of important things in life, like family*

Some boring facts:

1) *The length of the course in a straight line is 21,823 nm*
2) *The GPS says we have covered 11,128 nm through the water, but have only covered 10,338 nm of the course (47%). The extra*

> distance through the water is, for a variety of reasons such as adverse current, occasionally going backwards (not a good look), having to tack to windward, etc.
> 3) Half way should arrive at approximately 93 days, so if the same average is maintained, the trip should take about 186 days.

One of the things that gets at you now and then is that your body is in perpetual motion. At no time, even when asleep, are you still. Sometimes I think it would be nice to sit still in a lounge chair for 10 minutes, however, if you gave me the chance, you would get a huge knock back.

I am keeping all of my rubbish on board stowed down the stern. A few days ago, I was standing in the cockpit and got a whiff of what I thought was the rubbish.

I was wrong, 'twas me.

Once again, it was time to shift focus and look for our next rounding mark, St Peter and St Paul rocks. Also, on this leg I would arrive at the halfway point, which I eagerly anticipated. It would be a massive milestone.

Don't you love Wikipedia:

"The St Peter and St Paul Archipelago is a group of 15 small islets and rocks located 55 nm north of the Equator. It lies within the intertropical convergence zone, a region characterised by low average winds, punctuated by local thunderstorms. The nearest mainland is NE Brazil, 500 nm away. Tuna fishing is the main economic activity around the islets. The highest elevation is 17 metres and collectively the 15 islets only cover an area of approx. 3.75 acres."

They shouldn't be too hard to find in a fucking gigantic ocean.

The main electric bilge pump was causing me grief. When bilge water, (the water that gathers at the lowest point of the hull inside the boat) rises to a certain level, the pump is supposed to kick in automatically and pump it dry. Alternatively, it can be activated manually. Mine was not keen to kick in on Auto anymore but was okay on manual.

The main bilge, under the engine, had a fair bit of cruddy old engine oil and general gunk floating around in it, so I gave it and the pump a thorough clean to no avail. The stainless steel propeller shaft exited the hull through a round stern gland housing. The tension of the gland is adjusted so that where the prop shaft exits the boat it remains essentially watertight but should still allow a small drip of seawater to lubricate the shaft when the engine is running, and the shaft is turning. The shaft was locked off to keep it from turning because I would never run it in gear. I had run out of adjustment on the gland and even though the shaft was immobile I had a constant trickle of water coming in which was more pronounced as the boat surged on waves and pressure increased.

The leak was a pain in the arse.

With water accumulating in the main bilge, and the auto mode failed, I had to be constantly mindful of activating the pump manually, otherwise, if left to its own devices, the boat would eventually sink.

Of course, that was something to be avoided.

Logbook:
12th Jan
7pm

Just gybed to port and now heading straight at St Peter/Paul rocks. Sighted lights of a vessel to my East but no response when I called on VHF.

Then, out of nowhere, I had BOATS EVERYWHERE!

There is an imaginary circle with a radius of 180 nm around Ascension creating a sanctuary, and commercial fishing is strictly forbidden within it. I guessed that the commercial fishers gathered on the edge of the sanctuary, hoping to enhance the quality of their catch.

It was dark. Other boats always come out to play at night, and out of nowhere I had the lights of a heap of fishing boats ahead of me, which I had to dodge. They weren't a stationary target either, as they continually trawled, making my task of avoiding them more difficult.

I had made a conscious decision to not have a radar and to some, this might appear reckless. A key problem with radar is that it gobbles battery power at an alarming rate, and I simply would not have been able to sustain the power required to operate it every night. Also, when reading about others that had gone before me, with radar, their units often failed early on, for a variety of reasons.

I got bugger all sleep that night, setting my alarm clock for 45 min intervals until clear of them. Just when daylight approached and

I started to think I could rest easy, a cargo ship steamed by silently, another agent of stealth, on my port side about 1 nm away.

My run in with the fishing vessels marked the start of a long period of heightened concern, where I had to be constantly on the lookout for other vessels. Russian Roulette of the marine variety was alive and well.

For the first 80 days, I had seen ridiculously few vessels. Now there was a bloody plague of them.

Some time, for days on end, I would set the alarm clock for 1 hour intervals, stagger on deck, scan the horizon, then stagger back to the rack if clear.

Sleep deprivation is a real bitch.

Logbook:
13th Jan
8.20 am
311 nm to half way

Still rolling along poled out making some good miles. Spoke with Craig Hamilton on ABC radio last night plus home and Mum. Just spent a few hours rearranging the main cabin to clear the Starboard lower bunk so I can sleep there during the day to see if it's cooler. My bunk is like a fucking hot house.

I had just finished my latest book which was excellent. "One Crowded Hour" is the biography of one of the world's greatest combat cine cameramen, Australian Neil Davis (1934 - 1985) and a stunning read. I was now on to Joshua Slocum's "Spray".

Logbook:
14th Jan
1.30 pm
278 nm to half way.

Heat slows me down big time during the day. Must do my jobs in the early morning. I have rigged the rain catcher tarp over cockpit for some shade and it works well.

If it wasn't gonna catch rainwater, then it may as well serve some purpose.

Sunset

Bourbon and Coke. Beautiful Sunset. Glorious. Not a cloud in the sky. Some of the best sailing of my life

That evening, I was minding my own business, came on deck for a quick scan of the horizon, and was taken aback to see a ship going away from me, meaning that it had passed and I had no idea it was there. Another agent of stealth out to get me. No one on watch. Their radar either not turned on or not monitored.

By far, the most commonly question about the trip is, "Did you fish much?"

For the first two months, I was deep in the Great Southern Ocean where there were very few, if any, surface fish. The air and water temperatures were so bloody cold it would snow from time to time, and the wind chill factor was massive, dictating gloved hands most of the time. One of the last things I wanted to do was expose my hands and get them wet cleaning fish, so the line stayed in the locker.

In the warmer Atlantic waters, I was tempted to troll a line but was concerned about seabirds swooping on a lure close to the surface and hooking themselves. Eventually, I rigged a line and caught some fish and no birds.

Unfortunately, every time I cleaned and filleted a fish, I would find ugly white parasites embedded in the flesh and this concerned greatly. I was vaguely aware of Ciguatera fish poisoning and knew it was dangerous, but just how dangerous was not clear.

I have since learned that it is caused by a toxin found in tropical and sub-tropical fish, and the illness occurs when eating the infected fish. Symptoms may include nausea, vomiting, and neurologic symptoms such as tingling fingers or toes. Ciguatera has no cure, and symptoms usually go away in days or weeks. However, they can last for years.

Really?

I, and so many others, had a massive investment in this trip emotionally and financially, and the last thing I wanted to do was threaten a positive outcome for us all by eating some fish that might make me ill. I had enough food anyhow, so the decision was made to put the fishing line away.

I'm sorry to disappoint the avid anglers.

Update #65
15th Jan
488 nm to St Peter and St Paul Rocks
131 nm to the half way point

The Equator is now only 179 nm north and it's bloody hot. It is always in the mid to high 30's. It's impossible to sleep during the day but okay at night. We made good progress this week, racking up 988 nm, our 2nd best week thus far. The best one was week # 4 at 1006 nm. Our worst was week # 6, when we had our chainplate problem, but still remarkably logged 727 nm.

Every day seems to present a new challenge out here. The current challenge is that the motor will not start.

With 3 months to go, we are in reasonable shape but there are a lot of hard yards still to be covered. It will be good to get to St Peter and St Paul Rocks and turn for home.

Update #66
15th Jan
We are half way.

It may be noted that at 11.29 pm AEDST on Monday 15th January, 2001 Solo Globe Challenger was at position 01 deg 48' South of the Equator, 24 deg 30' West of Greenwich. It has taken us 92 days, 10 hours, 29 minutes to get here. The total straight line course length is 21,823 nm and we have completed 10, 911.5 nm at an average of 4.92 knots. We have sailed 11, 731 nm on the GPS log at an average of 5.29 knots.

It was half time. Who brought the quartered oranges?

Reaching halfway had taken me longer than anticipated, having lost a fair bit of time with rigging problems, however it was a massive boost and allowed me to think that we were making real progress. Still, there was no time to rest as there was a long way still to go. The next box to tick was crossing the Equator.

The Intertropical Convergence Zone (ITCZ) is better known by most people as the Doldrums. Generally speaking, it is the area around the Equator where the trade winds from the northern hemisphere converge with the trade winds from the southern hemisphere, creating a monotonous vacuum of windless weather.

Because of the restless and constant jostling of North and South, the Doldrums can be volatile and are typified by rain squalls where wind direction can vary wildly and wind strength can rocket from zero to 25+ knots, then back to zero, in a "caught with your pants down" moment. The violent storm cells are fast moving in generally random direction, each typified by a jet-black cloud as the ceiling of the cell, from which rain can bucket down. Throw in the occasional lightning bolt to the mix, and one begins to see how it might be a bit of a crazy place.

I was keen to get there.

I slid north, with the wind directly behind me, getting closer to the Doldrums, looking forward to more firsts. This would be my first visit to the Doldrums coupled with my 1st crossing of the Equator. As I got north, rain squalls were becoming more frequent but try as I might, I couldn't coax one my way. I was on deck filming a massive squall, congratulating myself on having recorded it and being the world's best cameraman, when my gut instinct told me something wasn't quite right.

Lowering the camera, I realised that the southerly breeze pushing the squall away from us had suddenly done a switchback and this massive, seething, blue, black and purple dark cloud was bearing down, about to clobber us.

I had not seen a switchback happen previously and scrambled to ready myself. I'd had quite a few unproductive practice runs/skirmishes thus far and as a result refined my rain catching method, and hoped it would pay dividends this time.

Quickly I banged the first reef in the mainsail and furled the headsail. The squall hit, the boat heeled a little and it began to piss down. You bloody beauty!

As I'd hoped, the rain hit the angled mainsail, ran down and gathered in the folds of reefed sail on the boom, which formed a small valley that allowed the water to run aft toward the cockpit where I was armed with buckets, containers, cooking pots and anything else I thought might hold water. I frantically caught as much as I could as it cascaded off the end of the boom.

I frantically captured 48 L of what I looked upon, and still do, as pure nectar from heaven, delivered straight from the "factory".

Water is the staff of life. I felt so in tune with my surroundings and at one with nature. I treated myself to a cup of tea without adding salty water to it.

Luxury Lovey.

That 48 L meant that I could increase my 24 hr ration to 2 L, unfortunately still having to mix in some "bad" water, but with a higher ratio of fresh, the salt taste was not so apparent.

Logbook:
17th Jan
St Peter and St Paul 152 nm away.

Very quiet night. After the rain squall disappeared yesterday arvo the sea flattened out and with not much breeze I just flopped along. There was a glorious sunset and then a light Westerly filtered in. "Droobed" along, only knocking over 67 nm in the last 24 hrs but that's OK.

We inched toward and finally, crossed the invisible equatorial line of 00 deg 00 mins. It was very hot and humid, and we had another rain squall collide with us. Collecting water now not as important, although I did collect some more. More poignantly, I was able to have a nude shower in the cockpit including shampooing my hair. Soaked to the skin.

As I washed myself, I was so overcome with emotion that I let rip with several "war cries" sending them off over the horizon for no one to hear but me. I was overflowing with pure unadulterated joy.

I've previously mentioned that a lot of people had asked me "Why?" Why do the trip?

When I was holding the buckets and cooking pots etc. at the back end of the boom, catching every drop of pure fresh unadulterated rainwater that I could, I felt it. I was soaked to the skin, thousands of miles from anywhere, with no television, no phones, no newspapers, no bullshit and I didn't have a job to go to.

I felt REALLY alive!

A massive piece of the jigsaw dropped in to place.

Crossing the Equator and slipping into the Northern Hemisphere was exciting new territory. The world continued to get smaller for me.

Update #67
18th Jan 5.34 pm local time
Position 00 deg 00' S, 27 deg 43' W
THE EQUATOR IS CROSSED.

It's been slow going since we hit the "wall" of the doldrums but we're getting there.
 No wind, SW, SE, NE, rain, hot. A real mixed bag
 St Peter and St Paul rocks are 107 nm away.

As we inched forward, to within just 40 nm of our next rounding point, the order of the day was more of the same. There were lots of big black ugly rain squalls circling us, with the occasional one giving us a tickle up. The wind was completely unpredictable in direction, but rarely exceeded 20 knots. It was a very confused place.

Another ship passed me, possibly heading to Brazil. I tried to raise him on VHF unsuccessfully. I reflected, that in Australian waters, 90% of shipping when called on VHF, respond. In the Atlantic, I was astounded to find that virtually no one responded. I found this very disconcerting, leading me to wonder if their bridges are manned, do they keep a look out and at what level is their seamanship?

It was bloody scary.

Logbook:
19th Jan
3 pm

Making very slow progress in bugger all wind. Running square and gybing lots to try and get there in daylight. Been trying to see the islets on the horizon but I can't.

 Finally, I picked up the jagged outline of the rocks when about 10 nm away. Being so low on the horizon and small, they were difficult to spot. They were much more stark and smaller than I had imagined.

Update #68
19th Jan
Position 00 deg 26' S, 29 deg 23' W

Saint Peter and Saint Paul Rocks were rounded at 8.35 am AEDST, Friday 19th January 2001 when Solo Globe Challenger crawled her way to the northern side of the rocks in the absolute grip of the doldrums. We approached the rocks in a light following breeze managing to squeeze out 3-4 knots of boat speed, but alas it fell dark whilst we were 3 nm short, so we bobbed and drifted for hours in darkness and showers of rain with the flash of the lighthouse to keep us company. I was extremely tired, (matchsticks in the eyelids job) and worried about drifting in too close as we were only about 1 nm off at one point.

There was a presumed fishing boat anchored near one of the islets. We flashed torches at each other. I let rip with a few "Cooee's" and "Aussie, Aussie, Aussies" across the water and we attempted to talk on the radio, but they could only speak Spanish and I am limited to "Peso" and "Gringo", so a conversation didn't get off the ground.

Rounding the rocks provided me with a buzz and sense of achievement similar to rounding the Horn. Not as big of course. Having first read about the rocks in Kay Cottee's book, I hadn't realised how much mystique they held for me. I spent a long time deriving simple pleasure from just staring at the reassuring and comforting flash of the lighthouse being first one I had seen at night on the trip.

I spent a lot of time coaxing Solo Globe, inch by inch, around the rocks in no wind and at times, very heavy rain. One minute I was worried about drifting onto the rocks, and then I would be worried cos we were drifting the opposite direction, to the north, away from home. It was a real roller coaster, and I ended up extremely tired. When I couldn't hold out any longer, I would grab a quick snooze but with the alarm set for 30 minutes.

Being a marine sanctuary, the waters were teeming with sea life. Prior to rounding, whilst still light, I was tracked by a pod of about 12 bloody big whales. They came to within 2 metres at times and it seemed as if they were shepherding me to safety.

"Head this way Tony", they seemed to be saying.

CHAPTER 27

Hard on the wind

By the time the first slivers of light appeared in the eastern sky, ushering in the new day, the jagged outline of the rocks had disappeared astern and the bow was pointing south. My strategy was to get south ASAP to escape the clutches of the Doldrums.

It was now time to go find our old friend, Tristan da Cunha again. Rounding her a second time would close the "loop" and bring to an end our antics in the Atlantic.

Logbook:
19th Jan
9.00 am
Tristan 2,459 nm.

Been very slow progress since rounding the rocks with bugger all wind from every direction of the compass. Didn't get much sleep last night and it will catch up with me today.

The next day, a lovely breeze filtered in for a few hours, allowing us to make good time. It kicked originally from the SE but quickly worked its way to a S headwind meaning that we were getting pushed to the right, taking us towards Brazil, where I did not want to go.

Then it dropped out to nothing again.

Logbook:
20th Jan
7.00 pm

Just had the most spectacular dolphin show I have ever seen. There must have been 150 of them jumping and doing tricks that you would only expect to see trained ones do at a tourist aquarium.

It was truly majestic and I was 100% captivated.

Logbook:
21st Jan
11.30 am

The doldrums have me firmly in their grip. Last night was a shocker, going nowhere or backwards. Since rounding the rocks I've only managed about 50 nm in 34 hours. It could be worse.

Last night I crossed paths with 5 or so ships, needing to set the alarm clock for 30 min intervals. One time, I woke suddenly, sat bolt upright in the bunk and smashed my head into the underneath side of the deck nearly knocking myself out. You should see the lump. When I jumped up into cockpit I hit my head on the fucking boom.

Fair Dinkum.

It was a very frustrating night however I now have a nice steady SE breeze and am making some miles south with full Main and big headsail, hard on the wind.

"Hard on the wind" is a term that means the wind is generally coming from where you want to go, so you have to sheet your sails on as tight as they can go, and then there is a lot of tacking (zigging and zagging) to get to the ultimate destination. It can be uncomfortable, take longer, and wetter, plus can take you way off course.

Generally, it is a pain in the arse compared to other angles of sailing.

I had a sneaking suspicion that the leg from the Rocks to Tristan was going to be "hard on the wind" a lot of the time.

Later on
Hard on the wind. (**See what I mean**)
Ships everywhere.

Later, later on

Hard on the wind, still! Getting pushed off course. I want to steer 176 deg S but can only manage 210 - 240 deg SW. We can only tough it out and see what happens. I don't want to get much further West if I can avoid it.

At night, it seemed like every ship in the world came out to hunt me down. I wasn't paranoid at all.

The black thunderous squalls continued, requiring lots of increasing/decreasing sail area to keep speed up. I was fortunate that my racing background had equipped me with the skills to "change gears" seamlessly, plus the work we had put in designing and installing the sail handling systems was really coming to the fore and the boat kept moving forward, albeit, at times slowly.

Solo Globe was in pretty good shape but I was apprehensive about the rigging issues. When beating to windward in a lumpy bumpy sea, I nursed the boat but had to keep moving, so I compromised a lot of the time.

The Satcom C now decided to throw its arse in the corner. Fuck!

I had taken 3 laptops, planning to use one as the primary and two backups. The 1st laptop had malfunctioned about 3 weeks prior. I had connected the 2nd and emailed Electrotech, who gave me, what I suspected at the time, may have been a Band-Aid solution, however, the system fired up again so I let it go. That was a big mistake.

Now, the same problem occurred with the 2nd one.

Fuck.

I connected the 3rd and it wouldn't send or receive.

Fuck, Fuck, Fuck! (repeat a lot)

Suddenly, the only communication link I had was through Capetown Radio. I was now sailing "blind" with no quality weather information and very unhappy about it.

I rang, looking for John at Electrotech who had been my salvation on previous occasions, but had been on holiday when I emailed about the 2nd laptop. I hoped like crazy that he was back on deck and could get us going again. The fact that Christopher Columbus didn't have satellite email or weather forecasts was cold comfort.

Even though I had a long way to go I had started to ponder a possible arrival day and the 25th April, Anzac Day, seemed a pretty good bet.

I still was gobsmacked by the number of ships that I was encountering. It seemed that there was a cycle, or that it was somehow predictable, but I couldn't identify a pattern, if there ever was one.

They didn't appear every night, but the problem was that I didn't know which nights they would come out to play so I had to be on guard EVERY night. I set the alarm for naps of an hour or so but often for 30 minutes. There was almost a bloody traffic jam some nights. I reckon they needed stop/go signs, and I definitely needed my own special lollipop lady to get me across the pedestrian crossings. It was bloody ridiculous.

I was still dumbfounded about shipping's lack of response to my radio calls. It was mind boggling. I couldn't work out whether their radios weren't turned on, or no one was on the bridge, or they didn't speak English, or they just didn't care. I was fucked if I could figure it out. Of all the ships called, unbelievably ONLY 3 had responded. I was extremely disappointed and surprised.

In spite of this, I felt pretty good mentally. (I can readers laughing) I was content however there were some things that I had started to look forward to with great anticipation. For example, it would be nice for someone to cook me a meal.

I had not used a knife and fork simultaneously since the start of the trip, eating nearly everything out of a bowl with a spoon, so using a knife and fork at the same time and eating off a plate, set on a stationary table, would be a treat.

My favourite breakfast in the tropics was either Muesli or All-Bran, with extra sultanas and long life milk. Lunch was often a tin of salmon mixed with diced tinned beetroot, 3 bean mix, potato salad etc. or just a tin of fruit. My evening gourmet delight might be more of what I had for lunch. Occasionally I would have rice or pasta of which I still had ample, as I had not eaten anywhere near as much as I thought I would.

I was knocking over 1 Lt of long life milk every 2-3 days. Running the engine to cool the fridge down was never part of the plan, so once I opened a carton it had a limited life of about 12 hours so I made sure to use it in that time. I'd tried various methods of slowing down the souring but in the end, after opening I would simply sit it in the coolest spot I could find on that day. If it started to curdle, I wouldn't waste it, mixing it with some juice from a tin of fruit or whatever. It was a bit "custardy" at times.

On 23rdJan the drama with the Satcom C email/weather system continued. I spent ages on a HF/phone call (via Capetown) with Chris at Electrotech, who felt that the email part of the system was buggered because he thought that the antenna had partially failed. I was very unhappy but there wasn't much I could do.

Fortunately, we had managed to resurrect the receipt of the free weather forecasts from Argentina.

I was despondent at the thought of no more email contact with home, let alone Clouds or close supporters. Greg Searant had done such a great job updating the web site and it was distressing that that would need to cease. I felt more isolated and vulnerable, but I figured I would get used to it.

I had to, as there was no other choice. I still had a boat that was in pretty good shape and my mission was still a living breathing thing. That had not changed.

That night, my time, I rang Lorraine and asked her to buy a handheld tape recorder. The plan I had devised was that I would ring home at least once a week, and at the end of each chat she would hold the recorder to the phone so that I could record a website update for Greg.

Where there is a will, there is a way.

Logbook:
23rd Jan
Evening

I was very tired and frustrated by the email saga and just as I was about to go to bed a control line on the Monitor broke so I engaged the Coursemaster and went to bed. Will rig a new control line today.

Shipping has disappeared all of a sudden?
We are still hard on the wind making slow progress.
I'm still being pushed toward Brazil.
Tristan is 2130 nm away.

Logbook:
24th Jan

Lunch was potato salad, 3 bean mix and a tin of prawns with an orange juice popper to wash it down. I knocked over a few pages of Sir Donald Bradman's book and then had a snooze, waking in a lather of sweat.

Later on

Completely and TOTALLY unexpectedly, the email system came alive and we were back up and running. I was ecstatic. Talk about fucking with one's emotions.

I noticed that the yellow "log in" light was fixed, instead of blinking as it had been since the problem developed. A fixed light meant that we were connected to a land earth station, so I fired up the laptop and fuck me if Perth wasn't "shaking hands" with us, to use computer parlance. We were back.

Emails flowed, including one from A Current Affair who wanted to do a story on me for Australia Day, two days hence. I thought, I'll give 'em a "Little Aussie Battler" story if that's what they want.

My demeanour was much improved.

Logbook:
25th Jan
Tristan is 1967 nm away
Another day hard on the wind.

It's dark and it is magnificent. No cloud, bright, bright stars. A gloriously brilliant evening. It's so good to be alive and be here. Shipping has disappeared

Update #69
25th Jan
270 nm east of Recife, Brazil

What a meteorologically confused place the doldrums are. I am glad to have experienced them but will be happy to leave.

Mark Schroder emailed, suggesting that I need to seriously think about my future and what I'm going to do when I get back.

I replied, telling him that the very first thing I am going to do is drink all the beer in the world.

I spend ages, day or night, standing in the cockpit, braced with feet apart, hands on the back edge of the spray dodger, fixated, watching the bow of the boat work her way through the ocean. No one wave strikes or is deflected by the bow as any another. Solo Globe continually pushes and forges her unique passage through the ocean.

It sort of hypnotises me and I love it.

When I look astern I realise that any evidence of us ever being here disappears almost as soon as it is created. 60 seconds after we have passed there is no sign of our visit.

On Australia Day, 26th Jan, I had great sailing conditions with a fresh breeze allowing us to head straight at Tristan at good speed whilst I cooked some bread mix with added raisins. The result was something akin to rock cakes, and as I baked I listened all the while to an AM radio station that had to be at least 360 nm away. I couldn't understand a word they said but I liked the music.

I was a happy camper.

Later on, I did some interviews including one with Tracey Grimshaw on A Current Affair. Interviews presented a challenge at times. The time difference with Aussie meant that I would often be perched in the Nav station, by the HF radio, late into the evening or way past midnight my time, trying to be an interesting "subject". The quality of the call was not always good, so some tweaking was often required which included trying different radio frequencies or a new call, all carried out with good grace by the Capetown Radio crew.

Logbook:
27th Jan
Very early am

Averaging 6.2 knots headed at Tristan, ticking the miles over. 1 reef in Main all the time and the big headsail in and out as the breeze comes and goes. I hand steered a couple of times today and it was very enjoyable.

8.15 am

The breeze cranked up to 25-30 knots with a short sharp sea. We were still bashing to windward and I reduced sail to 2 reefs and the small headsail, nursing the boat.

5.45 pm
Ditto, ditto.

Logbook:
29th Jan
7 am

Slept a lot last night but it was very fitful as the bunk is a hothouse. Pillows soaked with sweat.

I thought that I maybe should wash my pillowcases as they had been on the pillows for 3.5 months and were starting to get a bit "average".

For the first 2 hours of the previous evening, I had a tiny sliver of a new moon for company. I eagerly anticipated it getting bigger until whole. Some nights, a full moon was so bright that I could read a book by its light.

To try and get a reasonable rest at night, I sailed with a conservative amount of sail, to accommodate fluctuating breeze strengths. I knew that I would eventually break back into the robust weather systems to my south, and once I hooked into them they would send me scuttling for home. In the interim, I had to keep chipping away.

I was acutely aware of Solo Globe's nuances and idiosyncrasies. Down below, the movement of timber gave forth to various squeaks, creaks and groans as a byproduct of the boat's perpetual motion. I zoned out to virtually all of those noises except one incredibly annoying one that developed in the Nav area in the tropics. It was a squeak squeak, squeak squeak and a fucking squeak squeak again! Try as I might I could not stop it. I knew where it was coming from but couldn't get at it.

Through the night and cool of the early mornings, there was not a peep to be heard. As the day heated up and the timbers expanded, one piece would rub against another and off we would go. The hotter the day, the louder and more often it squeaked. It nearly drove me mad. Some would say it succeeded.

Update #70
30th Jan
Air temp 30 °C
Water temp 27.1 °C
240 nm off the coast of Brazil
Tristan 1,335 nm away

Since rounding the Rocks 11 days and 1,300 nm ago, we have been sailing hard to windward. Initially, the breeze pushed us off course towards Brazil however, last Friday, it shifted allowing us to head directly at Tristan. The breeze has mostly been 15-25 knots and occasionally 30 knots. This should be my one and only, long term "uphill" stint.

Only another 300 nm and we leave the tropics. The antifoul paint seems to be holding up well, however, the hull has some developing ugly black growth on it under the stern.

Shipping has disappeared for now and the new moon made its entrance two nights ago and beautifully complements glorious star laden nights.

Fun fact: I am still using my first 9kg LPG gas bottle. If it ran out today, I have enough gas to last me at least 491 days. I estimate 185 days out here so I have ample.

*What I don't have left is any of that bloody beautiful **Bi-Lo** light fruit cake. I'm just about out of Jatz and similar savoury biscuits as well, but overall, supplies are okay.*

The medium term weather forecast was for NW to NE following breezes which would be a welcome relief.

The previous night's dinner was a tin of vegetable soup mixed with a packet of 2 min noodles and dessert, a handful of sultanas.

Mark Schroder emailed back offering to help drink all the beer in the world.

Logbook:
31st Jan
12.15 pm

A stop/start affair so far today. Had about 6 rain squalls one after the other. Some days they all miss you but on other days they all clobber you. Not much wind in them. Each squall sucks the breeze away leaving us flopping around. I hope I pass into a new weather zone soon.

3.40 pm

Lately I've developed the habit of sitting on the port side teak pad on the high side of the cockpit for the last couple of hours of each afternoon as the heat of the day subsides. I sit, almost transfixed, watching the boat powered up, cutting through the water doing 6-7 knots.

I am exhilarated and revel in the freedom.

1st February was Mum's 78th Birthday and I hoped like heck that she had a lovely day. Mum had been an extra hard toiler all of her life. The hard work had been bookended by a rare inner strength and determination. I see a lot of her in my makeup and am so grateful for her passing on to me her never, ever, give in attitude and strong work ethic.

Later that day I could stand it no more. I washed 3 pillowcases, 2 towels, 2 shirts and a pair of shorts. It was only 3.5 months since they had been washed. Talk about a clean freak.

Yet again, I climbed into the recesses of the cockpit locker to inspect and grease the steering cables and whilst I was on a roll, tightened the mounting bolts on the Monitor.

There was a gale warning issued for about 450 nm south of me with strong NW to SW winds, so I figured it wouldn't be long and we'd be back into the rough, tough stuff.

Logbook:
2nd Feb
3 pm

Log registered 17 nm in 12 hours. Average speed 1.42 Knots

Yesterday and today have been the two hottest days of the trip. It is absolutely oppressive and I tip buckets of sea water over me to try to cool down. Did a part food inventory and I have plenty of tinned soup, veges, spaghetti sauces etc. and a reasonable amount of salmon, ham and prawns. Oodles and oodles of noodles, pasta and rice. I will not starve.

Update #71
2nd Feb
Air temp 35 °C
Water temp 27.7 °C
1,040 nm to Tristan

1,000 nm and 10 days straight down the coast of Western Australia in 1994 was my previous longest continual period of working to windward. That record has now been eclipsed as I've just come off 12 consecutive days and 1,400 nm working straight into the wind.

The stop sign was hung out yesterday after the breeze finally backed to the E then NE for a time, before departing completely. Progress in the last 24 hours has been very slow. After the breeze died yesterday it became incredibly hot and I was very, very pleased to see the sun set. Early this morning, just before sunrise, the ocean was like a mirror. I put one reef in the mainsail to minimise "slatting", furled the headsail and left the helm unattended. This morning we are inching forward at 2-4 knots.

53 nm more and we'll cross the Tropic of Capricorn, exiting the tropics. A number of boats are "Capricorn Dancer" and the words are featured in a beaut song. I really like the way the two words go together.

I left the tropics and celebrated with cereal, tinned peaches and two mugs of tea whilst reclining in the cockpit reading John Grisham's "Pelican Brief". The next couple of days were replica cut outs, making steady progress during each day with a gentle breeze behind us, then becalmed at night.

I was able to pick up Radio Australia on the HF, opening up a new avenue of entertainment dovetailing nicely into the books I was getting through which at that time included an Inspector Wexford novel by Ruth Rendell, "Some Lie and Some Die" and another by John Grisham, "The Firm".

I calculating estimated arrival dates more often and eventually it became addictive.

Sunday 15th April   Average required 5.2 knots
Monday 16th April   Average required 5.13 knots
Saturday 21st April   Average required 4.8 knots
Sunday 22nd April   Average required 4.73 knots
Average to date, 4.87 Knots

Logbook:
4th Feb
5 am
792 nm to Tristan

New day dawning. Had full Main and big headsail out all night. Broad reaching aiming straight at Tristan doing 5.5 knots. Hot night but good progress relative to the three previous becalmed nights.

4.15 pm

Been a good day's sailing. Pleasant consistent breeze. Hot again. Just crossed into the South African weather area. No ships. Bugger all of anything. Just ocean. Very peaceful.

Update #72
5th Feb
Air temp 30 °C
Water temp 26.8 °C
649 nm to Tristan

I was all set to tell you that the weather "gate" was behind me, but now I'm not so sure. Progress is stop/start. I've had three successive nights of being becalmed followed by lovely days. The temperature persists in the mid to high 30's, even though I am out of the tropics, on the same latitude as just south of Brisbane.

As I type, a shroud of absolute calm has enveloped us again. Our progress this week was just 745 nm, not much more than our worst week of 727 nm.

On the evening of the 6th Feb I saw my first ship in about 10 days and managed to raise it on VHF. They were bound for Capetown. Within 15 minutes of sighting, their lights had vanished. There one minute, gone the next.

Logbook:
7th Feb
5.45 am
597 nm to Tristan
Becalmed all night again. That's the 5th night of the last 7.
Please release me.

In the last 9.25 hrs we covered just 17 nm. As the sun peeps over the horizon, a light Easterly has just arrived so let's see if it has any substance.

Logbook:
8th Feb
5.45 am
487 nm to Tristan

What a difference some wind makes. Breeze freshened and curled to the E with good pressure allowing us some nice reaching last night with a near full moon. In and out of bed about 8 times. Have knocked over 98 nm in 15.75 hrs. for an average of 6.22 knots. What a huge difference to being becalmed.

As the day progressed, the breeze freshened, and the sea got quite lumpy and confused. I ended up with only the small headsail and double reefed Mainsail.

For the first time in a while, waves were occasionally breaking over the cabin, so I generally confined myself to below decks. Because of the sea state, I switched to the Coursemaster to be able to track a straighter course and have less wear and tear on the steering cables.

I was bored. When I read, my eyes would get sore as if I were tired, but when I tried to sleep, I couldn't. I thought that perhaps all the reading I had been doing had affected my eyes adversely.

Since the new breeze had filtered in, it had incrementally inched its way behind us, settling in from the NE. I was now able to pole out the small headsail and with 2 reefs in the main, Solo Globe was much more stable without anywhere near as much rocking and rolling. We were now "flat and fast", trucking along, making 232 nm in the previous 34.75 hours for a 6.68 knots average. For the last 12 hours, we'd averaged 7 knots. It sure beat being becalmed or bashing to windward.

The air temp was dropping quickly. One evening, in the bunk, I searched for a blanket for the first time in a long time. With the wind now behind us, light rain was blowing into the cabin, so I had the hatch slides in and sliding hatch closed. I was back to being cocooned below and I felt that there was a fair chance I would generally live like this until the finish.

The first 9kg gas bottle finally ran out after lasting an unbelievable 115 days.

Logbook:
9th Feb
2.40 pm
261 nm to Tristan

Just dropped Main. Boat was yawing off course and loading up steering system unnecessarily along with the rest of boat. Looks like frontal cloud moving across.

6.15 pm

Very "ordinary" day at the office. Just toodling along trying to keep big loads off everything. Ugly afternoon. Rain, cloud, wind, big seas around 20-25 ft.

I am asked a lot, "Have I ever had a run in with pirates?"

Pirates are like the rest of us, in that they don't like harsh cold conditions and gravitate to warmer, tropical climates like the coast of Somalia, The Straits of Malacca, the Gulf of Guinea etc. For some weird reason, I am attracted to hostile cold environments so I haven't come across any.

That evening the breeze died off. I didn't have much sail up as I had been dealing with the afternoon's shenanigans. I was scheduled to do a media interview around 11 pm my time, and I decided to keep reduced sail so that the interview would have a good chance of not being interrupted by me having to go on deck.

I ended up below for about 2 hours, focused entirely on setting up for and doing the interview, while the boat bobbed along. When I clambered on deck around 1 am, I was shocked and stunned to see the lights of a vessel about 1.5 nm away.

At first, I thought it was a fishing boat and that it would be reasonably simple to skirt it. I hoisted more sail to gain speed and changed course to avoid it.

It sped up and changed course to parallel me.

I hoisted more sail, sped up more and changed course again.

It sped up and changed course again.

It was stalking me.

The VHF burst into life with an aggressive Spanish speaking male. I very firmly explained that I was just a young bloke from Belmont and could only speak English. I think he wanted to compare mother-in-law's. I was very concerned.

I dived back on deck, raised more sail, piled on more speed, and they sped up yet again. They shadowed my every move.

Back at the radio, I gave them a real angry serve, telling them in no uncertain terms to "Fuck right off!" More indecipherable Spanish "yabber" was the response, as they continued to stalk.

I had read that when solo, in instances such as this, that others had changed their voice when transmitting to try and create an illusion that there were multiple crew. Being prepared to try anything to shake these fuckers, I gave it a go with a couple of different "character voices", but I don't think they were too convinced.

In the end, I was sailing flat bikkie with too much sail up, heading due west, over 90 deg off course, and for 3 hours they sized me up. For that 3 hours, I was very fearful.

The hair on the back of my neck was at full attention and I was genuinely concerned that they might, at the very least, board me, seize the yacht, rob me or even murder me.

Without warning, at 4 am they peeled off and disappeared as if they had never been there. To say that I was left drained, would be an understatement. Shattered might be more appropriate.

Logbook:
10th Feb
8.15 pm
99 nm to Tristan

Lots of cloud came in from the West this morning. Breeze up and down during the day at 15-30 knots. It has finally settled on SW. A lot of changing of gears today to keep speed up. Trying to get to Tristan before sundown tomorrow so I can film and see it.

Was on edge with breeze coming and going so didn't do much except stand in cockpit and watch for squalls.

Lunch was tinned tiny taters sliced and cooked like hot chips and they were bloody beautiful.

Moon up and not a bad night except the breeze lightening off.

On the morning of 11th Feb, Tristan was 73 nm away. Would I make it in daylight?

It was starting to get quite cold and generally rougher, so I retrieved my heavy duty wet weather gear and boots. The "party" was over. It was time to get kitted up and rodeo again.

When 52 nm from Tristan, it was blowing its arse off and was a total pain. I was hard on the wind, getting smashed.

I lamented the fact that when I rounded Tristan the first time, on Christmas Day, I'd had to battle in a very strong headwind and now, when approaching from the opposite direction I was battling headwinds again.

Bastard!

Out of 10, the level of enjoyment that day was a 4 at best.

Logbook:
11th Feb
5.30 pm
Has blown its arse off all day.

Tristan is 25 nm away. I think we'll skirt the land if the breeze direction holds. Sunset will be in 2 hours so forget filming for the doco. I can see the Island shrouded in mist and cloud.

I've been on edge all day.

Just received an email from Lorraine saying it was 3 am and she couldn't sleep, worried that I was okay cos I hadn't replied to an email from a couple of days ago. It's been much too rough and uncomfortable to sit at the computer but I did send her a brief reply to let her know I was OK and that I'll send a longer one when I round.

Update #73
11th Feb
Position 37 deg 16' S, 11 deg 12' W
Air temp 17 °C
Water temp 19.6 °C

Tristan da Cunha was finally rounded at 9.45 am AEDST on Sunday 11th February, 2001 and I am now heading to Tasmania, 7280 nm away. Tristan proved a real challenge to get around. Last Wednesday I finally got breeze with a bit of "grunt". Throughout Friday I had a day of 40 knots from N to NNW with very ugly seas, about 25 ft, as a result of cross swell and wind generated waves.

For the last 100 nm, I was in the grip of a 30 knot SW, hard on the wind with a triple-reefed main and small amount of headsail toughing it out. I finally rounded the island in the dark, with 40 knot rain squalls. Great!

How it all changes. Just a few days ago it was 30 °C and the sun was out with light winds. Now I've dug out the thermals, blankets and wet weather gear for the last "test".

CHAPTER 28
The Indian Ocean is a Beast

South East Cape, at the bottom of Tasmania, was 7,280 nm away, and I set course to go find it.

I had a hunch that this leg was gonna be a heck of a ride.

Vinny Lauwers is one of Australia's absolute sporting heroes and a bloody good bloke to boot. Most Aussies would not have a clue who he is or what he has achieved. In 2001, Cathy Freeman and Tiger Woods won the International Laureus sports awards for the International Female and Male Athlete of the Year, respectively.

At that same award ceremony in Monte Carlo, Vinny was the recipient of the International Disabled Sportsperson of the Year award. That means, the best in the whole bloody world. Vinny is a paraplegic, having broken his back in three places when hit by a car at 22 years of age, confining him to a wheelchair. Vinny would argue that he doesn't have a disability and I agree.

Soon after his accident, in the late 80's, Vinny was drawn to sailing and competed in two Sydney to Hobart races as part of a "Sailing with Disabilities" program. He got totally hooked on the sport. Vinny set about building his own 47 ft yacht, christening it "Vision Quest". As a warm up to the main bout, sailed with my now great mate, Grahme Rayner, 5,500 nm in the 2 × handed Melbourne to Osaka yacht race.

In December 1999, Vinny left his wheelchair on the dock and using his backside and palms of his hands, shuffled aboard "Vision Quest" and spent 233 days continuously at sea to become just the 5th Aussie to sail solo, nonstop, and unassisted around the world, arriving back in Melbourne in early August 2000.

He was the first Paraplegic in the world to achieve it.

Vinny Lauwers is bloody living legend!

As Vinny crossed his finish line, it was about two months before my departure. My schedule was crazy but I felt a real need to meet him, if he would be so gracious. When I made contact I found him incredibly accommodating, urging me to come to Melbourne to meet. I did so, and whilst with him he passed on many pearls of wisdom.

Amongst a treasure trove of great "stuff" that I took away there was one particular thing he really wanted to impress upon me.

I'll NEVER forget his words.

"The Indian Ocean is a beast"
"Tony, the Indian Ocean is a beast."

As I flew home, his words ricocheted around inside my head.

After rounding Tristan, Clouds wanted me to dive south to latitude 45 deg, to clear South Africa by about 600 nm and skirt a high pressure system, which if trapped in, would result in headwinds, slowing me down considerably.

Logbook:
12th Feb
5.30 pm

Have spent the whole day getting whacked by breaking waves. Hardly been on deck. Living below again, like a hermit. Slept this arvo, finished current book and had 2 cups of tea in the bunk because I can. Breeze slowly fading.

Logbook:
13th Feb
7.20 am

Last night I dreamt that I was batting for the Australian cricket team and I skied a hit really high and West Indian test cricketer, Viv Richards missed catching me out.

Starting yesterday arvo the wind has progressively lightened and in concert, I have increased sail however, every now and then we get a 2 minute micro burst of breeze. It is easy to get caught with your pants down.

Picking up Radio Australia on the HF quite clearly now in the mornings.

Later that morning the breeze fizzed completely, and I was becalmed again. In the afternoon, I amused myself by playing patience and eating my last packet of Jatz crackers smothered in peanut butter.

It was a crappy arvo with a big uncomfortable residual swell, but late in the game a new NW breeze arrived that freshened in the evening, climbing toward the forecasted 35-40 knots.

That afternoon, I couldn't get with the program. I had a sleep hoping to get my equilibrium back but that didn't do the trick. I felt a bit lost.

Late in the evening, we were scooting along with three reefs in the main and the small headsail poled out. We were flat and fast, as the opposing residual swell had been ground away to nothing so there wasn't much of a sea running.

However, I was on edge, waiting for more breeze

Logbook:
14th Feb
Midday

Just dropped Main as the speed was above 8 knots and the boat was loading up too much.

6.50 pm
40-50 knots?
Make it 50 knots!
BASTARD!

Been blowing a right mongrel with big seas getting bigger. Existing with a small part of the small headsail poled out. Not much to do but close the hatch and hang on. Surfed some big waves and been bashed on Port side. Testing the chainplate repairs yet again.

Update #74
14th Feb
Air temp 19 °C
Wind NW 40 knots
6,932 nm to Tasmania

Here, in my 43 ft. fibreglass cocoon I sit
   Storm boards in, hatch a good tight fit
   Down here where they make the wind and waves best
   We have returned for the final 8,000 mile test
   'Tis a good steady 40 from the north-west
   A small amount of headsail is best

The mainsail is down, to the boom is tightly lashed
BANG!! Another wave hits, I'm getting used to being bashed
My singular small isolated world exists down below
The bunk, the stove, the charts, the radio
So onwards we push to Tassie and up the East Coast
Headed toward Newcastle, and the people we love the most.

Through the night, it blew 40 knots from the WNW as the pre-frontal breeze gave us a pasting. The seas were increasingly difficult to negotiate and on two occasions we were knocked down flat to 90 deg with the head of the mast "kissing" the ocean. There were heaps of other "pretender" waves vying for a "kiss" as well.

It was yet another crap night.

The new day dawned and the big seas continued to give me a work out. Finally, in the afternoon the predictable shower of rain arrived, announcing the imminent arrival of the change. Finally, the WNW reached its zenith, the new SW front rolled in and the process started yet again.

Life went back to "normal". Whatever the fuck "normal" was.

Update #75
15th Feb
Ode to Solo Globe Challenger

In a Cole 43 named SGC
He left his home and his family
For 180 days she will be his home
His lover, his life, he will not be alone

With help from his friends we bade him goodbye
Pato and Chappy and of course Barry Rae
And don't forget Keir and Vicki and Gus
Then Steve and Phil ….. And the rest of us

We went to the sea to wave him away
And prayed for his safe return one day
To Newcastle Harbour he must persist
For a more beautiful place does not exist

NEVER, EVER GIVE IN!

Guided by Badham and modern e-mails
He sets his course and unfurls his sails
And heads west to east a man alone
Around the globe on a journey to home

He has worked for this time over the years
His destiny this journey - whatever his fears
South to New Zealand and around Snares Island
Left to the Horn 'Cross the great Southern Ocean

He is looking for sponsors - there are never enough
To share his vision for the kids doing it tough
In John Hunter Hospital they lay there sick
And Mowbray inspires us to all do our bit.

We share his quest with weekly updates
Via radio sessions we still hear our mate
Plugging away at each of life's chores
Until he gets home to peaceful lake shores

Station 12 is his lifeline to Holly and Jordan
And the outside world to relieve the boredom
He sits at the Nav table, keyboard in hand
Writing a poem - too far from land

We can only imagine his hours awake
Forever aware of the dodgy chainplate
Nursing his girl on into the fray
And knowing that failure is not far away

At 56 south where so many have perished
He turns to the left - a thought he had cherished
A dream he had dreamed for too many years
Had finally come true - though at what cost he fears

On to the Atlantic with warm ocean currents
With doldrums and rain, the sun and quiet moments

He plods on his way one step at a time
To Newcastle Harbour round Easter time

The cold and the wet a brief memory away
But they will be back in a few short days
Rounding Tristan Da Cunha a rock on the map
At 37 south to make his way back

By the light of the moon and a wind nor west
Again he turns left - the last leg of his quest
By now the journey is 2/3rds over
And on the next chart is one last ocean
The Indian it is - this final test
Before he can lay his dream to rest

Of sailing the world - to conquer the ocean
Of rounding the Horn and feeling the motion
Of mountains of water rolling under his feet
A challenge not many are game to meet

His family awaits with arms open and smiles
Steadfast she sails - it's only 7000 miles
To greet all his friends (we will shout and cheer)
And help him to drink the world dry of beer!

By: **Mark Schroder**

The boat was rocking and rolling around and the shock loads proved to be too much for one of the short 6mm spectra ropes on the Monitor, so I reeved a new pair and we were up and running again. I reflected that the pieces of rope had helped steer the boat 17,000 nm, so were entitled to a rest.

Update #76
16th Feb 4.58 pm local time

Solo Globe Challenger just crossed the Prime Meridian of Longitude, taking us from WEST to EAST of Greenwich. We crossed the

International Date Line on day #14 and it is now day #126, so we have been paddling around west of Greenwich for 112 days. It's new territory for me. In another 25 nm, our journey will be exactly 66.66% complete.

The weather has settled now after our 36 hour paddy whacking courtesy of the 40-50 knot NW. The last 36 hours we've had a SW breeze of around 20 knots. Just ducky, thank you very much.

Lorraine emailed, telling me that Jordan was crying a lot for me and poor Holly had a panic attack at school. It was 2 weeks since we'd had voice contact and worryingly, in that call, Jordan had got very upset, crying, not able to speak.

I thought about how we might be able to reduce their stress and came up with a couple of ideas.

I rang and spoke to Jordan, who wanted to explain why he had cried so much two weeks prior and in the process of trying to explain, the poor thing lost it again, getting very emotional and crying terribly.

I told him that he didn't have to talk and asked him to hold the phone to his and Holly's ear and for them to just listen. I told them that their Mum was going to get them a calendar each to hang in their bedrooms. I suggested that they draw a prominent circle around my ETA, Easter Saturday.

I suggested that every morning they put a big fat cross through that day's date. I hoped that as the crosses accumulated and the days left until Easter Saturday visibly reduced, it might help them, particularly Jordan, realise that it was gonna come to an end sooner rather than later.

As they listened, with Jordan virtually mute, I reminded them of how much they had enjoyed their first snow skiing experience not quite two years prior and told them that upon my return I would make sure that the four of us headed to the snow for a week. Did they think that might be a good idea?

I heard a muffled "nod of approval" from Jordan and was greatly relieved, thinking that we might be on the right track. I knew that I would have no money for an expensive trip to the snow but there was no way in hell that I was not going to take them.

Get me home!

Logbook:
17th Feb
Midday

Slow old morning just ticking 'em over. Forecast is for another front going NW to SW 25-35 knots. The sky tells me that it is close.

Lazy morning reading a Readers Digest compilation of 4 stories borrowed from Snapey and Alana.

Been thinking a lot about Jordan but not much more I can do except get home and be a good father.

Opened a bottle of a 98 Cabernet Shiraz Merlot last night and it was absolute piss but I still drank a glass of it. Will knock the rest off when I'm really desperate.

We were making good miles. In the previous 24 hours, we had averaged 6.64 knots and since rounding Tristan 5.5 days prior, our average was 6.08 knots. Having a 6 as the first number of our average speed was much better than a 5 or a 4. I was uplifted. Every mile sailed was a mile closer to home.

In the early hours of the following morning Solo Globe "tripped" on a wave that she was going much too fast on, and got knocked down flat with the top of the mast in the water again.

Fuck me! Give it a break.

Vinny's words echoed in my head.

"The Indian Ocean is a beast."

Logbook:
18th Feb
7.50 am
6,216 nm to Tassie

Blowing an absolute bastard again. Been hit by some big 'uns. Just like a canon going off when they hit. Have just about no sail out. Shouldn't blow any harder? Not much to do except make sure the boat is steering a good angle to the waves, put hatch boards in and ride it out. You just exist in these conditions.

1 pm

SW change just arrived. Sea very confused. Let's see what happens.

They are BIG.

Update #77
18th Feb 2001 10.55 am local time
Air temp 15 °C
Water temp "Getting cold"

The Cape of Good Hope, near Capetown, South Africa is aptly called the "Cape of Storms". I am 700 nm SW of there and it's blowing 45-50 knots from the NW.

Some quick impressions from the last 12 hours:

Ugly seas, curling, lipping, breaking, see that magical clear bit of the breaking section, now 30 ft high, steering 135 deg magnetic, seas on port quarter, mainsail lashed to the boom, tiny amount of the small headsail out, speed 6 to 8.5 knots, everything on deck tied down, a real big fucker just got me, like a canon going off, I hope repairs hold good, checked 'em for the 1,000th time, gotta keep the rig in it, sea boots/wet weather pants on, ready to go on deck if something breaks, listen to BBC, play a cassette, take your mind elsewhere, drink lots of tea, no sun, bleak, grey, I'm back down here where they make the wind and the waves, solar panels not pumping out power, wind generator off its head when let loose in this wind, storm boards in, hatch shut tight, Hang On!, another one, no leaks except chainplate, sink full of dirty dishes, will wash up later, other things to worry about, weather forecast from Capetown, no improvement for at least 12 hours, can't blow forever, chip away at it minute by minute, wave by wave, hour by hour, make little rocks out of big rocks, keep chipping, film the action, never looks as big on film, (except '98 Hobart), heaps of rain, flattens sea a bit, brings more wind, seas building more, thinking about deploying the drogue, not yet, will slow her down too much.

It was getting very cold again. My hands were burning, so I broke out the gloves, balaclava, beanies and thermal clothing, readying myself for the final assault.

Logbook:
20th Feb
10 mins past Midnight
5,964 nm to Tassie.

Just tried to make some phone calls for media commitments and after 45 minutes of mucking around getting the right frequencies and good reception, Capetown Radio advised that some computers were down and no international calls could be made. I was all dressed up with nowhere to go.

Dinner was a tin of pea and ham soup.

Today I ate my head off. The hunger must be because I'm back in the cold.

6.45 am
5,914 nm to Tassie.

Just got out of bed. Not that much breeze around but I don't like the looks of it. Overcast, drizzly, very grey and dark in areas. I don't have a good feeling.

Sailing a Great Circle Route between two points essentially means following the curvature of the earth to sail the shortest distance possible.

Heading South, as Clouds had me doing, was akin to sailing the Great Circle Route to Tassie, which meant I was reducing the distance to go relatively rapidly.

I ruminated, that at this rate, I might actually be home by Easter.

As the 21st day of the month progressed the barometer dropped yet again, heralding a new cold front. How many fucking more would I endure?

Being the gourmet chef that I am, I cranked out my famous "Sweet Breads" for lunch. Water (with a blend of saltwater), reconstituted raisins and some packet bread mix, fried in hot oil. Absolutely bloody beautiful.

By early evening, the seas had built significantly. The speed was regularly over 8 knots with bursts of 10's and 12's. The jury rigged port chainplate was creaking and groaning.

C'mon baby! You'll be right! Hang in there!

I reduced sail area to a minimum to take some load off it.

I did NOT want the mast laying in the ocean.

Update #78
22nd February 1.00 pm local time
Air temp 14 °C
Water temp 11.1 °C

Cape of Good Hope Rounded. At 9.34 pm AEDST 22nd February, 2001 Solo Globe Challenger was 555 nm due South of The Cape of Good Hope, on the same Longitude. That's three capes down, two to go.

We are now 71% complete.

Solo Globe is in good shape but showing signs of wear and tear brought about, in part, by the incessant movement and high loads. You are only as good as your weakest link and it is a continually evolving list of weak links which I have to continually monitor.

A suntan and sunglasses are mere memories.

It's a game of inches. The paper navigation chart that I am using was called to action way back on the 18th Dec and will be in play for another week or so. By the time that it has done its job it will have been in use for approx. 73 days straight. It lives on the navigation table and if I had a dollar for every time I've looked at it I'd be a billionaire.

To celebrate rounding the Cape I put together another "message in a bottle". "Sailing Vessel BUNDY", the glass "hull" of which originally contained Bundaberg Rum, took off on her maiden voyage with a note inside however S. V. BUNDY has not been heard of since.

The cold was back with a vengeance. One night, in bed with the usual mountain of mouldy, smelly blankets over me, I was still cold. I got up and pulled my snow ski pants on over the top of Gus' extra thick lamb's wool thermal pants. I then threw on my extra warm grey woollen top before burrowing back in under the blankets. The cold permeated deep inside every bone of my body. Another day, another dollar.

Logbook:
23rd Feb
4 pm
5,438 nm to Tassie.

Just mixed my daily ration of good/bad water. It will be good to turn a tap on and have a cup of tea that doesn't taste salty. Starting to run out of good books to read and will soon read some a second time. Just christened a new tube of toothpaste and a new gas lighter for stove lighting. The old lighter lasted 4 months.

If you know what to look for there is a predictable cookie cutter sequence of events that take place prior to the arrival of each new cold front in the Indian and Southern Oceans. Each is generally a carbon copy but with variations.

Initially, a pre-frontal breeze will fill in from the N quadrant. It will probably increase in strength and might also "clock" a bit in direction from the N back through to the NNW NW or WNW as it intensifies. The strength of the pre-frontal breeze can be a relatively moderate 20-25 knots but can also "smoke" you, climbing the Richter scale to 40-50 knots. The stronger the breeze and the longer it blows the bigger and nastier the waves become.

The barometer falls in tandem with the general rule that the faster it drops and/or the lower it goes, the more severe the system is going to be.

Then the pre-frontal breeze may drop out completely, leaving an almost zephyr. A shower of rain generally passes over, accompanied by some dark cloud, and then the new cold front from the S-SW quadrant will arrive. Sometimes, it blasts in with all guns blazing or may roll in, building in strength progressively.

When the front arrives, the wind direction is usually about 90 deg opposite to the pre-frontal, which can create a very confused cross sea until the new wind-generated waves become dominant some hours later. Sometimes, if you're lucky, the new front has less breeze in it than the pre-frontal.

About 6 hours after the new front arrives, the barometer will start to rise and about 12 hours after its arrival it generally starts to dissipate.

There will generally be a settled period until it starts all over again maybe 2-3 days later. It never, ever, ever stops!

I am thoroughly intrigued as to how many tens or hundreds of thousands or millions of years these frontal systems have been on their relentless march around the southern extremities of our planet.

Nature is amazing.

CHAPTER 29
Oh Dera!

Logbook:
26th Feb
3 am
5,111 nm to Tassie.

Just heard on the BBC that Sir Donald Bradman has died. I've read a book about him on this trip and began to understand not only what a great sportsman he was, but what a great Australian as well.

Have nice steady breeze now and making up some lost time. Stars are out. Good night. Just had 6 hours in bunk even though up and down 3 or 4 times. Baked beans and sausages for dinner followed by a cup of tomato soup.

Update #79
26th February 3 pm local time
Air temp 14 °C
Water temp 12.5 °C
5,044 nm to Tassie

I've just transferred to a new chart with exotic sounding places on it like, The Seychelles, Madagascar, Mauritius, Zanzibar, Mozambique and Swaziland HOWEVER the most interesting feature for me is the thin slice of Western Australia. AUSTRALIA. YES.

Today we have a long loping West swell with a fresh NNW breeze around 25 knots. The swell reminds me of when Morrie and I went around Oz when we encountered swells 200 metres apart, 40 ft and higher. Today I reckon they are 125 metres apart and about 35 ft high. There is nothing dangerous about them, but they do take a bit of getting used to. Majestic, is how I would describe them.

In a previous update, I spoke about "magnetic variation" that affects the steering compass. The amount of variation differs as one moves around the earth. Soon I will be in an area that has a huge 45 deg of West variation, meaning that to head due East (90 deg) we have to steer 90+45 = 135 deg.

A couple of afternoons ago, coming off the backend of another bagful of breeze, I was in the hatchway facing aft but looking down into the cockpit when I got the fright of my life. A huge whale surfaced not more than 25 metres directly astern, heading at right angles to our track. There was only one "blow" from this beautiful creature and he/she was not to be seen again. What a pity.

We're now getting down to the business of this marathon. Easter looks good.

Logbook:
27th Feb
6.20 am
4,936 nm to Tassie.
Just woke. I love my bunk.

That morning my friend, the whale, paid me another visit. I was below decks, heard a blow, and bounded up into the cockpit like a startled gazelle. (read: lumbering baby elephant) There it was again, a mere 15 metres from the boat, swimming in parallel and harmony with us. I could have almost stepped from the boat on to its back and a big part of me was wanted to. It swam in joyous unison for 15 minutes before peeling off to leave me alone yet again. It was like a dear friend was shepherding me safely toward home.

How could you kill or harm one?

Never. Never. Never.

That afternoon I was back in fog yet again, with an opaque curtain of white sitting constantly 500 metres ahead that we never got to.

I knocked up a banana cake for lunch to comfort myself. Very naughty, I know!

The next day I tried to ring KOFM for a scheduled interview. It took an hour of mucking around, including inconveniencing the good folk at Capetown Radio and running the engine for an hour to charge batteries. Then the message came through that KOFM were busy that week and couldn't fit me in.

Really?

I did some filming with the camera taped to the boathook for some "off boat" footage and when reviewing the tape, I discovered that the marine growth on both sides of the aft waterline had now morphed into truckloads of ugly black trailing "weeds".

Prior to departure Solo Globe's underwater surface been liberally painted with an antifouling paint to inhibit unwelcome growth including barnacles and a vast range of other marine organisms.

Yachts are coated every 12 months on average but hot/warm water speeds up degradation of the protective paint allowing growth to attach exponentially as the paint loses its effectiveness. As the growth multiplies, (think 2 × rabbits breeding) boat speed drops off in proportion, as if a handbrake is progressively applied. The warm water of the tropics had not helped our cause and the result was now becoming apparent and would only get worse.

My book of choice that day was Wilbur Smith's, "The Seventh Scroll."

Then I SCORED!

I was rooting around in a cupboard, that I had rarely looked in of late, and lo and behold I discovered some beautiful, vacuum sealed, cured smoked ham sausages, of which I thought I'd eaten the last of ages prior. You fucking beauty. I was overly excited. About food of course.

Update #80
4th March 2 pm local time
Air temp 11 °C
Water temp 10.5 °C
4,282 nm to Tasmania
230 nm NW of the Crozet Group

We've been sailing for 140 days and are 77% complete.

I've been feeling okay but sleeping like a log. Last Friday morning I was scheduled to be interviewed by Luke Grant. I thought I would grab a couple of hours in the rack beforehand. For the first time in my life I slept through an alarm, finally dragging myself out of the rack after an unbelievable 11 hours. Needless to say, I don't think Luke was waiting by the phone.

Last night it blew 35 knots with a shocker of a sea, exerting big shock loads on the chainplate repairs but they continue to hold on and with the added concern of the steering cable chafe, I'm a little worried.

Each day rolls into the next and I've had this desire to make up a sign with my name, DOB and current date, hang it around my neck and take a photograph of "Prisoner Mowbray".

On the morning of 5th March, I was recovering from another bastard of a night where the boat had been tossed around mercilessly with accompanying big shock loads on the mast. The barometer had bottomed out and I hoped that we would get a reprieve.

I had 2 big bowls of porridge with raisins, dried apple with lashings of honey for breakfast.

That day I took some time to whittle down a list of unanswered emails. Varied topics included a jazz fundraising night, Ashley at Sony wanted a review for a journalist and I thanked Bi-Lo's Richard and Darren profusely for having arranged for Lorraine and the kids to go to the Newcastle Show at Bi-Lo's expense. Luke got an email as well discussing my arrival, which he was helping organise. It looked like the welcome home reception was gathering momentum.

Speed needed in Knots to finish by:

Saturday   14/4   5.11
Sunday   15/4   4.99
Monday   16/4   4.87
Current average for trip = 5
Since leaving Tristan = 5.82

Logbook:
7th Mar
8.45 am
4,017 nm to Tassie.

Pasta for dinner last night followed up by a big serving of indigestion.

Breeze has quietened right down. Is a glorious day, sun and blue sky.

Tried to raise Perth Radio last night on the HF. They are still 3,000 nm away. Nothing heard.

6 pm
3,962 nm to Tassie.

Email from Snapey. I asked him to fire the finish gun and he will be proud to do so.

Update #81
7th March 10 am local time
3,850 nm to Tassie
250 nm NE of the Crozet Island Group
Psst!

Kevvie and Frankie Babe here. You know, the big fella's imaginary friends. He's asleep and he's not even cute now. We've been watching him on this computer and we thought we'd sneak a go.

Frankie Babe and I have had an "interesting" trip with him. We have to do all the night watches plus if it's over 20 knots he sends us on deck for sail changes. He was on deck a fair bit in the tropics, as it was nice then but he just swanned around whingeing about the heat and kept asking us to get him a drink.

Frankie Babe wants me to tell you about the "wind". We're not talking about the NW gales on deck but the "southerly busters" down below. That poor Gary Telford lent him his woollen thermal pants and we reckon Tony's absolutely blown 'em to bits. There's no doubt he's world class, although he says his brother, Trevor, beats him hands down.

What about his table manners? There is no conversation whatsoever when there's food around and he's really going to have to stop using his fingers when he gets back. Last night he told us one joke for the 7th time. Poor guy can't tell a joke to save his life so we just politely laugh and act like we haven't heard it before. Probably a lot like you guys back home have to act with him. Cecil B de Mille he is not. Always shoving that **SONY** camera in our faces even though we keep reminding him that we're invisible to everyone else.

One trick we really like playing on him is when he goes up the bow to change sails and we're down the back. We hook a rope over a cleat or tie it off again after he has checked that they're all free. After much colourful language, he comes clomping back, unhooks it and goes forward again. It really is good fun.

I think I just heard a yawn from that "pit" he calls a bunk, so we'd better pack up.

This is Kevvie and Frankie Babe signing off.

Logbook:
8th Mar
6 am

Something is brewing. Barometer dropping. Breeze increasing. I'm very uneasy. Can't sleep. Still making good time. No sea running. Thinking so much about home and finish but still a long way to go.

Logbook:
9th Mar
3.40 am

ANOTHER SW FRONT JUST GOT ME. *Why do fronts like to hit at 3.30 am? Bugger all sail out. Handling it well at present.*

11.20 am
3,694 nm to Tassie.
Front losing its bite now. Was ferocious for a few hours.

Baked beans and spaghetti for brekky. Back to triple reefed main and small headsail.

Every day rolls into the next. I find it difficult to focus on anything, except the distance to go, how long until home etc.

Now only a 6 hr time difference to home.

The weather conditions tested not only my sailing skills but continued to test my mind as well. When it was calm, I found myself impatient to get moving, using my race skills to extract incremental increases in boat speed. At the other end of the spectrum, when it was blowing and I was getting my arse kicked, I slowed the boat down.

What a head fuck.

The cycle never stopped.

The Indian Ocean is a beast.

I tried to raise Perth Radio again and "Bingo", I got through, so called home. Even though reception wasn't too flash I was encouraged as it would only get better the closer I got.

South Africa was disappearing in the rearview mirror and sadly, the quality of my link with Capetown Radio, was diminishing.

I retired to the cockpit to knock back a mug of tea, and enjoyed a star laden night sky. I generally avoided hanging out unnecessarily in the cockpit in those latitudes as it was usually too cold, wet or windy, however I felt really excited about speaking to Perth and my spirits were lifted. Life was good.

Logbook:
10th Mar
7 pm
3,527 nm to Tassie.
Boring, Boring, Boring.

Blowing its arse off again. Barometer dropping, frontal rain, getting dark, just a tiny bit of small headsail out, hatch slides in, getting whacked by a bastard of a sea. Front after front after front. The next one should be here soon I hope.
It's best not to look out of the windows.

10 pm
3,509 nm to Tassie.
SW change just arrived.

The next morning, I pondered that the previous 24 hours had been a right royal pain in the arse and it was continuing that way. I was struggling with a very rough sea, creating an extreme motion. I had only managed a couple of hours of fitful sleep.

Breakfast was porridge and raisins with honey. I was overly concerned that I only had half a packet of raisins left. I loved them. I had enough food to get me to the finish line but it would be interesting to see how much was left.

Logbook:
11th Mar
2 pm
3,419 nm to Tassie.

I cannot believe how much I am urinating today. When not urinating, I sit for hours staring at the GPS or stand at the stove staring out the window, contemplating.

Update #82
11ᵗʰ March 1 pm local time
Air temp 12 °C
Water temp 11.9 °C
3,296 nm to Tassie
2,250 nm WSW of Perth

We are 90 nm further south than the bottom of Tasmania. Since rounding Tristan 4 weeks ago, we've racked up 3,984 nm for an average of 5.85 knots. Another SW cold front barrelled us early Saturday morning, preceded by the usual 30-40 knot NW breeze, frontal rain and very ordinary seas. Clouds wanted to know if I was keeping count of the fronts. Bloody hell, I've had some.

A week ago, I was in "sleep" mode where I couldn't get enough. Yesterday I was entrenched in "eat" mode. I could not fill myself.

Hurricane DERA is 1,800 nm back over my left shoulder, generating 75 knots near the centre and "phenomenal" seas. Lovely!

I find it difficult to comprehend that I've been out here for 5 months. It just seems like I've been for a good long sail.

We're 82% complete now and I've got to keep it solid and straight for the last 18%.

Hurricane "Dera" is mentioned for the first time.

Crouched over my laptop in the gloom of the navigation concocting that update, not for a second did I realise the impact that "Dera" would have on us.

Vinny was right. The Indian Ocean is a beast.

The next day the weather forecast reported that "Dera" had a pressure of 960 Hpa with winds of 67-75 knots and phenomenal seas within a 20 nm radius and 50-60 knots within a 40 nm radius.

In other words, it was real mongrel of a system.

I ruminated that we were lucky that it was 1800 nm behind us.

Logbook:
13ᵗʰ Mar
7 am
3,172 nm to Tassie.
The dawn of a new day.

Email from Schrodes: *"You are on the final leg. Don't lose sight of what got you to where you are. Keep plugging away and do all the little things. Check and cross check. Be careful"*

Email from Trevor: *He had built a skateboard ramp for Jordan.*

I searched for ways to occupy my mind and that morning, with religious fervour, I whittled away 45 minutes by patiently getting rid of the lumps in some mouldy damp bread mix from which, I then made my internationally acclaimed "Sweet bread cakes".

As I wolfed down these gastronomic delights, I tuned in to one of my favourite stations, Radio Singapore. I loved their music playlist.

3.15 pm
3,112 nm to Tassie.

Just received weather forecast. Another front imminent. Hurricane "Dera" is moving South to South East. Very strong winds of 55-65 knots, not that far behind me. Let's get out of here.

A Hurricane. That raises the bar to a new height.

"Dera" originally formed in the tropics, in the Mozambique Channel between Madagascar and Mozambique on the East Coast of Africa. She whizzed around there for a while, wreaking havoc, and then moved out of the tropics, intensifying and morphing into a deep low pressure system.

Originally, a long way behind me, I didn't rate her much of a chance of affecting us. 36 hours after I first became aware of her, I realised that she was heading in my direction at speed, closing in. A little bell started tinkling in my head.

That afternoon, as usual, it rained before the arrival of the latest cold front, but something wasn't right. When the front got to me there was no "sting", was short lived and the barometer didn't drop very far before climbing again. I couldn't put my finger on anything in particular but there was a distinct uneasiness percolating.

Logbook:
14th Mar
11.40 am
3,051 nm to Tassie.

Painfully slow progress today. The "go slow" sign is out.

"Dera" is heading this way, generating 60 knots. It might affect us.

I wondered if this lovely sunny day might be, the "calm before the storm?"

I got some sleep that evening waking at around 2 am and as I crawled out of my bunk I had no idea that it would be a very long time before I burrowed my way back in.

Logbook:
15th Mar
4.20 am
2,945 nm to Tassie.

There is ANOTHER front due soon. It's dark with light rain and fog. Charming weather. Sitting around waiting for the front to arrive or sunrise, whichever happens first. "Dera" still heading my way bringing plenty of breeze.

1 pm
2,888 nm to Tassie.

Breeze been freshening throughout morning and sea built. Just dropped Mainsail and only small headsail now. Forecast is for 40+ knots and with Barometer dropping as it is, I think it might get ugly.

Rice and spaghetti sauce for lunch listening to Radio Australia.

8 pm
2,844 nm to Tassie.
Been blowing hard all arvo. Seas getting really big.
Forecast 50 knots tonight in my area.

Having not slept for 16 hours I was getting very tired, as I was generally sleep deprived to kick off with. Then, throw in the mental and physical energy I had expended throughout the day added to the energy sapping cold plus my increasing concern for my wellbeing as conditions went downhill and it would be fair to say I was feeling fucked, both emotionally and physically.

However, there was no time to rest, as the wind continued to pump in.

Would this ramp up to a replica of the 98 Hobart drama?

9 pm

It was now blowing an unrelenting 50 knots with very steep 30 ft breaking waves crashing onto the boat regularly.

At times, she was overcome, wanting to lay beam (side) on, 90 deg, to the advancing walls of water, a definite "no go" or "death" zone. I needed to change the set up, and in a hurry, otherwise, something dramatic would happen for sure. I decided to switch self-steering systems so I powered up the Coursemaster in "standby" mode. A cloak of foreboding surrounded me as I waited tensely for the right moment, then, in between breaking waves, I flung open the sliding hatch, ripped out the hatch slides and launched myself into the cockpit at the steering wheel and disconnected the Monitor. I then scurried back to the hatch and flicked the Coursemaster to "pilot" mode, and held my breath as I fine-tuned the settings, assessing the outcome of the new tactic.

I set her up to steer down the waves with a bias, keeping the oncoming waves around 150 – 160 degrees to the stern. The situation was relieved for the minute, but I was living on the edge and whilst it continued to blow it would only worsen for us. I retreated below to my cocoon.

Circumstances can change quickly, requiring a spontaneous adjustment of goals. As conditions spiraled, I adjusted my immediate goal to one of survival.

All this and "Dera" was still lurking.

Logbook:
16th Mar
8 am
2,774 nm to Tassie.

What a mongrel of a night. Blew a solid 50 knots from NW then 35 or so from the WSW with the change. Result was a completely fucked up sea. The cold was vicious. Boat and I got tossed around in a violent motion but the Sun is up now and it MIGHT start to abate but, of course, the cycle will re-commence.

Vinny Lauwers is right. The Indian Ocean is a beast!

By midday I had not slept for 34 hrs.

It was blowing its backside off again with a constant power packed, 50+ knots and we were taking a lot of big waves on board again. Solo

Globe and I were toughing it out. I was willing the Barometer to rise to no avail. There was the occasional patch of blue sky that would give me hope, however as quickly as these brief patches of hope appeared they disappeared, to be shrouded by dark grey ominous clouds again.

It generally was an extremely average day. Things were not good. Solo Globe was once again being pushed 90 deg to the oncoming waves from time to time and the Coursemaster was taking a fair while to get her back on course. As each correction took place the off course audible alarm reverberated around the cabin.

Beep, beep, beep, beep, beep, beep.

I was on a knife edge. I didn't want to adjust course to steer her down the waves on the opposite, what I felt was the more dangerous, bias.

Beep, beep, beep, beep, beep, beep.

One small change to the course setting or altering just one of a myriad of other factors that go into the equation can make a huge difference. It can be the difference between continuing to teeter on the edge of the precipice or falling headlong into it.

Beep, beep, beep, beep, beep, beep.

The breeze ratcheted to and sat on 60+ knots with breaking, "cliff face", 40-50 ft waves.

I had to regularly activate the main bilge pump as more water than normal made its way into the boat, flowing to and accumulating in the bilge.

Talk about fucking stressful.

At that point sleep was definitely not on the agenda. Once, I had a "feeling" that I was on collision course with a ship, so there I was on deck in 60 knots, waiting until I was on the crest of one of those big bastards, straining to see through the salt misted gloom, looking for the faintest glimmer of the light of a non-existent ship.

Dera had arrived!

7.10 pm
2,710 nm to Tassie.
Been blowing 60+ knots all afternoon

Today, and particularly this afternoon, has been the roughest and windiest part of the trip.

I have not had a good time today. Very strong wind all the time and absolutely pumping in the cloud squalls. Very big seas. I'm not game to let her line up straight on a wave.

I got very close to deploying the parachute drogue to try and stop her getting side on and to slow her down a bit. I got it out of the locker and set it up. It's ready to go now if I decide to deploy.

8.10 pm

I was standing at the hatch looking out into a dark cockpit about 20 mins ago when a wall of green and white seething water engulfed us. Under massive pressure some burst inside around the hatch surrounds and sprayed a large area around the galley. It threw a hell of a lot of power at us. It ripped the outdoor camera from the solar panel frame so I went on deck to retrieve it. As I came back below, the main bilge alarm went off. The sound of the alarm strikes fear into my heart. I activated the pump manually, yet again, emptying the bilge, allaying my fears that we were going to the bottom. Thank Christ for that.

I have a real dilemma on my hands. I'm not sure what to do to settle the boat down. She's okay for a while and then some big bastards come along and upset the show. The Barometer is rising ever so slightly and I am wishing like hell for a reduction of wind and waves.

I can only hope.

My options had been VERY limited but one had been to deploy the drogue to slow her down and try to stop her from surfing down the face of those monsters. Deploying would probably have stabilised her, however I was reluctant to do so because we had already been engulfed a number of times from the stern and I felt that slowing her down would increase the frequency of being inundated.

I hoped conditions were about as bad as they were going to get, as the barometer had started to rise slightly.

By 1 am I had not slept for 47 hours

I was almost beside myself with tiredness. My mind and body screamed for a rest and I rationalised my decision to hop into my bunk by telling myself that thus far we had "weathered the storm" and it looked like we might get though unscathed.

I was still kitted up my wet weather pants and sea boots as I "backed up", on hands and knees into my bunk when, with no warning, it happened.

Ka "fucking" boom!

Another bloody freight train got us square on!

Update #83
16th March 1.00 am
Position Approximately 45 deg 20' S, 84 deg 30' E

Knockdown! Big time! Stuff everywhere. The mast is still intact as well as most other deck gear. The spray dodger is a mess. The GPS is out but I have spares. I'm okay. Running bare poles and streaming drogue. More later.

In a micro second my world is upside down.

One half of my brain saying "This is not good, you're in trouble!" The other half is wondering:

"Are we going to go to go all the way?"

"A full 360 deg roll?"

"Are we going to come up at all?"

"Am I going to get out of this one alive?"

Water is pouring into the cabin under monumental pressure.

After what seemed like an eternity, she righted herself and as she did so water rushed to the low point of the boat and the dreaded shrill of the bilge alarm pierced the cabin.

Has the hull been breached?

Has the propeller and shaft been ripped out?

Have I pushed my luck once too often?

Am I going to the bottom?

I frantically ripped up the floorboards and discovered a large volume of water, alarmingly lapping the underside of the motor and, it was STILL rising.

In a panicked state, I grabbed a portable bilge pump, plugged it in and thrust one end of the hose into the bilge and the other into the galley sink.

As the pump got to work, the bloody bilge water continued to rise!

Christ, we are going down!

Then, almost imperceptibly the level seemed to stabilise and then, miraculously, it seemed to start to fall.

NEVER, EVER GIVE IN!

Eventually, I realised that the belly of the boat was not going to be overwhelmed.

After deciding that we would continue to float, at least in the short term, I went on deck expecting all sorts of carnage but found the only major casualty was the spray dodger that had been torn from its attachments and its stainless steel frame fucked up and bent. Repairs would have to wait. The GPS antenna was buggered as well. A little later I set up one of the spare handheld units to navigate with from then on.

There was no doubt that I had to do something different. I launched the drogue in 60 knots with waves between 40-50 ft. We were still swamped by some bloody massive mountains of water but the drogue, supplied by Alby "bloody" McCracken of Para-Anchors Australia did a fantastic job of saving my bacon. I rode it for 11 hours while I dusted myself off, tried to get my head together and tidied up a bit.

Three times I went on deck determined to retrieve the drogue but on the first two occasions, I retreated. I was extremely gun shy and very wary. On the 3rd go around I went for it, as the breeze was down to 35-40 knots and it was time.

The catapult effect of the knockdown was crazy. So many items in the cabin, big or small had become projectiles, hurtling around at warp speed. There were many marks and indentations on the cabin roof and timber fit out, when tins of food and other things had cannonballed around. Many cans of food were dented.

The Nav table lid had lifted and its contents of books, charts etc. got wet or damp. Luckily, my last operational computer stayed dry.

The places some items came to rest was ridiculous. The toolbox, stowed on the cabin floor, ended up in the top Port bunk spewing out its contents along the way. The square plastic washing up container that sat adjacent to the galley took off, with its contents of cutlery, cups and dishes dispersed everywhere. I mean EVERYWHERE!

It was bloody crazy stuff.

In the end, I went 60 hours without sleep and was completely physically, mentally and emotionally fucked.

Clouds reckoned that the area is the worst on the globe. Worse than Cape Horn and I 100% agree.

Vinny said it, "The Indian Ocean is a beast"

The period leading up to, and just after, the knockdown was by far the worst set of conditions I had encountered in the five months thus far.

The whole episode had left me very shaken, however I had ventured out there to be tested on my abilities and preparation, so I had to keep at it. The knockdown had to now transition to a memory.

I hoped that it would be a long time before the experience was repeated.

Oh "Dera", if only wishing made it so.

Tarp for catching rainwater doubling as a sun shade. Note, pillows, book, orange safety harness tether (on left).

Starboard side support system for more rigging problems.

Rainwater catcher/sun shade, top view.

The dreaded alarm clock.
30 minute naps.

Glorious sunset in mid Atlantic Ocean.

Day after day of pleasant conditions in the Atlantic. Note, bird perched on bow rail.

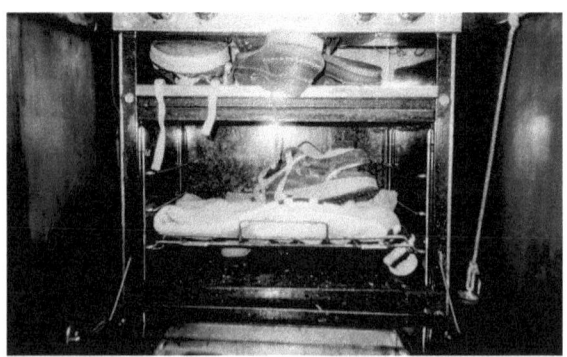
Drying shoes in the gas oven.

After the knockdown caused by
Dera. Crushed spray dodger.

Another perspective of damage caused by Dera.

During knockdown "stuff" hurled around cabin. Picked
up and thrown into a bunk for future sorting.

In the freezing Southern Ocean, heading to Cape Horn.

In the heat and humidity of The Doldrums.

Near Tasmania and home. What a transformation, but not in a good way.

CHAPTER 30
Hunting Down Tasmania

Later on that afternoon, I re-hoisted a small amount of mainsail for the first time in about 4 days. I rang home and as we chatted, some blue sky appeared through a cabin window, lifting my spirits immeasurably.

The knockdown had allowed a huge amount of water into the cabin, so I spent time drying out pillows, pillowcases, blankets, socks and a whole lot of other gear. Some items I rested on the warm stovetop and others I put inside the lit oven. I overdid a pair of shoes, tempering the rubber toes so that they ended up like steel toecaps.

When I could finally get to my bunk for a sleep, my crazy dreams continued. The latest one took me back to my newspaper run when I was a kid. The problem was that I never had a newspaper run when I was a kid.

After a sleep, the post knockdown clean up continued. In the Nav area, paperwork, calculator, pens, pencils, erasers, books and assorted sundry items were wedged in all sorts of nooks and crannies caused by the slingshot effect of the wave that had taken us out. Eventually, I got the area close to normal. Whatever normal was.

I decided to see if the engine would start, in case I needed it to charge the batteries. Of course, I wouldn't use it in gear as that would disqualify me. It was a tad slow to fire up, but fire up she did, and I ran it for an hour, to blow away any damp cobwebs, so to speak.

As we inched closer to Australian soil, I began to receive Radio Australia as clear as a bell and on a Sunday afternoon was able to relax, tuning in to a Melbourne Storm vs Wests Tigers rugby league match. I also listened to some of the 1st day of the 3rd Cricket test in India between Australia and India.

All in the day of the life of a solo sailor.

Logbook:
19th Mar
5.30 pm
2,332 nm to Tassie.

Big afternoon. I've just repaired the spray dodger as best I can. Got rid of the bent and twisted stainless steel front hoop. The back hoop is badly bent as well but is still sort of doing its job. The boom must have compressed down onto it when we swam. The dodger looks terrible but has brushed up not too bad. It will do the job until home.

My hands are a mess with cuts, abrasions, swelling and stiffness.

When repairing the dodger, I belted my left ring finger with the hammer TWICE in the SAME spot, within 10 minutes of each other, in an air temperature of 6 °C

I think said something like, "Oh, dash it all, gee golly gosh, I've hit my finger". I am a bloody idiot.

Logbook:
20th Mar
9 am
2,248 nm to Tassie.

Very overcast and drizzly rain but made good miles in the last 24 hours. I am pleased I tidied up the dodger yesterday as the wind driven rain is being kept largely at bay by it but would not have, otherwise. The storm boards are in and the hatch has to be closed in any event but the dodger gives some protection, getting in and out of the cockpit.

Logbook:
20th Mar
9 pm
2,169 nm to Tassie.

Had a fairly brisk 12 hours sailing, knocking out a really good 79 nm for an average of 6.58 knots.

Was getting close to another edge but the breeze backing away now.
Barometer dropping though.

AUSREP was a reporting system designed to contribute to the safety of life at sea. It was operated by the Australian Maritime Safety Authority

(AMSA) in Canberra. Participating vessels logged their position, course and speed daily, allowing AMSA to maintain a "helicopter" view of vessel movements in Australian waters.

I was invited to join and every 24 hours I emailed my position. A return email advised of any participating vessels within a 300 nm radius, alerting me to any possible dangerous interactions. This system was a great comfort, however I still had to be very cautious 24/7, as not all vessels participated.

After more than 5 months of needing to be continually "on guard" and sleeping with "one eye open" I was starting to wilt a tad.

I was gonna be bloody glad to get to the finish line.

Logbook:
21st Mar
11.20 am

Blowing a bastard again.
Just gotta get through it as gently as possible.
Just received today's AUSREP. Nothing in my area.

6.10 pm

Another fucking SW Front arrived 10 mins ago.
This one was ONLY about 10 hours ahead of The Australian Bureau of Meteorology's prediction.
I should have picked its arrival as I had the shower of rain just prior.
It sounds crazy but I'm always glad when the cold fronts arrive because it takes away the anxiety of not knowing how severe the new breeze is going to be.

The next morning found me wondering when in the bloody hell it was all going to stop. It had blown "dogs off chains" all night. Yet another cold front had blasted in, building to 45 knots and it had been very cold again. That morning was groundhog day, as the vicious and repetitious cycle continued as the Barometer rose and the breeze started to abate. Seas were still 30 ft and breaking but with the back end of the small headsail out, she was handling it pretty well. Yet again, I willed an improvement in the weather.

Speed *needed in Knots to finish by:*

Wed   11/4   5.29
Thurs   12/4   5.05
Fri   13/4   4.83
Saturday   14/4   4.63
Current average for trip 5.08
Since leaving Tristan = 5.82

I had this growing, almost overwhelming feeling that the sea and mother nature was testing me exponentially more each day, the closer I got to the finish.

Was I good enough? Was I worthy?

I was going to be very glad to get around the "corner" at Tasmania. That day, I started on a new navigation chart and was overjoyed to see the whole of Tasmania on it.

Bring it on.

Update #86
22nd March 3.00 pm local time
Position 45 deg 21' S, 105 deg 00' E

Down to the business end of proceedings now. Tassie is 1,780 nm away and I'm 900 nm SSW of Perth. Sliding through 105° 00' E, so the time difference with the east coast of Aussie is now just 3 hours and down to 2 hours on Sunday morning when daylight saving finishes. I am now working off a chart that shows all of Australia and I can actually see Lake Macquarie and Newcastle.

Since the last update, there has been plenty of windy, wild conditions to keep me occupied. I've hardly had the mainsail up lately.

It's been relentless.

With the latest cold front the cabin temperature dropped to 5 °C. There is lots of condensation down below and twice, in the last few days, it has hailed at night.

Like I've said before, "I'm not gonna die wondering."

This morning the safety tube broke on the Monitor for the 2nd time. The purposely designed safety feature had absorbed huge loads over a long time. It took a couple of hours to fit a spare and it's ready for war again. It's all part of the unassisted component of the challenge having to have everything on this 43 ft yacht to sustain me. It is finite. Nothing from the outside world.

When a bigger wave than normal is set to smash you sometimes you get a warning. Sometimes you don't. A warning might be the "hiss" associated with the approaching wall of water.

If you hear it three times in succession, you know you are going to get clobbered.

At night, down below, storm boards in, you hear the first hiss.

Then you wait for the second one?

If you hear the second, then you wait for the dreaded third.

It still beats mowing the lawn or going to work.

Logbook:
23rd Mar
7.30 am
1822 nm to Tassie.

In sleep mode, again. Got real cold since new front arrived a couple of days ago. I get into bed about 9 pm and don't get out until about 7 am which is shameful.

I get up occasionally to check our course and go to the loo but get straight back in.

With just 3 weeks or so to go, welcome home plans were apparently taking shape. Keir's role at NBN Television allowed him to morph into my honorary PR person, keeping the public informed with updates through news broadcasts and other avenues.

NBN had been very kind to me over the years and extremely supportive of our fundraising efforts. They had been "on board" from Day 1 of this project and that support continued by allowing Keir free rein.

I had no real idea what was happening as I still had a lot of arduous sea miles to tick off and that had to be my main focus. When Keir emailed asking for information or some input, I responded and then went straight back to concentrating on getting the boat and me home. I still had the equivalent of 4 Hobart races to sail.

3.10 pm
1,780 nm to Tassie.

Excellent run of 149 nm in last 24 hours. Ate the last of the raisins this morn with porridge. Sultanas finished ages ago. I despair.

6.20 pm
Good steady running breeze. Go, go, go. 'tis good.
   Baked a loaf of bread for lunch.

Logbook:
25th Mar
4.45 am
1,551 nm to Tassie.

Sitting here in the dark, listening to ABC broadcaster Trevor Chappell talk about the 6 degrees of separation, home brewing and playing some good music. I am about to try and get through to Craig Hamilton for an interview. Coconut and pumpkin soup with a packet of 2 minute noodles for tea last night. Just had a tin of peaches interspersed with lots of cups of tea.

   21 days until the finish. It's hard to believe that it's nearly over. I am very keen to get back and get stuck in to all the things I want to do. The future is promising.

Update #87
25th March 2.00 pm local time
Position 45 deg 13' S, 115 deg 15' E
Air temp 9 °C
Water temp 10 °C

The fourth Cape is rounded. At 3.09 pm AEST Sunday 25th March, Solo Globe Challenger crossed longitude 115°10' E, 650 nm south of Cape Leeuwin, Western Australia.

   SE Cape, the last one, is 1,353 nm away.
   Today is the anniversary of my father's death in 1982. William (Bill) Henry Mowbray lost the battle one day before his 76th Birthday.
   I dedicate my rounding of Cape Leeuwin to Dad. I hope he's watching from some place and is proud of me.
   It's been kinder weather in the last few days with steady running in SW-W-NW breeze, which has contributed to Solo Globe racking

up her highest week's mileage of 1,010 nm, just topping the 1,006 nm from week # 4.

For the last few days there has been an ugly low pressure system just ahead of us, pumping out 55 knot southerlies and a slow moving high pressure 400 nm north of us. I've been in the middle of them with the "hammer down" trying to take as much advantage as I can and squeeze through the gap.

Tassie here we come.

Logbook:
26th Mar
8 am
1,387 nm to Tassie.

A new front just arrived but much weaker than I thought it was going to be. No argument here. Am broad reaching with small headsail and double reefed main with a kindly sea. Slept well during night.

Today is Dad's birthday. He was born on 26th March 1906

He was a gentle man and would not do you a bad turn. Being not quite 50 years old when I was born, there was an age gap but I'm so lucky that in my early twenties I realised he wasn't going to be here forever and was able to really appreciate him while he was still alive

10 am

144 nm in last 24 hrs. You bloody beauty.

Logbook:
27th Mar
9 am
1254 nm to Tassie.

Breeze died right down about 12 hours ago.

Listening to ABC Adelaide broadcast a very moving tribute to Sir Donald Bradman. He was a great man. I like tuning in to Trevor Chappell's excellent morning show and this morning he was on song, being very entertaining. Varied topics included the history of flight in Western Australia, how to set up a Bed and Breakfast and interviewed a member of the 1970's band "Daddy Cool".

Logbook:
28th Mar
7 am
1,153 nm to Tassie.

Just crossed longitude 120 deg E so now just 1 hour difference with home.

5 pm
1,092 nm to Tassie.

Working to windward. This is not right. The High pressure to my North East affecting us. A quiet, non-descript day today.

Then I had a pretty ordinary night compliments of the High pressure spitting 30-40 knots of NE breeze at us. As the system inched East, the breeze backed off a tad and the wind angle opened up and it became manageable. Sunrise revealed a monotonous steely grey and overcast sky. I had not had much sail out, so progress was slowed as I concentrated on a steady, steady approach. Later in the morning, I did an interview with David and Tanya which was the first for a while, but as always, great fun.

Logbook:
29th Mar
8 pm
964 nm to Tassie.

Been a very ordinary day. Big unpredictable swell from the North along with an overcast grey sky, rain and fog thrown into the mix. Now broad reaching in a smooth sea. No sign of the new front.

I now have a gloriously beautiful evening with all cloud gone, clear star laden sky and a new moon. It's wonderful to stand in the hatch looking out and take it all in. What a contrast to 12 hrs ago when I wasn't enjoying myself at all.

Logbook:
30th Mar
7 am
896 nm to Tassie.

A good nights sailing. Up and down a lot to urinate but it is a good alarm clock. Back to all grey, overcast and mizzly rain. That doesn't matter so long as I have a favourable breeze pushing me to Tassie.

Last night's dinner was pasta, tuna, tinned carrots and a packet of seafood bisque soup all combined in one pot.

I had leftovers for a midnight snack and I had breakfast from it as well.

There is enough left for lunch.

Later that morning I was pumping out quick miles as I cranked up the volume on a Barry White tape and cleaned the galley a little, promising myself to do a better job another day. Keir emailed a script for me to record a voice over for a TV ad so I spent time rehearsing.

In the same email, he told me that it looked like he had managed to arrange for world renowned Tasmanian photographer, Richard Bennett, to fly over at SE Cape and photograph us. The reality of getting close to home was starting to get very exciting.

It turned out to be a nice afternoon for a sail with a smoother sea, full sail, comfortably broad reaching.

That evening, apparently, Keir, Biggles and Luke met to fine tune arrival plans. All three had waded headlong, without a second thought, into the deep end of the pool in a variety of ways to support us. Luke was applying himself, organising speaking evenings and other events for me to attend. They were all super keen and whilst I had to temper my enthusiasm, I was getting very excited to move to the next chapter of my life, whatever that may be.

Thoughts of Holly and Jordan invaded my mind so much now, imagining what it was going to be like hugging and kissing them for the first time. From day #1 I had forced myself to compartmentalise my thoughts of the two most important people in my life, but now the dam wall had an irreparable breech in it, as thoughts flooded in. (I cry yet again) Regardless of who might be at the finish, my kids HAD to be the priority.

I found it hard to believe that it might nearly be over.

It seemed that my whole life was meant to be on that boat sailing.

That evening, at around 10 pm, I was getting ready to hit the rack but thought I would jump up into the cockpit for the millionth time to check our path ahead. Swiveling my head, scanning the horizon I was horrified to see the lume of two boats BEHIND us meaning that I had passed them already without knowing they were there. Bloody hell.

It had me tricked, as I was 800 nm from land and no boats were supposed to be anywhere near the area.

Who would be so stupid to be there?

Just me!

Then another bloody lume jumped up on the horizon on the bow, directly ahead. I knew it was some way off, but I was not at all keen to get too close so I altered course to pass with a liberal safety margin. It took about an hour to draw abeam, passing 2 nm off what was a brightly illuminated large fishing boat that resembled a floating block of flats.

It turned out to be a very average (read: fucking terrible) night as I encountered another three fishing boats. By the time the new day dawned, I had managed just two 30 minute naps and was exhausted.

Seeing the boats was incredibly surreal because for the previous 47 consecutive days, I had only seen my beautiful whale and ocean.

Logbook:
31st Mar
11 am
732 nm to Tassie.

Another SW cold front arrived 45 mins ago.

Before it arrived, we had very, very heavy pre-frontal rain. Swell has been all over the place but settling a bit now.

I rang Keir to do a news interview and record the following for the welcome home TV ad:

"Hi, Tony Mowbray here and I'm nearly home. Lots of emotions starting to flow now. It's been an incredible trip for me so far and I'm so pleased that many of you have been able to follow my progress on the net, radio and TV. You've shared the highs and the lows with me, the scary bits, the cold, the heat and the loneliness.

Well, I'm nearly there and I would love to see you all on the foreshore on Easter Saturday when "Solo Globe Challenger" crosses that finish line.

I will have travelled right around the globe non-stop, sailed 22,000 miles and spent 181 days continuously at sea.

You might even be the first person I see since leaving and we might even have a cold beer to celebrate.

I'm coming home!"

NEVER, EVER GIVE IN!

It felt surreal to be in the bloody Southern Ocean, in the "Roaring 40's", narrating a TV ad. Who does that? An Idiot? You're right again!

After my "Media Commitment" it was time to get back to the sailing bit. Around mid-morning the new front ripped in increasing quickly to 40-50 knots yet again.

Fucking hell.

The sea got fucked up very quickly and I had a VERY tense time. I spent the whole arvo staring at the deteriorating conditions through the clear acrylic hatch slides. At its peak, it was pretty ugly, and I contemplated deploying the drogue again. Fortunately, by late afternoon the barometer started to rise, accompanied by a slight softening of the breeze with a clearing sky with lots of blue. I felt I had been tested enough and that I deserved to get to Tassie and home.

Unfortunately, it wasn't done with me yet.

That night I went to bed about 10 pm, setting the alarm for 11.30 pm to enable a quick check of our course and sure enough, there were the lumes of two more boats straight ahead. Fuck me. Here we go again!

I rushed below, hurriedly donned my wet weather jacket, pants and sea boots as it was wet, wild and woolly on deck with a strong breeze and very cold. I bounded back up into the cockpit and saw that there was a boat either side of our course, with the starboard one closer.

I initially adjusted course to sail between them but then changed my mind, deciding to leave them both on my right side. It took 2.5 hours to get near the first one and as I got closer, I realised that we were on a likely collision course. Unless I changed something, it would be a very close call, so I adjusted course to our left. Despite this, we were still converging and in my paranoid state, I was sure that it was doing it on purpose.

I needed more horsepower out of Solo Globe to speed up, so I unfurled more than the desired sail area for the prevailing 25 knot breeze. We were now hard pressed and to say I was worried would be a vast understatement. Crapping my pants would be an apt description.

With our deck lights on, to illuminate us, I frantically called them on VHF and as usual no one answered or they didn't have their radio turned on. BASTARDS.

In the end, when the other vessel was only about .5 nm away, I finally drew clear. Then I had to circumvent the next one which had its own set of fucking challenges, though I eventually got past it as well. As I finally left the second boat in our wake, we were able to resume normal course and set about getting our Mojo back, wherever Mojo had gone. Day break arrived, thank fuck. I was shattered and totally drained.

I went below and slumped in the Nav seat, leaning forward in an almost trance like state with my head in my hands, staring almost unseeingly at the floor and my feet, clad in sea boots. They were extremely comfortable and as I sat there staring, I realised, to my wry amusement that I had spent the whole night, in what seemed like a fight for my life, with my boots on the wrong feet!

I was exhausted, having had just 2.5 hours sleep in the last 54 hours.

I was set to go to bed when I received the latest weather forecast and bugger me if there was not another bloody cold front due 3 hours hence, so I decided I could not go to bed with it bearing down. I could not believe how many fronts had hammered me.

In my daily AUSREP report, I mentioned the fishing vessels which resulted in an immediate frenzied response from AMSA who were particularly keen on information. The consensus was that they were foreign and fishing illegally.

Legal or illegal, they had to be absolutely, fucking stark raving mad to be hanging out in that part of the world.

Logbook:
1st April
7 am
521 nm to Tassie.

It's April bloody fools day and I'm toughing it out big time.

The NW built to about 30-40 knots and the front arrived with the biggest, blackest cloud formation you have ever seen with heaps of rain. It settled in from the SW blowing 40-60 knots with fierce rain squalls with nil visibility. It was very unsettling with the boat wanting to climb beam on so I set the vane slightly off square and sheeted a tiny bit of the small headsail on the wrong side to keep the head away. She managed to run fairly square and as comfortable as you could hope for.

I have not been happy.

I just want to get to Tassie.

I was worried about more fishing boats and kept checking every hour but didn't see any.

Just received an email hoping it was from home and guess what?

Another fucking front near WA on its way to me.

BLOODY HELL!

Update #88
1st April 1.00 pm AEST
Position 44 deg 30' S, 135 deg 23' E
Air temp 11 °C
Water temp 12 °C
497 nm to Tassie, 500 nm south of Adelaide

We are now 94% complete. We've crossed 135°00' E and are now on the same time as the East Coast of Australia.

The other night I scribbled some thoughts:

A venting of anger, brutal, a game of inches, confused seas, not having fun, cold front after cold front. When will they stop? Never! Pitch black, More fishing boat? Testing, testing, testing, Is Barometer rising? Mantra: soft, soft, soft, gentle, gentle, gentle, calm, calm, calm. I've got a headache, light the stove to heat cabin, very cold, out here nature doesn't ask you, it demands and orders!

Anyhow, the sun has risen on another day and we are battling along in 30 knots and a more manageable situation. You may deduce from all of this that I haven't had much sleep of late and that Tasmania will be a welcome sight.

Easter Saturday, 14th April, is looking good for our finish, so mark your diary.

Logbook:
2nd April
8.30 am
396 nm to Tassie.

Had tinned prawn and potato patties for dinner which were left over from lunch. Had some good sleep while the boat slid along on a relatively good sea.

It's amazing the difference 24 hours makes.

I would really like to get around Tassie before the next front arrives so I can get into the relative protection of the land.

I did an interview with Luke this morn, and the plan is to be interviewed by him each morning until the finish.

Early morning on the 3rd I had just 281 nm to Tassie.

There was a large high pressure to my north blocking and pushing an approaching cold front to the SE away from me. I needed the high to hang in there for another couple of days, continuing to block so I could sneak around the corner and head for home. I cajoled myself that I must do some filming as for the last week or so I had not been motivated to do so.

I had chosen to do the trip with virtually no insurance on the boat. When I had crossed an imaginary line, 200 nm off the coast of Australia after departure, my cover had been suspended. Now that I was closing in on the 200 nm line again, it would kick back in.

I could not have cared less about insurance. My view is that if your uninsured boat sinks from underneath you and you are lucky enough to get back to land alive, then it's a fantastic bloody day to be celebrated.

Logbook:
3rd April
Midday

Sliding along at about 7 knots. Might be a bit of current helping us.

Getting very excited now. Should see land tomorrow arvo.

That next bloody front is bearing down on us. I hope we can turn the corner before it clobbers us.

Update #89
3rd April 9.45 am
Position 44 deg 07' S, 140 deg 55' E

I'm hunting miles down in my search for land. It's been 51 days since I last saw land. It is 259 nm to SE Cape and we should be there about lunch time on Thursday. If I'm lucky, I might see Terra Firma on Wednesday afternoon. I'll have to be extra vigilant for other boats now.

Update #90
4th April 4.30 pm
85 nm to SE Cape

I haven't sighted Oz as visibility is a shocker, combined with the wind direction which is pushing me away from land.

The NW breeze freshened throughout the afternoon yesterday, and at 4.00 pm I dropped the mainsail (it's still down) and spent the night getting paddy whacked by this 40 knot NW. Today it has continued at the same strength as a new cold front is approaching, working its way around to the west and then SW. It has been another wild night and day. I'm sure the big fella that doles out the cold fronts checks me every now and then, and if I appear to be vaguely enjoying myself, he slings another one my way.

I last saw a piece of Australia on the day I departed. It's just up ahead. Bring it on. Show it to me.

Logbook:
5th April
5 am
28 nm to SE Cape.
Matsuyker Is. Lighthouse sighted to Port.
Australia!
I'll see land soon!
I'm ready for my big day.
Fuck yeah!

For the previous couple of days, I had been able to pick up some AM/FM Radio stations which were thoroughly enjoyable to listen to after so long of just my favourite half a dozen or so cassette tapes interspersed with various HF Radio stations in France, Germany, Africa, the BBC, Voice of America, and Singapore.

It was pre-dawn, that magical part of the new day, as I closed on Matsuyker Island. The Lighthouse was like a southern sentinel, blinking at me unerringly. I felt it beckoning me to turn left and head north, telling me that home is just over the horizon.

I was elated at the prospect of rounding. I turned on the radio and thanks to an atmospheric skip I picked up a Brisbane station which unbelievably right at that very moment was playing a song by Aussie band, Men at Work, their iconic and almost unofficial Australian anthem, "Down Under".

It is a song that stirs patriotic fervour in any red blooded Aussie and so it was with me. There I was, standing in the cockpit with the lighthouse blinking away, the first rays of light were appearing in the east and we had a beautiful steady breeze allowing Solo Globe to heel a little, leaning into her work in a steady canter.

I do not have an artistic bone in my body and nor can I sing for nuts but there I was belting out "Down Under" at the top of my lungs.

Do you come from a land down under?
Where women glow and men plunder?
Can't you hear, can't you hear the thunder?
You better run, you better take cover.

And he said

I come from a land down under
Where beer does flow and men chunder
Can't you hear, can't you hear the thunder?
You better run, you better take cover, yeah.

I was just giving in to it.

Life was pretty bloody good.

In revisiting the leg from Tristan to Tassie through the course of writing, it has been difficult to not sound like a broken record and in the back of my mind have been thinking that I could not have had that many fronts pummel me.

I went back through my logbook and was taken aback and completely blown away by the following statistics.

I had new fronts arrive on the 15th, 18th, 22nd, 25th February followed by 1st, 4th, 8th, 10th, 13th, 15th, 20th, 25th and 30th March.

The last two rolled in on the 1st and 4th April.

I had a staggering total of 15 fronts hit me in 53 days for an average strike rate of one every 3.5 days.

In other words, I had been battered and nearly had my ass handed to me by mother nature many more times than I ever imagined.

They are absolutely stunning numbers and leave me shaking my head in disbelief. No wonder I was exhausted.

Update #91
5th April 2.40 pm
Position 43 deg 43' S, 146 deg 49.5' E

At 9.49 am this morning, Solo Globe Challenger was at position 43°43' S, 146°49.5' E. South East Cape has been rounded.

I still have a reasonable sea running, but in comparison to where I've been this is like sailing on a calm Lake Macquarie.

Richard Bennett has just flown over and snapped a heap of photos. A big thank you to Lake Macquarie and Newcastle City Councils for funding Richard's work and a massive shout out to Keir for organising it.

I had rung Richard to set up a rendezvous time and location and bugger me if not 30 minutes prior to his arrival we were, unbelievably, completely becalmed. Then, with just 10 minutes to go, a beautiful Westerly breeze filtered in and Richard managed to get some good action shots of Solo Globe powered up in full flight.

When the plane departed, I found myself a bit "fragile" having had my insular world shaken. In a huge test of the mind, this leg of 53 days, had been the longest of the trip without seeing land, eclipsing the 50 days from the start to Cape Horn.

From Tristan to Tassie I had seen just one whale and 8 fishing boats.

Then I saw land AND an aeroplane on the same day.

The trip was now approximately 96.5 % complete, but statistics show that many car accidents happen within a very short distance from home so now was not the time to take my eye off the ball.

CHAPTER 31
It was lunacy out there that night

That afternoon saw a mixed bag of fluctuating, land affected breeze resulting in a series of stop/starts. As nightfall descended, the breeze dwindled to a consistent "bugger all", as did our speed, leaving us becalmed, at times.

With low or no speed, maneuverability was minimal and on more than one occasion Solo Globe wanted to do a 180 degree turn and head back from whence we had come.

No way Jose!

I want to go home.

Email to Jordan:
Hi there "Big Fella" and how are you going? Your excursion sounds like it was fun. Did you go into Newcastle? I will be home in time to watch your next game and I promise to come and watch. I hope you're looking after Mum and Holly. All my love, Dad

Jordan was just 8 years old so emailing wasn't a priority for him. I guess sitting at the computer communicating with me may have been too confronting as well, HOWEVER, the following one from him is a classic and I loved it, although I desperately wanted more.

Email from Jordan:
Hi Dad, lost 3-0 at soccer today. See ya.

What can I say?

Paralleling the coast fairly closely, I needed to be extra vigilant as the proximity of land and increased shipping presented a higher level of danger. That night I slept for an hour at a time, keeping a keen lookout in between.

The 50 mm wide thermal printer worked overtime, spitting out congratulatory emails on our rounding, and, being so close to achieving our end goal.

In the dawn light of the new day, I was south of Tasman Island, in the mouth of Storm Bay, toodling along quietly. Adjacent to the island, ahead, was an Australian warship.

I jumped on the VHF and received an immediate response from the radio officer on what I learned was HMAS Noarlunga. To our utter amazement, we discovered that he had been the radio officer on HMAS Newcastle when Cyril and Keir had been taken aboard in the deadly '98 Hobart.

Are you kidding me? What a hell of a coincidence. We laughed about my possible stalking of him. Later on, in an interview, Luke asked if the radio operator's attitude was, *"Oh no, not you again."*

Logbook:
6th April
Midday

Very slow progress. There is a High Pressure system sitting over Bass Strait and I am trapped by light winds flopping around. Yuk. The sun is shining brightly though and I've got shorts and sunglasses on.

I had always assured sponsors that we would finish at a "media friendly" time. I would not sail to the finish line at 2 am with the media tucked up in bed. As the trip progressed, I had become confident of being able to sail up the Harbour on Easter Saturday, 14th April and that date was now locked and loaded.

When I committed to that date with the shore team, I had a massive safety buffer, needing to achieve a mere 3.32 knots on average, having achieved 5.66 knots for the previous 2 months or thereabouts.

One would be forgiven for thinking it would be easy.

It should have been a walk in the park, as the stats reflect.

Speed *needed in Knots to finish by:*
Thurs	12/4	4.42
Fri	13/4	3.79
Saturday	**14/4**	**3.32**
Sunday	15/4	2.95

Current average for trip = 5.
Since leaving Tristan = 5.66

If I were to arrive early I would simply "stooge" around in big circles, washing time away, BUT if I were late, that would be a bit of a fuck up.

Update #92
6th April 4.00 pm
Position: NE of Tasman Island

Progress has been dramatically slowed caused by anywhere between "not much" and no wind. A NNE breeze arrived about 1 hour ago making us work to windward but at least some progress is happening. In the last 30 hours, we have only reduced the distance to go by 82 nm for an average of 2.73 knots although it has been a beautiful day with 22 °C air temp which, for me, is tropical.

If I can keep on the pace it leaves just 8 days to go.
See you all soon.

Just over a month prior, I had filmed the aft waterline with a camera strapped to a boathook and had discovered "truckloads of an ugly black growth attached to the hull."

Even though we had bugger all breeze, which to boot were headwinds, our boat speed was way below par. I leant over the side and using a mirror I was aghast to discover that the "ugly black growth" had transformed into a bloody forest, and we were now carting around our own personal aquatic research project.

A plethora of 40 cm long black bushy weeds had attached to what resembled half oyster shells, that had grown on the hull. The result was huge drag and a massive loss in boat speed. It had grown exponentially since I first discovered it and was now a huge impediment, but there was not much I could do about it except get in the water to try to scrape it off and that was not about to happen. I had to push on regardless.

Logbook:
7th April
7 am
594 nm to Home.
Going bloody nowhere. Just sideways.

NE breeze came in yesterday arvo and I ended up with a full Main and small headsail on Stbd tack sailing toward land, a long way off my desired course. I ended up very close to the Tassie coast south of Maria Island then tacked back out to sea heading almost sideways to the rhumb line.

I tried the tack back toward land again but the angle was still crap so I headed back out to sea and have been doing so all night.

The breeze has swung a little favourably through the night but I'm not reducing the distance remaining.

I'm almost going up and down on the one fucking spot. There must be a lot of adverse current and when added to the drag that the research project attached to the hull is creating we are going fucking sideways.

It is a pain in the rear.

Please let the breeze kick from the NW sector and allow me to head for home.

Midday
579 nm to Home.

Blowing hard and still beating to windward with 3 reefs in the Main and small headsail making painfully slow progress.

Logbook:
8th April
3.15 am
546 nm to Home.

A front is coming. We are so slow it is bat shit crazy. Just dropped the Mainsail. The Barometer is falling. I wish the front would hurry up so I can point for home.

At this rate, I will not make it on Saturday or even bloody Sunday

I have to play it safe this close to home. 33 nm in 15.25 hours = 2.16 knots.

It's bullshit.

Midday
539 nm to Home.
Bloody hell.
I've backed right off, going nowhere and waiting for the front.

The breeze must go NW soon. I dropped the Mainsail at 2 am, hoisted it at 7 am and then dropped it again at 10.30 am.

This is stressing the boat and me far too much. It's not worth it and if I don't finish until Sunday or later then so be it.

The new front mowed us down at 8.30 pm that Sunday evening with a 40 - 50 knot hammering. For the earlier part of the night it was brutal, but after the initial clobbering it moderated to a fresh 20 - 25 knot breeze which served up a wet, bumpy ride but generally, we were able to head in the desired direction.

It was very rough and very cold and for a time I lay down on the cabin floor to get some respite. I was fully kitted up in my wet weather gear in case I had to go on deck in a hurry. Wedged between a cupboard and the engine box, in the foetal position, I pondered the question, "Is this any way to live? Or exist?"

Update #93
Sunday 8th April

Each day from now until the finish I am writing a daily diary for the **NEWCASTLE MORNING HERALD**. *This is my first effort.*

It is Sunday afternoon and we are 120 nm east of Tasmania, level with Bicheno. Since rounding South East Cape 3 days ago, our progress has been agonisingly slow. No wind initially gave way to strong headwinds, adverse currents and big breaking seas that are hurting my beautiful boat that has looked after me so well for the last 175 days.

The finish line is 539 nm away and is so close compared to the 21,284 nm we have travelled, yet it seems light years away as we grind out each remaining mile slowly and painfully. I am awaiting the arrival of a cold front this evening that will provide us with a much needed boost if we are to round Nobbys next Saturday morning, bringing to a close an adventure that I committed myself to nearly 4 years ago.

I have been put to the test in so many ways including loneliness, isolation, separation from my family, the legend of the Southern Ocean, sailing in the 'Furious Fifties' for 42 days straight and rounding Cape Horn. The cold, huge seas, high winds, pea soup fog and worrying about hitting icebergs have all left their imprint on me.

My logbook on Day #7 records in part, "The furthest south I have been is 43 deg 41 minutes and here I am at 44 deg south, quickly heading to 48 deg and then to the big one, Cape Horn at 56 deg. We are now getting into the realm of what I have thought about for so long, listened to people talk about and read about. Sailing in the 40's and 50's on my own is going to be special. Take it on. **Never, ever give in**. What a test. 6 months out here. Am I good enough? I'm not going to die wondering, am I?"

Last Thursday morning, I was a very, very proud Aussie and Novocastrian as I sighted the bottom of Tasmania amidst the salt spray generated by yet another gale that was the hallmark of the 53 day leg across the Indian Ocean from underneath South Africa. Rounding our famous landmark, Nobbys, and aiming Solo Globe for the finish line is going to be very special. More tomorrow.

Update #94
Monday 9th April
460 nm to home

Monday afternoon finds Solo Globe 180 nm east of the NE tip of Tasmania. We are now making good progress and in another few hours we will cross the 40th parallel of latitude finally emerging from the roaring 40's after 8 weeks. This coincides with entering Bass Strait which vividly brings to the fore many mixed emotions as I close in on the spot that my seven crew and I met with our problems in the 1998 Sydney to Hobart race.

As I type, the breeze is increasing and I have been on deck to reduce sail as it's shaping up to be a wild afternoon. My poor old girl has been in perpetual motion, and me too, for 6 months now, with both of us under great stress, at times. Just as we are now.

The Tasman Sea is providing the final test.

Update #95
Tuesday 10th April

Early afternoon Tuesday finds us two thirds of the way across Bass Strait, approximately 120 nm SE of Gabo Island. We are making steady progress towards home, 330 nm to our north. The wind has lightened off considerably, and I am trying to coax from Solo Globe every little bit of speed she can give me. With close to 30 crossings of this infamous stretch of water, I've seen most of its moods. Today is one of her better ones.

My satellite email decided this morning that it has had enough and has shut up shop. I have carried out various checks, and have decided that from now until the finish my only form of communication with the outside world will be via RadPhone calls using my High Frequency (HF) Radio. My trip *is about many things, but one very important aspect is that I'm trying to raise as much money as I can to buy vital equipment for the* **NICU** *at* **The John Hunter Children's Hospital.** *Have you ever seen a premature baby? They are amazing. Why don't you put your* **Newcastle Herald** *down briefly and go and find something that weighs 500 grams, and try to imagine it as premature baby fitting into the palm of your hand. Help me in my quest to give these precious wonders an improved chance of life by coming to Queens Wharf on Saturday, and signing a special sail that's just been around the world. It already carries the signatures of thousands of Novocastrians. Add your name and make a donation.*

My feeling of anticipation grows hourly, and I cannot wait to be home. It has been a long time coming.

Update #96
Wednesday 11th April

Bass Strait is a crazy stretch of water. Tuesday night saw us bobbing along on a gentle sea with that brilliant full moon that we are experiencing at present. It can be such a beautiful place, yet at times can be absolutely brutal.

I was very happy to exit the Strait and enter southern NSW waters.

Wednesday afternoon finds us 100 nm east of Merimbula, and we have not had a good day. People often ask me "Why?". It is a question that cannot be answered easily and today I have been asking myself the same thing again. Fierce rain squalls, very solid headwinds, lightning and the barometer dropping like a stone have been the focal point of my existence today.

One must be patient, however, I will admit that earlier in the week I threw my patience into the bilge but had to retrieve it and dry it out for possible future use.

We are not far off being hammered by a very strong SW change that will provide even bigger seas than we have at present, but will also provide a slingshot effect, ensuring our finish on Saturday. With 22,000 nm covered, the Tasman is throwing one final test our way in the last 1% of our journey. It's taking me right down to the wire, but what it doesn't realise is that boys from Belmont just don't give in.

Frank Rigby, a man I have a great deal of respect for, said that it is amazing what I will do to avoid mowing the lawn.

Logbook:
Wednesday 11th April
11.15 am
250 nm to home.

SW front just arrived. It's been 25 –35 knots from the North clocking progressively to the NW, W and now from our old friend, the SW.
   Here we go again.

Since rounding the bottom of Tassie, I had been plagued by calms, strong headwinds, adverse current and greatly reduced boat speed due to the growth on the hull. I had become increasingly frustrated at my lack of progress and I had been pushed way further off the coast than I had ever planned for, which would consume valuable time getting back in. The 3-4 day safety buffer I had up my sleeve had all but evaporated. Despite the positivity I espoused in the updates, there was a very real chance that I would not make the finish on Saturday.

At 11 am on Wednesday, the latest cold front arrived as forecast. I thought it would be no big deal for us, as we had been on the wrong end of more than our fair share of them over the preceding 170 something days.

It progressively ramped up so that by mid afternoon we had 50 knots, which was sort of manageable however at 4 pm it doubled down on itself and burst through the 60 knot barrier and kept on going. Conditions deteriorated disproportionately as night approached.

The water temp was 25 °C, indicative of a fast flowing southerly set which was colliding head on with the 60 + knots of wind. This caused the waves to build incredibly quickly to about 40 ft with near vertical faces, dangerously close together and wildly unpredictable breaking crests.

Suddenly, for the second time on the trip, and within a month of the first occasion, I had my back to the wall, clinging by a gossamer thread to life, in full blown survival mode.

Later on, I realised it was a version of the 1998 Hobart bomb.

I put the drogue out late arvo, setting the boat up for it to work in concert with the Coursemaster and a micro amount of the small headsail to try and have her navigate us through the mayhem. It was not pretty. I had a hell of an afternoon and as night closed in it got worse.

Much fucking worse.

I had one of the worst nights of my life.

We were knocked down repeatedly, gouged sideways through the ocean, regularly broached with the top of the mast driving into the ocean water at 90 degrees and then further. It was a pitch black freezing cold night, and unbelievably I ended up with water in the boat where I had never had it before.

It was lunacy out there that night.

It was so very tough emotionally as the finish line was just 250 nm away. I had racked up 22,000 nm with just a tad more than 1% to go.

Talk about a mind fuck!

"PLEASE, just let me get this thing done. Just let me get to the finish line. You've got to test me again, haven't you? Test me one more time. Am I not good enough? Am I not worthy? Just one last test?!"

And test me she did, as we were engulfed, knocked down, broached and skull dragged through the ocean like a rag doll.

The Coursemaster's audible off course alarm was going off its head again.

Beep, beep, beep, beep, beep.

The course was generally what I wanted it to be, but due to the constant violent movement of the boat, the Coursemaster, sometimes didn't know which way was up. Neither did I.

Beep, beep, beep, beep beep.

The beeping was driving me insane, so I moulded damp toilet paper into earplugs and rammed them into my ears. The insanity was relieved a little, but only a little.

Throughout the night, monstrous waves rolled down on us engulfing us from astern. I stood below, at the hatch, for hours craning my neck, looking out through the transparent acrylic hatch slides, watching the white boiling breaking section of the top of some waves thunder down on us. When the really big ones were about to hit, I would back up further and further down below until I was clinging to the mast, waiting for the beast to completely overwhelm us and do with us what it wished.

It was just like the 1998 Hobart, only this time I was on my own!

Anyone that says they have spent a lot of time at sea on a yacht and has never been scared is either a liar or has never been there. It's that simple.

I've been scared plenty of times.

I was very scared that night.

When the waves slammed into the hatch slides, seawater sprayed inside as if someone was outside with a firehose turned on full force.

In an effort to reduce the ingress of water, I wadded more toilet paper and packed it in the openings. This worked reasonably well, but whenever a particularly big wave thundered in it would blast the paper out, on to the cabin floor, from where I would patiently pick it up, squeeze out excess water, and wad it back in place.

Through the night, the rope towing the drogue chafed through and the drogue was lost. In one way, this was a benefit as we sped up a bit outrunning some waves, but it made the side on broaches wilder.

Amidst all of this chaos, mayhem and insanity, around 3 am, I was mentally worn out and at an extremely low ebb. I needed to recharge my mental batteries and get a second wind, so I lay down on the floor of the cabin, very cold, soaking wet and fearful.

I curled up on the floor with my sea boots, wet weather jacket and pants on in the foetal position physically, but NOT mentally.

I lay there with my eyes closed thinking, "have a look at yourself. You've got shit paper in your ears, soaking wet, freezing, you're scared, and you may not live to see the sun come up. Why the fuck, are you doing this?"

After at least two luxurious minutes, I got my second wind and started to push myself up off the floor to resume the battle. As I raised myself to my hands and knees it hit me.

I didn't know why, but I told myself that I needed to remember as much as I could about that night.

There was something there, but what was it?

Why did I need to especially remember this night, as distinct from so many others?

That night was a night of pure survival.

That night was a night from hell.

By going from wave to wave, minute to minute, we got through it somehow.

CHAPTER 32

This was my home turf

O n Thursday morning I was at my equal lowest ebb of the trip. Equal to the severe knockdown a few weeks prior.

Following is part of a radio interview, verbatim, with Luke and Chief on Thursday morning 12th April 2001.

Luke: "Hi Tony!"

Tony: "G'day mate, how are you?"

Luke: "Well we're alright, but we want to know how you are importantly"

Tony: "Mate, I've had the equal worst night of the whole trip last night and it's continuing."

Luke: "Okay, so we know that the winds have been 40 to 50 knots, but I suspect worse where you are? Are they mate?"

Tony: "Yeah mate, I've had about 60 knots plus and I've had, and got, some very big seas. I'm 90 miles off the coast. I keep getting pushed further out to sea and I can't get in. I'm 90 miles ESE of Jervis Bay."

Luke: "Okay so what are you running I guess no sails at all I guess?"

Tony: "Oh Mate! No sails. I put the drogue out. The front came through about 11 o'clock yesterday morning and it was fairly timid to start off with. It freshened around 3 or 4ish in the afternoon and got quite fierce

I put my drogue out…like I had no sail up… put the drogue out…

I lost it during the night…It's chafed through and it's gone. Ah mate, I've been knocked down…engulfed… Umm I've had the worst night. The stove won't work…I've got water where I've never had water… The boats soaked …you name it mate it's happened last night."

Luke: "Okay, so do you have any idea when it might improve for you Tony?"

Tony: "Well, it is a bit better now as I look out the window here I've probably got swells…. God damn, I've got a rainbow would you believe… I've got swells here of about 30 to 35 ft and wind of about 40 knots still I suppose"

Chief: "The temperature has dropped a fair bit too. I'd say it would be cold out there."

Tony: "Very cold last night…particularly when you're wet."

Luke: "Tony, you've just mentioned to us that you've got water in the boat where you've never had it before? Is the boat still riding high or are you suggesting that you dropped closer to the water?"

Tony: "No, No, the boat's dry in terms of what's in the bilge. I've just had water like…the force of the water…when I've been knocked down and knocked over. It's like a fire hydrant, it just sprays in and it's just gone everywhere."

Chief: "Prior to this front coming through, obviously, you would have been starting to have a few thoughts of coming home, but right at the moment you're just worried about where you are in getting through that weather?"

Tony: "I'm just worried about the next minute, and the one after that."

Luke: "Fair enough mate. You said you are being forced out further away from Australia, so ideally what weather are you looking for, and is that possible for the next couple of days?"

Tony: "I'm 150 miles now from Nobbys. I just want this to moderate a bit more. The barometer is rising slowly. I tried to get a weather forecast this morning and haven't got one. I believe, you know, that it should continue to abate. It should be okay later on today I believe. Basically, even if the wind stays in the… It's blowing from the south-west so basically when you're running with it with no sails up, you're running North East… so you're running away from the coast. If it just abates a bit I can sort of head north or slightly west of North, and you know, the seas coming on my side won't be so bad."

Luke: "Did you get sleep last night? Because I know how important it is to have some rest and be able to handle this kind of weather. Have you had any sleep mate?"

I sighed deeply. Exhaustion had worn me away and I was getting close to the bottom of the barrel resolve wise. I wanted it done!

Tony: "Na mate. No sleep. Just hanging in there."

Luke: "Boy oh boy mate, we're all thinking about you, you know that."

I was genuinely grateful at his and Chief's kindness and concern. As the interview eventually came to a close I was left quite emotional.

However, this wasn't over yet.

Most observers would be forgiven for thinking that the closer I came to achieving my overall goal, that the pressure on me would progressively reduce, and I would become more relaxed each day.

It was completely the opposite.

As the trip unfolded, day by day, the pressure of the emotional and physical investment made by me, and others, over nearly 4 years, increased until it was nearly unbearable.

What I knew, but NEVER EVER shared with anyone, was that if it all came unglued, I would have to go back and start again!

If the boat sank underneath me, 1 nm shy of the finish, and I survived, I would have failed.

No matter what the toll, I KNEW I would have to start afresh.

Crazy huh?

I needed it to be over!

Throughout most of Thursday, the winds weren't quite as bad but it still blew 40-50 knots with 35 ft waves, giving me cause to be very cautious.

Finally, at dusk on Thursday, the weather backed off enough to allow me to slowly alter course back toward the coast, ending my errant ways.

Heading in from sea, I was a massive 90 nm off the coast when abeam of Wollongong. At midnight, as I continued to angle in toward land, incredibly I was 75 nm ESE of Sydney Heads.

When off the southern Tasmanian coast, my plan had been to casually saunter north, close to the coast and enjoy the scenery. I had planned to pass by Sydney Heads, a mile or two off, soaking up the sights of the big smoke. How different it had turned out to be.

The leftovers of the front were now a steady 25 knot breeze, allowing for fast reaching, pointing exactly where I wanted to go. Home! Life was on the up and up.

At 5.30 am on Friday morning, I started on my final navigation chart. At midday, I was 10 nm ESE of Norah Head and smokin' to Moon Island at 7-8 knots.

I had last seen land just south of Maria Island. That morning, my first sighting of the mainland was Bird Island and Wybung Head, about 22 nm south of Newcastle. It was extremely emotional, and as the outline of land, I unashamedly cried. (Again!)

I still had a little bit of "golf to play", but I knew I was home.

Moon Island is a small dome shaped rocky islet about 12 nm south of Newcastle. It is only .5 nm off the coast and sits like a sentinel, guarding the entrance to Lake Macquarie.

It was fitting that 32 years prior, when I was 14 years of age, I had for the first time felt the irresistible hypnotic pull of the ocean at Moon Island, when I ventured out for my inaugural blue water trip. It was an incredible feeling of attraction and back then I instantly knew that I wanted more of "that" feeling.

At 2:30 pm on Friday, 13th April 2001, I arrived off Moon Island to the very same spot that I had first been at 32 years prior. Over the preceding six months, I had self-administered a monumental, industrial sized dose of "that" feeling. It felt pretty bloody good.

Adjacent to Moon Island is Blacksmiths Beach, a typical Australian coastal surf and sand mecca, popular with swimmers, surfers and sun lovers alike. With the finish just 12 nm away and arrival scheduled for the next day, I finally had time to kick back and enjoy the moment.

The feeling of quiet self-satisfaction, inner peace and serenity that I experienced at that time was my personal reward.

It was my reward for having "taken it on" and for having endured.

It was my reward having **never ever given in.**

I was at peace.

I furled the big headsail, tucked three reefs in the mainsail and hove to, essentially parking the boat in the now gentle sea breeze and smooth seas, about 1nm off the beach.

Jeff "Mowie" Mowbray is a distant relation. He, and Tony "Bull" Steers were my age and real Aussie larrikins. Jeff and I navigated high school together, however both of us mainly went there to eat our lunch and look out of the window, with neither applying ourselves academically.

"Bull" didn't go to our school, but I really liked him when first met, as we both attended the apprentice training school at the BHP Steelworks, as 1st year electrical apprentices.

"Bull" sadly passed away a couple of years ago.

Mowie and Bull worked as professional lifeguards, and for many years their "office" was Blacksmiths Beach.

On this Friday arvo, they were lounging around doing nothing in particular, as usual, keeping an eye on the beachgoers, when they looked out to sea and saw what they thought may have been Solo Globe bobbing around.

Aware of my imminent arrival, one said to the other "I think that might be "Mowie" out there?" They decided that it probably was, and they should investigate.

They launched their inflatable rescue boat and scarpered out.

I was down below, completely unaware of them drawing near, when I heard a yell, "Hey Mowie are you there?" Startled, I jumped up into the cockpit and there, quite close, was the two of them, grinning away like Cheshire cats.

In the previous 180 days, I had not seen a human being, so these two rough heads were my first in person human contact in 6 months.

It was absolutely bloody incredible.

I warned them not to touch the boat, as that would be deemed outside assistance and I would be disqualified. They kept a close, but safe distance, as we chatted.

I had talked so much on the radio over the past 6 months, saying "over" at the end of each sentence was now natural. I absentmindedly and regularly said "over", many times during my meeting with the boys, to indicate that it was their turn to talk. I inadvertently had Mowie and Bull in stitches!

A half cabin powerboat had been commandeered by Cookie and he arrived with Snapey, Biggles. Keith, Luke and Chief on board. Things were going swimmingly with our over water reunion, until Chief went green at the gills with sea sickness. He blamed the three meat pies he had knocked over on the way to the boat launching ramp.

Then someone realised that they hadn't put the bung (plug) in and they were sinking fast and might have to swim to the beach. They reckoned they knew about boats!

Later, the NBN chopper arrived and I broke out some sail to allow my cameraman mate, Glenn Cook, to get some good footage of us including a close-up vision of me looking about 100 years old.

By dusk, all had departed, leaving me alone again to spend my last night at sea.

Seeing my mates had wound me right up and I was chock full of anticipation for what was to come the next day. After all the trials and tribulations that we had been subjected to over the years we were finally there! (almost)

I was pumped and ready.

Luke put together the following update.

Update #98
Friday 13th April

I'm to spend one more night at sea before we make our entrance tomorrow. I can hardly wait. I can't express how eager I am to see and hug Lorraine, Holly and Jordan.

I'm very appreciative of all the people of the Hunter that have helped and supported me. This would not have been possible without the support of so many people throughout the Hunter Region. There is no way I can repay everyone, but I would like you all to know how much I appreciate your efforts.

I hope to see you all there.

I'm so proud to be a Novocastrian.
I'm so proud to be an Aussie.

Reefed down again, with the boat virtually, intentionally stationary for the 1st time in 180 days, I was no longer pre-occupied with making miles.

I had originally left with 48 stubbies of beer and unbelievably I still had 6 left, which my mates still cannot get their head around. I also had half a bottle of bourbon.

I spent a wonderfully contemplative sunset and early evening sitting in the cockpit, sipping a couple of beers, gazing at Belmont just across the way. This was my home turf. This is where I learnt to sail, swim, fish, catch crabs and prawns and do all the stuff that kids do.

It felt good.

It felt really good!

By 9.30 pm I couldn't keep my eyes open and so I collapsed into the bunk. Waking at 1.30 am, Kevvie, Frankie Babe and I started preparations for our big day out.

This was to be their last day on this epic journey with me and I wanted them to enjoy it. I could tell they were keen to get to land!

I was keen to turn on a tap and have fresh water on demand, have a cup of tea without a salt overtone, some freshly oven baked warm bread smothered in butter and vegemite, an apple, a cream bun, a cold beer with mates at the bar of the yacht club, a meat pie, the touch of a human being. The list was almost endless.

Amongst a number of tasks, I applied some fresh sponsor decals around the cockpit, being ever mindful that all of this came at a price and had to be paid for somehow.

Then it was time to eat. Menu options were limited by now, but a can of baked beans got me started and then I cranked out some of my much loved "sweetbreads" with honey and sultanas. I fried these Tony Mowbray specials golden brown and wolfed them down.

I salivate as I type.

At 5.30 am I had a rare shave, and an even rarer warm water sluice down with some remaining fresh water, which was now not so precious.

On Day #1 when underway, I had written:

After clearing the harbour, I changed out of my "street clothes" into my sailing attire. I placed my shoes, socks, long pants, belt and shirt in a white plastic shopping bag and knotted the top. I placed it inside another plastic bag knotting it as well. I then placed the package in a locker that I thought had a good chance of staying dry.

I now retrieved my "steppin' out" civvie clothes and found them in excellent condition. I put the same ensemble on as if I had taken it off just the day before.

The belt had come in a notch or two and I calculated that I had lost about 8kg, but only because of some restraint. I could have quite easily come back fatter than when I left, so losing 8kg was a major achievement. If I had come back a bigger porker, the ridicule from my mates would have been unbearable.

I had left with (what remained of it) my hair close cropped, compliments of a #2 comb on my electric clippers. The kids had never seen me with hair longer than about 10 mm. I had decided not to cut it on the trip, and I now had a bushy mane around the sides and the back, topped off by some long wispy stuff on top. The result was a zany, mad professor look. Combing my locks was a challenge and that morning I used a metal fork from the cutlery drawer. One has to be resourceful.

I was now booted and spurred, ready for our big day out.

Let's go get 'em!

CHAPTER 33
It's over, stick with me, it's going to be okay.

At 7 am there was bugger all breeze, which was a good thing for a change. I was 7 nm from Nobbys, slowly meandering, zigging and zagging, running the clock down.

Some boats came out from the harbour and one of the them was skippered by Darren Nicholson and Ricci. Darren is a world class sailor, a successful businessman and had always been an enthusiastic supporter. I was very pleased to see he and Ricci and eagerly participated in our, across water meeting, with me talking at about 100 mph. More spectator craft progressively gathered around, and at 10 am I decided it was time to go do it.

I drew a bead on the entrance and headed toward it.

On Easter Saturday, 14th April 2001, I was finally able to do what I'd visualised for so long.

I found my "breakwater", to which I steered and then entered the harbour mouth. I paused, looked to my left up the Hunter River, to where the finish line lay about 2 nm. I drew a breath, trimmed the sails and sailed my boat to the finish line.

I went looking for Lorraine, Holly and Jordan.

There was a gentle breeze, funneling straight down the harbour, necessitating a zig zag work to the line. Initially, I headed toward the northern rock breakwall which sits adjacent to the small, lightly populated suburb of Stockton. Under normal circumstances this breakwall would host just a few anglers and walkers, but on this morning, there were spectators by the thousand, waving madly.

Later, my brother Trevor, reckoned the fish were biting, and the fact that I happened to sail by at that time was purely coincidental.

If there are this many people on the Stockton side, I wondered how many there were on the more populated, more accessible Newcastle side of the harbour? I swivelled my head to look over my left shoulder and as the view came into focus I was utterly amazed to see the thousands and thousands of Novocastrians that had come out to welcome us home. I would later find out that 30,000 people had converged on the harbour.

It was a stunning reception.

I sailed close in to give the Stockton spectators a close up and then tacked across to the Newcastle side to give that mob a good view. On-water spectators multiplied, in or on, canoes, kayaks, surfboards, yachts, paddle boards and fishing boats.

The breeze incrementally faded in strength the further I sailed up the harbour, plus there was a slight adverse current which also slowed our progress. Spectators were able to walk in unison with us, allowing all concerned, including me, to thoroughly enjoy this once in a lifetime experience. Onlookers were cheering, waving, yelling out, holding up placards whilst I wildly waved back.

When I committed to the trip not quite four years prior, not for a millisecond did I ever imagine having all of those wonderful supporters there on that day to acknowledge our effort. It had been the furthest thing from my mind for all of those years and on this day, it was VERY special and meant a heck of a lot.

To anyone that was there, I thank you so very much for helping make the day so special for my family and I.

I will NEVER forget it

The 50 metre long finish line was between a red buoy and the end of a large and very substantial concrete wharf that formed one side of a small man made boat harbour. The onlookers were perched high up in various vantage points, and packed like sardines on the wharf, surrounding harbour side buildings and walkways.

As the breeze faded to bugger all, I positioned myself for a final run at the line. The soft breeze combined with the slight adverse current meant that I (stupidly) miscalculated my approach. As I got to the point of no return, I realised that my last manoeuvre was not going to be easy.

I had to do one more unplanned tack very close to the wharf, and as I turned the boat she responded sluggishly. For about 10 seconds or so I was 90% convinced that I was going to head butt the bloody wharf.

Imagine head butting a concrete wharf after 181 days at sea in front of 30,000 people. That would not have been a good look but would certainly have given them something to remember, albeit not the memory I/we were hoping for.

After some frantic spinning of the steering wheel, and swearing and cursing under my breath, I somehow managed to get the bow headed away from disaster and drifted across the finish line as the wind dropped to zero, becalming us at the perfect moment.

I stood in the cockpit, facing the crowd, and with clenched fists punched the air repetitively. As my beautiful boat had slid gracefully over the finish line, Snapey had let rip with a massive blast from an air horn to signal that it was over.

You fucking beauty!

The official finishing time was 11:28.40 am

Total time taken was 180 days, 23 hours, 28 minutes and 40 seconds.

There is not one thing that I would change about that day, except, I wish my Dad could have been there.

Maybe he was watching from somewhere.

I set about readying the boat to enter the small man-made harbour. I kicked the engine over, furled the headsail and dropped the mainsail. I was about to put the motor in gear for the first time in 181 days but before doing so I was compelled to take it all in again being almost mesmerised by the turnout.

As I looked around, taking in the scene that had been years in the making, my gaze came to settle on the closest spectator yacht, which, almost by fate, was the Butters' boat with Craig and Jenny, plus sons, Alex, Coen and Nic on board.

While I was away, Nic's brain tumour had sadly continued to take its toll but on this day, he was as excited as all get out.

On the morning that I left, Nic had presented me with "Billy" the Bear which I had cable tied to the mast, below decks. "Billy" was now a world circumnavigator, and along the way had seen and experienced things that would have left a lesser pint sized toy Koala Bear strapped into a mini straitjacket, but not our "Billy". Despite being a bit bedraggled, he still had plenty of get up and go left in him.

The Butters' mob and I exchanged pleasantries, and then I disappeared below deck and freed "Billy" of the 2 plastic zip ties that had held him in place since I had signed him on as 1st mate.

I manoeuvred Solo Globe alongside to return "Billy" back into Nic's care. As that small toy was passed from my hand to Nic's, it was the ONLY thing that mattered in my life right then.

It was a moment that I will never forget.

Nic occupies a special place in my heart, as he does with many.

It was surreal that all those people waited patiently whilst we chatted. On reflection, it seemed like they knew something special was happening and they were giving us time. Eventually, Craig suggested that I really should get a wriggle on and get myself into the harbour for the final welcome.

I dropped the ticking engine into gear and motored slowly through the narrow entrance of the small harbour, the perimeter of which provided shoulder to shoulder, packed in like sardines, standing room only.

As a scarred and battle weary, but still "tough as teak", Solo Globe Challenger and I (not as tough as teak) entered, the reception was unbelievable.

People clapped, cheered, waved madly and shouted. I was thrilled that Mum was there to witness and be a part of this incredible celebration. Whilst I had been away she had become a little unsteady on her legs, so Trevor had borrowed a wheelchair for her and they occupied a prime spot looking down as we entered. At the spot I was to berth at, Lorraine, Holly and Jordan were waiting and alongside them were my blood brothers, Biggles, Snapey, Keir, Keith, Cookie, Dave and Cyril.

After all this time, upon actually laying my eyes on the people closest to me in the world, a massive adrenalin rush hit me. I spontaneously started yelling at the top of my voice, leading the crowd in a series of "Aussie Aussie Aussie!" chants with them yelling back, "Oi Oi Oi!".

I manoeuvred the boat in close. Biggles was first to touch and steady her. Mooring lines were cast, caught and made good by he and the boys.

With the boat secure, it was all I could do not to leap across onto land, and hug those that really mattered. However, as is so often the case, bureaucracy had a part to play in proceedings.

Prior to leaving, I had made inquiries at immigration and border patrol and initially stumped them when I asked if I needed to clear out of the country officially, considering that I did not intend stopping anywhere and would be returning right back to where I started. Eventually, they decided to draw up paperwork as if I were heading to Auckland, NZ, which did of course, require official exit documents.

It did not matter that I didn't stop anywhere, I would still need to be officially cleared back in. Bureaucracy was, and is, alive and thriving.

It was decreed ahead of time that I was not to step ashore, and no one was to board the vessel, until we had been officially processed back in. I hoped for a super speedy process so that we could get on with the festivities.

Earlier on, when I wrote about returning from NZ prior to the world trip, I introduced you to the little customs man that I christened "Billy Bunter", to whom I technically still owed $187.

Who should emerge from the crowd at this moment? A bloody beaming "Billy Bunter" himself, in person. Presumably, he had the honour of approving my entry back into my own country.

Fuck me. Here we go again.

"Billy" was loving the attention as he hoisted himself on board and clomped along the deck in his polished black leather shoes, to make his way below.

Now, it was a MUCH different story from June 2000.

Now, he wanted to be my best fucking mate!

I reckon he would have sat there all day with me, his only mate, if I had let him. I politely answered a couple of questions about the trip after the official bit was done, then pointed out that there were a squillion people on the wharf waiting for me to step ashore, including my wife and children, who I was desperate to hold and kiss, and would he mind hurrying the fuck up? Considering the situation, I did ask him as politely as I could.

I know what you are thinking.

No money changed hands.

"Billy" was helped ashore and toddled off.

At this point, I had not yet set foot on terra firma and was determined not to do so until I embraced Holly and Jordan. I was concerned that if I stepped ashore, my long hoped for moment solely focused on them would be swept away, as others stepped into the frame.

I thought, "I don't care how many people you send, I want my kids first."

Video footage of the moment shows Jordan's little arms and hands wrapped around me, clinging to the left side of my neck. Holly was in symmetry, latched on to my right side.

We were as one!

Whilst thousands watched in silence, I whispered repeatedly in their ears, "It's over, stick with me, it's going to be okay, it's over."

Eventually, we released the grip we had on each other as the time to step ashore had arrived and I then made a beeline for Lorraine.

The four of us were swept up in a whirlwind of media grabs, photos, congratulatory slaps on the back, kissing babies and shaking hands.

We eventually climbed the stairs to the top level of the Queens Wharf Brewery, and from that vantage point various speeches were made which I generally can't remember much of.

I had decided that I would not have a beer that day as I wanted to try and remember as much as I could, however some of it is a blur so my abstinence was a partial waste of time.

One indelible memory however, is of Jordan shadowing me all afternoon, determined to not let me out of his sight again. Many times, I would be in conversation with someone, and I would feel his small, 7 year old hand slide into mine, grab hold tightly, vice like, determined to not let me go again, any time soon.

Our only means of transport was an old small family sedan, similar to a shoebox bolted to a roller skate. Unbeknownst to us, Mark Schroder had negotiated a sponsorship with Rob Dawes and the team at Hunter Subaru, Maitland, for the use of a Subaru station wagon. Late in the afternoon we were shown to the car and presented with the keys, and overly excitedly we four headed to good old Belmont and home.

Many aspects of that day and evening were surreal, including the fact that not only had I not seen a motor vehicle for 6 months but now I was actually sitting in one with my family and driving it on a busy road.

We walked through the door at home late afternoon, and I decided it was finally time for a beer, so I knocked the top off a stubbie and settled on the lounge.

The kids were intrigued that their dad actually had long hair and Holly amused herself greatly by combing and brushing it, creating small ponytails accompanied by ribbons and bows.

I lapped up the attention.

I wish I had a photo.

At 6 pm the local evening NBN News came on and in another totally surreal moment (not only because I hadn't seen a TV for 6 months), I was the lead story.

Bugger me if I wasn't watching myself on a TV, with my kids beside me and ribbons and bows in my hair. It's a crazy world at times.

Lorraine prepared a simple meal of rump steak, boiled potatoes and snow peas and at around 8.30 pm, after a second beer, I was totally buggered and needed to go to bed.

Freshly showered (another surreal moment), I pulled back the covers and stood there marvelling that I was about to rest my rough old head on a freshly laundered, crisp pillow case, wrapped around a beautiful fluffy pillow that was neither damp, mouldy, smelly, yellowed or repugnant.

What a reward!

Many have surmised that through that night I would have woken every hour or so, but the opposite was true. My head hit the pillow and I was gone for all money, getting in a solid 9 hours straight.

The next day, Easter Sunday, the four of us were VIP guests at a rugby league match between the Newcastle Knights and the Cronulla Sharks. Half time saw me on the centre of the ground being interviewed in front of 15,000 spectators. The kids and Lorraine were deservedly treated like royalty.

The perfect weather continued dovetailing into our publicised sail of Solo Globe back to Lake Macquarie, two days after finishing, on Easter Monday. I had a number of crew on board that day including Lorraine and the kids. Retracing our steps a little, we sailed the 12 nm back to Moon Island on a beautiful warm day, on a smooth sea with gentle SE sea breeze.

The Swansea channel that connects Lake Macquarie to the ocean is about 3 nm long and roughly, at halfway, there is a bridge. For marine traffic to navigate in or out of the lake, the bridge has to be lifted whilst 4 lanes of road traffic are halted.

When we entered the channel near Moon Island, we were taken aback by the number of vessels that were waiting there to accompany us. We didn't realise that this was just the first flotilla of supporters.

At the bridge we stooged around, waiting for it to open. Whilst doing so, we could, with limited view, see that there more boats on the lake side. As we passed through the open bridge, we were blown away by how by many boats made up the second flotilla. I was totally gob smacked as air horns were blasted, and people clapped and cheered.

Many of the houses that lined the channel were decorated with flags and banners with a typical message being "Welcome home Tony, well done."

It was extremely humbling.

Almost as one, we toodled along the narrow waterway toward the open, more easily navigable, lake waters. As we transited from the channel into the lake, we were almost engulfed by a third flotilla of boats. It was as if the surface of the water was carpeted with boats and one could have walked the nautical mile or so to the yacht club, stepping from boat to boat. It was a phenomenal sight.

I entrusted the wheel to Biggles and climbed the mast to the bottom set of spreaders to get a better view. I ended up launching myself into another sustained round of "Aussie Aussie Aussie" with "Oi Oi Oi" belted right back at me. I've never felt so alive.

We arrived at Lake Macquarie Yacht Club where it had first started for me many years prior, when I was just a kid under Snapey's and Jack's tutelage. We snuggled Solo Globe into a marina berth and I stepped onto the wharf to another incredible reception.

This group consisted mainly of my sailing friends and family, and was a large but intimate gathering. "The Legend of Lake Macquarie", Jack Morgan, was there grinning like he had won the lottery.

The closing 30 seconds or so of the documentary that was later made shows me standing on the wharf with my arm lovingly draped around Jack's shoulders, praising him: -

Tony Mowbray

"*This man taught me so much everyone. He is a legend. Jack Morgan. Don't forget the name. He is a legend. He's taught that many kids how to sail it's unbelievable*"

Then, as I wipe tears away: -
"*Tears in the eyes. I've come back in to Lake Macquarie. I've stepped onto the wharf here at Lake Macquarie Yacht Club and I'm home!*
   Its bloody good!"
   And it was.

Off Moon Island on day 180.

Less than 18 hours to go.

Off Blacksmiths Beach talking to Snapey, Luke, Chief, Cookie, Biggles and Keith as well as "Mowie" and "Bull". Note, black growth on hull. 11 nm to go.

My last evening. Sun setting directly above Belmont, where it all started for me. I was home.

Rounding the Breakwater, entering the harbour, headed for the finish.

Crossing the finish line and pretty bloody happy about it.

Lorraine, Holly and Jordan. Yahoo!

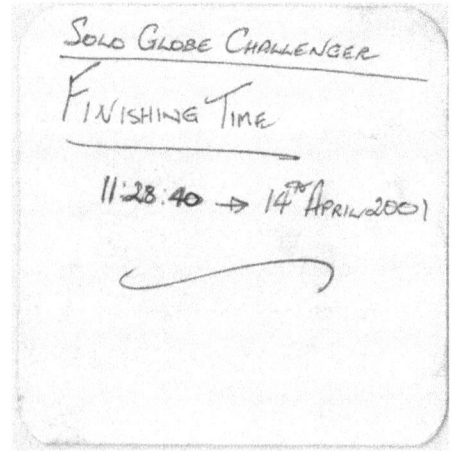

Snapey was my official finisher and appropriately recorded details on the back of a beer coaster.

30,000 supporters were there to welcome us home. Photo credit, Glenn Cook

I am kneeling at the bow embracing Holly and Jordan. I want my kids!

Finally, together. Snapey (fittingly) on right.

Mum with grey hair in wheelchair, brother Trevor behind, me in front in white shirt. Luke Grant looking at camera.

What can I say.

VIP guests at rugby league match the next day, Newcastle V Cronulla.

Job Done! It was finally over once we crossed the finish line of the 2001 Sydney to Hobart yacht race. Back row from left, Biggles, me, Keith. Middle row from left, Cyril, Dave, Snapey. Keir. Front, Cookie (kneeling)

CHAPTER 34
Back to Bass Strait after '98

I previously wrote:

I thought, "I don't care how many people you send, I want my kids first."

Video footage of the moment shows Jordan's little arms and hands wrapped around me, clinging to the left side of my neck. Holly was in symmetry, latched on to my right side.

We were as one!

Whilst thousands watched in silence, I whispered repeatedly in their ears, "It's over, stick with me, it's going to be okay, it's over."

I thought it was over, but it wasn't quite.

There was a little bit of unfinished business.

Before I set off on the world trip, I told the guys that I had no idea how it would pan out. I outlined a number of possible outcomes which included:

1. I might be financially screwed.
2. The boat might be buggered or sink.
3. I might die.

Yet, despite the crazy, quite likely possibilities, I had felt compelled to plant a seed when I posed the question to them, "*While I'm away, think about whether or not we should go back and do the Hobart race again?*"

Three weeks after I crossed the finish line, in early May 2001, we gathered at Cookie's for a private crew and family barbecue. It wasn't a celebration, but simply a need to be together in each other's company.

Before that day, we had prearranged to talk about the Hobart "question", and so after a while we guys went to my house, two doors down. We convened in a rough circle, a carton of beer in the middle on the floor, and let the question linger in the air.

"What do you guys think?" was met with a pause.

"I dunno… what do youse think?" summed up the collective reply. After a long hesitation, the reply came.

"I don't know… what do you think?"

For over an hour, we skirted the question. Some of us were in without any hesitation. Some weren't so sure. There was no pressure and no expectations. Just one thing was unanimously agreed to that day. If we went back, we would go back as one.

It had to be, all in, or none in.

A few weeks later, the "Bass Strait Eight" committed to sailing in the 2001 Sydney to Hobart yacht race. We were going back to finish the job.

75 yachts faced the starter. The weather couldn't have been more different from '98, but at times the ocean still reminded us who was in charge.

Cookie: *"One night, we were thumping to the windward, crashing off waves. I heard a very loud crack and felt myself lift clear off my bunk. That put the wind up me a bit."*

In a moment that felt like inescapable fate, Snapey navigated us to the exact spot where everything had come undone three years prior on 27th December at 4:03 pm.

Last time, it was chaos.

This time we were almost becalmed.

We rejoiced in being together and alive.

Keith reflected: *"The trust and the camaraderie between us is a beautiful thing."*

It ended up being a pretty slow race overall with generally easy conditions. On the last morning, as the new day dawned, we were adjacent to Tasman Island leaving just 40 nm to the finish. This meant that we would hopefully be able to sail the last leg in daylight, allowing us to collectively soak it all in and thoroughly appreciate the enormity of the moment. Slowly, but with purpose, the breeze carried us along as we inched our way forward.

The final 12 nm up the Derwent River was incredibly emotional.

Dave: *"The anticipation of getting to the finish line was at an all-time high"*

When we crossed the finish line, I felt a huge weight, that I hadn't fully realised I had been carrying, lift from my being. It was almost a physical experience as I felt it leave me.

It was an emotionally charged time for all of us and came about just 260 days since I had hugged and kissed Holly and Jordan in front of all those people, whispering in their ears that it was over.

Now, it was truly over.

Snapey wrote in the Logbook:

AFTER THOUGHTS:

"We logged 690 nautical miles.
We laughed 690 nautical miles.
In 690 nautical miles, we exorcised some of the demons of 1998."

CHAPTER 35
Nic, Billy the Bear and other matters

COMMUNITY RESPONSE

From the start, I always tried to refer to our endeavours as if "We", were doing it together, not "I".

I wanted people to feel a real part of it, perhaps vicariously living the adventure with me through interviews and email updates.

I am DEEPLY gratified and humbled to have received the following letter in 2001, of which I still have the original. It is representative of many sentiments, all of which I treasure.

Dear Tony, as you must know by now a thousand times, we all feel like you are "part of our family"!!

My husband would be at home in bed listening to you, as I did, whilst delivering newspapers for the xxxxx newsagency.

From the weeks you lived in those "smelly" socks, making us laugh, to the night you "fought" the storm, so close to home.

The report you gave the next morning made the tears roll down my cheeks. So close yet so far! The tone of you voice was not a "good one".

BUT, congratulations! Congratulations! Congratulations!

To Lorraine, Holly and Jordan, their strength and love must be congratulated as well.

In late 2024, more than 23 years later, I received the following message out of the blue.

Hi Tony, I am not a person that you know, but want you to know that I will never forget you.

As weird as this may sound, we share a special day for different reasons.

23 years ago, you sailed back into Newcastle and all I wanted to do was come watch you, however on this fine Easter Saturday my plans changed as my son decided that it was time to enter this world. Off to hospital we went for the beginning of the most exciting day of my life.

As I was only in early labour I asked if I could pop into town to watch you, then come back to hospital, to which I received a very firm, NO.

Early evening my son was born.

I was so very proud of what you did and was hoping to witness it.

Your achievement will forever hold a very dear spot in my memories and I hope you always remain proud of yourself.

Well done legend, and thanks for an incredible memory that up until now you didn't know you made.

I am INCREDIBLY humbled, yet again.

KEVVIE and FRANKIE BABE, (My imaginary friends)

As soon as we berthed they jumped ashore, disappeared into the crowd and haven't been seen since.

It turns out that they were only fair weather sailors.

SNAPEY

Robert Brown Snape very sadly passed away in May 2021

I salute you!

THE OTHER '98 HOBART CREW

As of 2025 the remaining 7 of us are alive and as close as ever.

STEERING CABLES

They got me to the finish line.

When I was knocking the boat back into shape after the trip, I removed the worn cables and replaced them with the set I had left behind in the garage. The wire strands on the worrisome cable had worn down to be razor thin. I twisted the removed cable in the opposite direction to which it was accustomed, and it sprang spikes like a porcupine before falling apart in my hands.

It just lasted, but last it did.

NICHOLAS "NIC" BUTTERS

Nic passed away on 8th December 2004 aged 14 years.

Nic was an absolute gem.

In July 2005 Craig and Jenny established the Nicholas Trust.

"The Nicholas Trust is committed to the care of children in the final stages of their young lives.

To support the provision of Paediatric Palliative Care services and facilities for children with a life limiting condition and their families. Over 400 children in our region, under the age of 18, have a life limiting illness and require access to paediatric palliative care services. 40-50 of these children will die this year."

www.nicholastrust.org.au

BILLY THE BEAR

When Craig and Jenny created the Trust, they asked me to speak at the launch and inaugural fundraiser. I was honoured to do so. My primary task was to motivate attendees to donate generously.

I asked Jenny where "Billy" was and she told me that he "lived" in Nic's bedroom. She retrieved "Billy" for me and that evening I went on stage with the pint-sized wonder bear hidden in my trousers pocket. At a poignant moment in the presentation, I pulled him from my pocket, introduced him and gave an emotion charged presentation as I shared his story.

I then sat him atop a piano on stage, telling the audience that "Billy" was going to keep a trained eye on all of them throughout the evening and report to me those that didn't dig deep into their pockets. He perched on the piano and had a fabbo time. Later on, he told me that he much preferred the top of a piano for a few hours as against being in the Southern Ocean with a grouchy old has been.

NICU

Fundraising for NICU continued up until April 2002. In total, we raised $180,000 which allowed them to acquire 10 new vital signs systems monitors. Fundraising initiatives can be varied and at times very unusual. Just after the world trip finished, I accepted the donation of a brand new Royal Enfield motorcycle from the Australian importer, who happened to live in Newcastle. He said that I could do whatever I wished with it, so long as all proceeds went to NICU.

It had a retail value of $5500.

What to do with a motorcycle?

We explored a number of options and eventually, through an amalgam of ideas, a plan was devised.

The motorcycle was painted gloss black with gold trim. I removed the fuel tank. The seat was upholstered with black vinyl. I removed the seat and took it to an upholsterer who made a new vinyl seat cover in the red white and blue colours of the very popular local Newcastle Knights rugby league team. I went to a Knights training session with my limp piece of red, white and blue vinyl and had the team sign it. I also had them sign the fuel tank as well with a gold leaf pen.

Cookie clear lacquered the tank to protect the signatures. The signed vinyl went back to the upholsterer, who attached it to the seat. The reassembled bike looked incredibly good, and it had cost bugger all to transform into what we hoped would be a collector's piece.

In April 2002, we held our last major initiative, a fundraising dinner and obligatory charity auction. We had three people enter into a bidding war and eventually the bike with a retail value of $5,500, sold for $13,500.

At the conclusion of the auction the donor was ecstatic. He'd had a few drinks (read: more than one and less than 100), and he excitedly rushed to me growling, "Mowbray, you bastard. I've got a container load of those fucking things. Let's go get 'em and we'll sell them as well!"

THE NIGHT OF LUNACY

I previously wrote:

I didn't know why, but I told myself that I needed to remember as much as I could about that night.

There was something there, but what was it?

Why did I need to especially remember this night, as distinct from so many others?

In the months after I arrived home, I would, from time to time, see snippets of TV news or current affairs shows that touched on the loss of a 10.5 metre charter fishing vessel, the "Margaret J" that had set out from Burnie on the NW corner of Tasmania.

The vessel had disappeared in a storm and three men had lost their lives.

The incident continued to make the headlines because the search authorities had refused to heed the advice of local fishermen who strongly advised that the search be conducted in a certain area.

Some time passed, the search was unsuccessful and finally the authorities begrudgingly searched the area that had been suggested initially. It was there that they located the wrecked vessel and two bodies.

When I searched the internet, this is a little of what I found:

> "*Ron Hill, and Kimm Giles, both of Ulverstone, and Robert Kirkpatrick had just left on a fishing trip in rough weather when their 10.5 metre boat sank off Robbins Island in western Bass Strait on 9th April 2001.*
>
> *All the crew probably reached a liferaft. When atrocious weather hit Bass Strait 11th April, it was likely that the raft overturned and the exhausted men died. An alarm was raised on 12th April when the men were overdue, but a four day search failed to find them. It was reactivated on 2nd May after pressure from local fishermen.*
>
> *The deflated raft and the bodies of Mr. Giles and Mr. Hill were found about 125 nautical miles away on Prime Seal and Flinders islands in eastern Bass Strait. The body of Mr. Kirkpatrick was never found.*
>
> *Fears that the fishermen were still alive when the first search was called off led to a rift between police and local fishermen that intensified when a Senate committee began an inquiry into the tragedy.*"

Watching these various short grab news items only gave small glimpses of what had happened and then one night I watched a longer TV exposé that dealt in more detail with what had occurred. When I pieced the dates together, it hit me like a ton of bricks. I sat bolt upright, transfixed by the program, the realisation hitting me like a sledgehammer.

Just prior to my night of lunacy and grim fight for survival, these three men had lost their lives in the same storm that steamrolled its way across Bass Strait to me.

Three more men perished so very close to me, just as six others had died just 2 years and 4 months prior in the 1998 Sydney to Hobart.

I was touched to my core.

DOCUMENTARY
"SOLO GLOBE CHALLENGE – LOOK IT IN THE EYE"

A goal was to make a documentary, but I had absolutely zero experience or knowledge how to go about that. I accumulated hours of raw footage courtesy of Sony and Ashley Roan but how to put it together was way above my pay grade.

Keir and NBN television were the solution and Keir worked tirelessly creating a beautiful documentary. NBN aired it once on their regional network NBN in late 2001. Channel 9 aired it nationally in early 2002

The opening and closing segments are on YouTube.
Opening:
https://www.youtube.com/watch?v=5ynriWfTaX8&t=4s
Closing:
https://www.youtube.com/watch?v=Er4xB4plIuU

PUBLIC/CORPORATE SPEAKING

Many people assume, quite reasonably, that after the trip I may have been reclusive but the opposite was the case. Our financial position was fairly ordinary and only vaguely manageable. I needed to go to work.

I needed to start to rebuild financially and to start and pay back Lorraine and the kids for standing by me for so long. I joke about it, but when I stepped off the boat on to the wharf, someone gave me a mobile phone and I was back in business. In my mind, that day I was a professional corporate speaker.

Being the "flavour of the month" only lasts so long. Probably a month?

I worked out pretty quickly that to achieve longevity I needed to have more than just an interesting story. One needs to weave in parallels and examples of teamwork, leadership, goal setting, planning to succeed, 100% commitment, overcoming adversity etc. and so I did. I was very proactive for a number of years and at my peak was completing approximately 100 paid professional presentations annually.

I've been fortunate to speak all around Australia plus I've flapped my gums in Canada, USA, Mexico, Hong Kong, Italy, UK, Japan, Malaysia, New Zealand, and Fiji etc.

A BOOK

Well, bugger me love, here we finally are!

I have not written seeking wealth or public acclaim, just in case it happens to be any good?

My hope is that people will find it interesting and informative. If someone can take something from it that can help them in some aspect of their life then I will be humbled and gratified.

I started collating my memories, logbooks, audio tapes, emails and other reference materials throughout 2001 when I first hit the keyboard.

I've had a few serious attempts at finishing it off since, but I am easily distracted.

As I type it is 2025

That didn't take too long.

CHAPTER 36
What happened to Solo Globe Challenger

Late 2001/Early 2002:

I knocked her back into shape after the circumnavigation.

December 2001:

Participated in the 2001 Sydney to Hobart race. Returned to Lake Macquarie.

April (early) 2002:

We replicated our 1996 7 day, non-stop sail around Lake Macquarie raising more money for the John Hunter Children's Hospital NICU.

April (late) 2002:

I sailed her to New Plymouth, NZ with 4 others on board.

May 2002:

Solo Globe and I competed in a Solo Trans-Tasman race from New Plymouth, NZ to Mooloolaba QLD, Australia. The race was only held every 4 years and was a 'bucket list" item.

June/July/August 2002:

Lorraine, Holly, Jordan and I cruised the Great Barrier Reef.

September 2002:

Sailed her from the Great Barrier Reef back to Lake Macquarie.

December 2003/January 2004:

Undertook a 7-week expedition from Sydney to Antarctica and return via Hobart with 4 others on board. We sailed to what is freely acknowledged as the windiest place on earth at sea level, "The Home of the Blizzard".

Winds have been recorded there up to 340 k/h.

We visited Mawson's Hut in Commonwealth Bay, Antarctica.

September 2006:

Sold her to a great guy, Peter, from Sydney, who aspired to sail long distances, solo. Over the ensuing years, under Peter's stewardship, Solo Globe sailed north from Sydney, across the top of Australia to South Africa. They then crossed the South Atlantic via The Caribbean arriving in Florida. It was there he met and married Cindy.

Together, they then sailed to the UK before arriving in the Mediterranean where they based themselves and Solo Globe for 4 years in Turkey and a further 3 years in Italy.

2017:

Peter very sadly passed away when they were in Sicily, Italy.

2017:

Apparently, Peter had always told Cindy that if "anything" were to happen to him that she should contact me for help as he knew I loved the boat as much as he did and that I would help her. The end result was that I purchased Solo Globe back from Cindy, sight unseen.

2017-18:

Under my totally unexpected new ownership, we cruised the waters of Sicily.

2018-19:

I sailed her back to Australia via Gibraltar, The Canary Islands, Caribbean, The Panama Canal, Tahiti, Tonga, Fiji and Brisbane before arriving back at good old Lake Macquarie.

2022:

I sold Solo Globe to a new owner who, as of 2025, has her in Hobart.

It's been a hell of a journey so far!

CHAPTER 37
Books Read

The following list is in the order that I read them.

1. *Lionheart* by Jesse Martin Good read, well put together. A remarkably short preparation time.
2. *The One That Got Away* by Chris Ryan
3. *Black and Blue* by Ian Rankin
4. *Life Is So Good* by George Dawson and Richard Glaubman
5. Very, very good book about George Dawson 102 years old American who learnt to read and write at 98yrs!
6. *Long Walk to Freedom* by Nelson Mandela
7. Brilliant.
8. *What's It All About* by Michael Caine
9. *Unnatural Exposure* by Patricia Cornwall
10. *Sirro Tales From Tiger Town* by Paul Sironen and Daniel Lane
11. *Water from the Moon- A Biography of John Fawcett* by Scott Bevan
12. *Most people That I Know (Think that I'm crazy)* by Billy Thorpe
13. *One Flew Over the Cuckoos Nest* by Ken Kesey
14. Brilliant!
15. *The Last Islands* by John Bates
16. *(The almost late) Gordon Chater* by Gordon Chater
17. *Schindler's List* by Thomas Keneally
18. *The Kon-Tiki Man* by Christopher Ralling and Thor Heyerdahl
19. *The Wrong Way Home* by Peter Moore
20. *The Remorseful Day (Inspector Morse)* by Colin Dexter
21. *One Perfect Day* by Paul Harragon and Brett Keeble
22. *Ben Lexcen, The Man, The Keel, The Cup* by Bruce Stannard
23. *Never Tell Me Never* by Janine Shepherd

24. *Dare to Fly* by Janine Shepherd
25. *The Falcon and the Snowman* by Robert Lindsay
26. *The Daughters of Cain* by Colin Dexter
27. *Peter Cook Biography* by Harry Thompson
28. *The Jewel That Was Ours. Inspector Morse Novel* by Colin Dexter
29. *The Chalon Heads* by Barry Maitland
30. *"Whiticisms", Confessions of a Left Arm Quick* by Mike Whitney
31. *Going Wrong* by Ruth Rendell
32. *Six Years with God* by Jeannie Mills
33. *Endurance* by Alfred Lansing
34. *South Pole 2000* by Caroline Hamilton
35. Thanks Mum.
36. *Out There* by George Day and Herb McCormick
37. *Off the Air* by Mike Carleton
38. *Kevin Costner - Unauthorised Biography* by Todd Keith
39. *Are you Somebody- The Life and Times of Nuala O'Faolain*
40. *Antarctica, a Traveler's Tale* by Jean Bailey
41. Found a postcard at rear dated 29/6/1980 from Stanno to Snapey.
42. *Deek, the making of Australia's World Marathon Champ* by Mike Jenkinson
43. *Nick Farr-Jones Biography* by Peter Fitzsimons
44. *One Crowded Hour. Neil Davis, Combat Cameraman 1934-1985* by Tim Bowden
45. *Sailing Alone around the World* Joshua Slocum
46. *Spy Catcher, Autobiography of Peter Wright* by Peter Wright
47. *Danzigers Adventures* by Nick Danziger
48. *The Don- Biography of Sir Donald Bradman* by Roland Perry
49. I would have liked to have seen him bat.
50. *Bob Woodward – Wired Short Life and fast Times of John Belushi* by Bob Woodward
51. *Compilation of 4 Short Stories- Readers Digest*
52. *Killshot* by Elmore Leonard
53. *Ruth Cracknell Memoir* by Ruth Cracknell
54. *The Pelican Brief* by John Grisham
55. *Some Lie, Some Die* by Ruth Rendell
56. *The Partner* by John Grisham
57. *All my Enemies* by Barry Maitland

58. *The Marx Sisters* by Barry Maitland
59. *Once were Warriors* by Alan Duff
60. *Road Rage-Chief Inspector Wexford* by Ruth Rendell
61. *Hornets Nest* by Patricia Cornwall
62. *Readers Digest Compilation* by 4 various authors
63. *Readers Digest Compilation* by 3 various authors
64. *Bustin down the Door* by Wayne "Rabbit" Bartholomew
65. *Readers Digest Compilation* by 4 various authors
66. *The Seventh Scroll* by Wilbur Smith
67. *Charlotte Gray* by Sebastian Faulkes
68. *Just Williams* by Kenneth Williams

At the conclusion of *Just Williams,* I had 32 days remaining. As if a tap were turned off, I suddenly could no longer focus on reading. Thoughts of home occupied my mind and I simply could not read anymore.

Therefore, the following statistics actually represent just 5 months reading, not the 6 months I was at sea.

I read what I thought was the best books first, and so by early March, I was left with the less interesting of the 100 books I had taken.

In addition to completed books, there were another dozen or so that remained unfinished.

Statistics:

Pages read = 21,094 (completed books only)
If averaged over 6 months = 116.5 pages per day
If averaged over 5 months = 140.6 pages per day
I read 62 books over 181 days for an average of 1 book every 2.92 days. 'twas heaven on a stick!

CHAPTER 38
Food and other supplies

Except for the first couple of weeks, everything I ate came from a tin or a packet plus some vacuum sealed 400g portions of various smoked meats like pork, chicken and sausages

I did have refrigeration, however for it to operate it was necessary to run the engine. With limited diesel, it simply was not feasible to operate the fridge except for the first couple of weeks, when I got stuck into fresh produce until it was gone. From then on, I didn't use the fridge except as storage.

HOW MUCH FOOD WAS FOOD LEFT?
I left with what I thought was 9 months of supplies.

I reckoned I could have gone another 1.5 months but what was left was generally the stuff I didn't like.

Having less left than what I thought I would can be put down to one or more factors:

1) I spent 4 months in the cold and needed lots of calories.
2) I ate because I was bored.
3) I possibly under catered a tad.

The following is a good overview of the supplies that I took. It is not exact.

PACKET FOOD:	QUANTITIES:	CLEANING, CONSUMABLES, TOILETRIES:	QUANTITIES:
Fruit cake Bi-Lo	45 (beautiful)	Paper towel	20 rolls
Other cakes	A lot!	Pens, pencils, ruler, erasers etc.	lots
Biscuits sweet	A lot!	Liquid baby bath soap	2 × 500 ml
Biscuits Jatz, Sao	24 packs	Alfoil	2 × 30 m
Rice crackers etc.	36 × 100g	Tissues	6 × 228 pk
Sugar	2 kg	Soap powder for laundering	1 × 1.25 kg
Breakfast cereals	11 × boxes	Sorbolene	2
Hot shots	36	Playing Cards	2 × decks
Cheese (long life)	6 × 500g	Paper bowls	2 × packs (10)
Milk in a tube (condensed)	2 × 200g	General cleaning items	Varied
Suimin	60	Cigarette lighters for lighting stove	6 × lighters, 6 × gasmatch lighters
Pasta and sauce meals	36 large sachets	Vitamins	6 × bottles varied
2 min noodles	96	Toothbrushes	6
Cup-a-soup	144 × sachets	Tooth picks	1 × 200 pack
Dried Egg	2 × 200g	Shaving cream	2 × 250g
Breadcrumbs	2 × 375g	Lemsip	2
Flour	2 × 1kg	Cotton buds	4 × 200 packs
Rice	10 × 1kg	Blank Cassette tapes	12
Pasta	6.75 kg	Torches and spare globes	6 × torches

Tony Mowbray

Deb instant mashed potato	10 × 350g	Toilet paper	72 rolls
Salt	500 gm	Pot scourers	4 × 5 pack
Cooking oil	2 × 750g	Glad Wrap	1 × 150 m
Peanut butter	3 × 375g	Washing up detergent	4 × 500 ml
Honey	3 × 400g	Wet ones	5 × 120 pack
Vegemite	3 × 235g	Soap	4 × bars
Jam	3 × 450g	Garbage bags	150 × L, 60 × S
Tomato sauce	3 × 500 ml	Notebooks A4	4
Bar b que sauce	2 × 375 ml	Batteries	158 assorted
Mustard	1 × 250g	Matches	1 × 250 pack
Chili sauce	1 × 500 ml		
Sultanas	6 × 1 kg		
Raisins	4 × 1 kg		
Dried apple	12 × 1 kg		
Dried apricots	12 × 1 kg		
Muesli bars	70		
Fruit bars	60		
Chocolate	A lot!		
Lollies	Bucket loads!		
Tea bags	2060		
Milo	3 × 450g		
Bread mixes	7 × 2 kg		
Cake mixes	8 × 350g		
Pancake Shake mixes	9 × 375g		
Long life custard	12 large		
Long life cream	24 small		
Long life milk	130 litres		
Mayonnaise	3 jars		

Long life fruit juices	18 litres		
Pasta and sauce sachets	47 assorted		
Snak Paks	12		
Fruit juice poppers	56		
Rice cream	12 × 440g		
Parmesan cheese	5 × 125g		
Curry powder	2 × 200g		
Parsley flakes	1 × 5g		
Mixed herbs	1 × 10g		
Chili powder	1 × 35g		
Nuts	9.6 kgs		
Bottled water	2 × 10 lt		
Cordial mix-up	6 × 750 ml		
Soft drink (Carbonated)	60 × cans		
Powerade drinks	33 litres		
Potato Chips	12 kgs		
Pickled Onions	18 × 150g		

FRESH PRODUCE:	QUANTITIES:	TINNED FOOD:	QUANTITIES:
Potatoes	10 kg	Fruit pears, peaches 2 × fruits apricots	72 × 415g
Eggs	36	Meats, Ham, Corned beef, chicken,	12 × 450g 24 × 340g
Yoghurt	7	Salmon	18 × 290g
Margarine	3 × 500g	Tuna	6 × 425, 4 × 95
Onions	2 kg	Prawns	18 × 200g
Carrots	1 kg	Soup	41 tins
Fruit Juice	4 lt	Peas	30 × 420g

Cookies, Rock Cakes, Slices etc.	7 packs	Corn (Including creamed)	35 × 420g
Cheese	2 kg	Potatoes	24 × 410g
Tomatoes	2 kg	Creamed corn	12 × 420g
Salami	5 kg	Seafood Mix	12 × 290g
Apples	2.5 kg	Mushrooms	6 × 220g
Bacon	.75 kg	Carrots	18 × 410g
Oranges	3 kg	Potato salad	12 × 425g
Bread	3 loaves sliced	Beetroot	8 × 450g
Bananas	2.8 kg	Bean salads	12 × 440g
Muffins	16	Hawaiian salads	10 × 440g
Milk fresh	3 L	Mixed salads	12 × 440g
Sausages	4 × packs	Pasta Sauces	16 × 425g
Sirloin Steaks	6	Tomatoes	10 × 400g
		Tomato paste	3 × 150g
		Baked beans	24 tins
		Spaghetti	6 × 420g
		Champignons	6 × 190g
		Smoked Oysters	24 tins
		Potatoes	12 × 410g
		Coffee	1 × tin

www.ingramcontent.com/pod-product-compliance
Lightning Source LLC
Chambersburg PA
CBHW041314240426
43669CB00024B/2982